Radiant Circles

Ecospirituality and the Church of All Worlds

Radiant Circles

Ecospirituality and the Church of All Worlds

Alder MoonOak

Winchester, UK
Washington, USA

JOHN HUNT PUBLISHING

First published by Moon Books, 2022
Moon Books is an imprint of John Hunt Publishing Ltd., No. 3 East Street, Alresford
Hampshire SO24 9EE, UK
office@jhpbooks.net
www.johnhuntpublishing.com
www.moon-books.net

For distributor details and how to order please visit the 'Ordering' section on our website.

ISBN: 978 1 80341 062 3
978 1 80341 063 0 (ebook)
Library of Congress Control Number: 2021950348

A CIP catalogue record for this book is available from the British Library.

Design: Matthew Greenfield

UK: Printed and bound by CPI Group (UK) Ltd, Croydon, CR0 4YY
Printed in North America by CPI GPS partners

Contents

Chapter 1

Introduction

We begin our journey in the night forest, weaving through the oaks and magnolias, following paths of candlelight towards a large circle cut into the ground, blazing fire in the middle, bales of hay for sitting, and twelve nude people, arms outstretched to the sky, watching sparks fly up and mingle with the stars. Drumming begins, willowy dancing, shadows twirling against the trees. The circle creates a vortex of energy, builds to a crescendo, then bursts out into the universe. Cakes and ale, storytelling, ritual magick – all to the ancient gods and goddesses with a history stretching from the molten genesis of the planet, through the ascent of primates, to the building of space stations.

NeoPagans – the naked people circling in the woods – have beliefs and practices originating from the grey mists of time. They see themselves as direct descendants of antique and medieval rural traditions of nature magick and earthy rites, synchronizing humanity to planetary rhythms and resisting the extremes of the Abrahamic traditions. Though it's one of the fastest growing religions in the West, nostalgia for pre-Christian nature rites and seasonal festivals, without the barbaric unpleasantries of yore, shapes its manifestation as a New Religious Movement in the 21st century.

I've spent decades studying, observing, and participating in this religion, and most of my life in the interesting world of speculative imagination in pursuit of transcendent visions, ecological wisdom, deep spirituality, and evolutionary knowledge, all in the cause of helping Earth's *Homo sapiens* achieve the paradisiacal future foretold in many sacred texts and teachings. And I'm not alone. A powerful but hidden minority of humans labor with me, our toils mostly confined to academia, small esoteric groups, and special writings. This has been my world, filled with astounding discoveries and precious visions – and this book is the result. So let's begin our journey with an explanation of a few basic ideas repeated throughout this book.

Visionaries

The human family has been blessed with visionaries for 100,000 years. Visionaries see beyond ordinary consciousness into the spirit realms – whether other levels of awareness, alternative spatial-temporal dimensions, or higher states of thought and being. Visionaries peer farther into reality, deeper into perception, and longer into the potential future, and so return with wisdom for the People. Shamans served the clan and tribe as the first spiritual guides. Later formalized priesthoods advised the pharaohs and performed specialized rituals, rites of passage, and various blessings, functioning psychologically, emotionally, and culturally. They delved into the darkness and found treasures that they shared, bringing comfort and consistency into otherwise painful and chaotic lives. This is what religions often still do.

Whether such religious functions emerge from human capacities for self-initiated transcendence or 'supernatural' sources means little in this book because either way, positive energy gets exchanged, healing occurs, and evolution advances towards visionary futures when tears are dried, lions lay down with lambs, the true Atman attains liberation and enters Nirvana, the saved enter heaven, perfection is attained, and paradise comes to Earth. States of love and bliss remain the goal, the reason for the struggles, the result of discipline and devotion, the end of the journey, if there is one. Visionaries see into the depths of reality and serve as guides to a potentially better future. When they write their visions, the modern result is often science fiction or other speculative literature, where possibilities are laid bare, explored, and refined, preparing the fields of the present for the harvest to come. But they can also be esoteric or mystical babblings, barely discernable by our mainstream society, forever at the edge of collective consciousness but profound in their eventual implications and slow but steady evolutionary application.

Ecospirituality

Ecology begins with *eco,* the Greek term for 'household,' and functions as a holistic science that investigates and exposes the complex interrelationships and interdependencies within the 40 mile swath, from ocean bottom to stratosphere, where life flourishes. It studies Earth not only in discreet parts, but also as a single, interconnected unity, each part dependent on and linked to every other in a web of mutually-sustaining bio-systems. Ecology has expanded from its scientific origins to include, and be claimed by, environmental movements advocating for the integrity of nature, both for its own sake and because human life obviously depends on fully functioning and viable ecosystems.

In addition, according to atheist apologist Sam Harris, *spirituality* refers to "the efforts people make, through meditation, psychedelics, or other means, to fully bring their minds into the present or to induce non-ordinary states of consciousness"[1] which is linked to ethics insofar as "we have ethical responsibilities towards other creatures precisely to the degree that our actions can affect their conscious experience for better or worse."[2] Harris' definition eschews tribal religious supernaturalism in favor of empirical neurological explanations, yet clearly defines spiritual matters as including physically transcendent experiences and moral constraints. Other nontheistic definitions suggest that *spirit* is another word for "consciousness" and *spiritual* refers to its expansion or deepening. *Spirituality,* then, is the quality or state of having or developing an expanded or deepened consciousness.

If *ecology* is the study of our household Earth, and *spirituality* describes experiences of transcendence, then combining the two suggests an expansion of both terms to unprecedented parameters of inclusiveness and integration. To do so, we must open our arms to bear-hug dimensions and our hearts to extraordinary magnitudes of potential because the act of (re)combining planet and spirit is itself an exercise in cultural evolution, and evolution is sometimes unpredictable, leading to novel and unexpected outcomes. So *ecospirituality* can be defined for our purposes as the confluence of planetary ecological holism and spiritual consciousness transcending human sensory perception (but not experience) into a meta-narrative wherein human and non-human worlds take on deeply held import and are thus imbued with ultimate value and consequently become worthy of protective care or even veneration.

In other words, ecospirituality is the story of the modern divorce and postmodern reconciliation between *Spiritus* (the transcendent and ineffable interior-subjective) and *Ecos* (the imminent and empirical external-objective), beginning with the ancient Greek symbol for Earth: a cross in a circle. The circle represents not only the cycles of life – from daily moods to the swirl of galaxies – but also the infinite and eternal. The horizontal line of the cross represents the physical/material plane of reality (which can be widened and broadened with experience), and the vertical line stands for the spiritual/mystic plane (which can be heightened and deepened). Humanity, and possibly all life, stands poised in the center where the two meet.

Religion

While our subjective spiritual experiences may be unique, they can be shared to create a lexicon of common experiences forming the basis of religious belief and practice; however, the religious definition of spirit is limited because the organizational-institutional structure of religion is constricting, so religion has been limited. Its purpose is to create a space-time context for accessing our 'higher selves,' and the exterior/interior energies referred to as 'divinity.'

Religion encourages the individual transcendent experience within a collective context and utilizes various methods for inducing this experience, including singing, dancing, words of wisdom, prayer, chanting, meditation, adoration of icons, ingesting psychedelics, contact with nature, and reading or studying sacred texts. The spiritual or religious experience is the falling away of ego-self and ordinary consciousness, manifesting as feelings of unity with all, intimate relationship with 'divinity,' or being one with the cosmos. Barriers drop and a profoundly open inclusiveness may result. Love pours through from a source of great benevolence, and joy from a never-ending source.

In the present scientific era, it's easy to see and acknowledge transcendence in technology – we're used to phenomenal breakthroughs and advances resulting in new, undreamed-of techno-marvels. But religion has usually been bound by tradition and xenophobia, allowing little or no growth. Some religions are proud of the fact that they've remained virtually unchanged for centuries. What a loss to humankind this has been. Religion often has been left to rot, condemned to the numbing repetition of historical events, stifling orthodoxy, and oppressive orthopraxis ossified by inflexibility.

Green Religion

Ecospirituality implies a relationship between three entities: spirit, humanity, and Earth. Forming such a relationship implies emotional and material connections between mutually respectful participants. Since holistic spirituality is one royal road to interconnectivity, religions can share in the project – and increasingly do so. However, an argument can be made that many religions have remained indifferent to the sacredness of Earth. To include the planet as a holy object violates the separation of Creator and Creation. Traditionally, a valuated hierarchy reigns, with God at the top, humanity in the middle, and Earth at the bottom.

Mining extant religions for ecological elements offers a few gems within established traditions and their millions of loyal adherents. Turning the great religions green certainly deserves serious support; passion for both faith and environment may prove an effectual combination worthy of solving global-sized tribulations. For instance, two models of valuating the Earth emerge from Christianity. *Creation stewardship* finds inspiration in the Bible for the belief that God is the true owner of the world and that people are therefore responsible to Him for the care and wise use of His property.[3] Some Evangelical Christians, otherwise noted for their support of the valuated hierarchy of separation, nonetheless have a model called *creation care*.[4] Other world religions also have green elements: Hindu approaches include *dharmic* ethics, *prakrti* (material creation), or *ayurveda* (traditional medicine); Islam possesses the concept of *hima* (inviolate zone); and Judaism contains the environmental initiative *ecokashrut*, celebrations of *Tu B'shvat*, and the principles of *halakhah* and *bal tashkhit*.[5]

New religions based on ecospiritual tenets don't usually carry the baggage of inerrant ancient texts, historically-stationary avatars, or mythologically-recalcitrant stories along with them into the 21st century. Their genesis is in the postmodern milieu, and they're immersed in contemporary vocabulary, somewhat like the advantages experienced by a child growing up with high technology over the elder striving to master it at an advanced age – it can be done, but more effort is required. Green religions and Earth spiritualities are authentic products of contemporary society.

> ...the greening-of-religions phenomenon is, in my opinion, a response to and an implicit affirmation of the more scientific evolutionary and ecological worldview so elegantly and

> attractively expressed by Aldo Leopold. If it weren't for ecology, we would not be aware that we have an 'ecologic crisis.' If it weren't for the theory of evolution, we would be both blind and indifferent to the reduction in global biodiversity. The world's newly green religions thus tacitly orbit around the evolutionary-ecological world-view.[6]

Ironically, the techno-scientific industrialism of modernity is mother of both ecological instability and its possible solution within an "evolutionary-ecological world-view." Such a paradigm shift emerges from evolutionary advancement, away from numbness about the interconnection and interdependence of life towards a deep empathic relationship with the living planet.

Dark Green Religion

One movement that sees itself as stimulating the re-valuation process by promoting ecospirituality has been categorized as 'Dark Greens,' a term which University of Florida professor Bron Taylor defines as "a religion that considers nature to be sacred, imbued by intrinsic value, and worthy of reverent care."[7] Taylor serves as editor of the *Encyclopedia of Nature Religions* and of the *Journal of the Society of Religion, Nature, and Culture,* and has written the seminal book on the subject: *Dark Green Religion: Nature Spirituality and the Planetary Future.* His disciplined passion for Earth religions appears in all his work, and from it arises what he sees as part of the solution to environmental issues: a new synthesis combining the fact-driven and immanent Earth sciences with the commitment-driven and transcendent spiritual arts.

In the Preface to *Dark Green Religion,* the scope of Taylor's investigation includes detailing "the emergence of a global, civic, earth religion" shaping the "worldviews and practices of grassroots social activists and the world's intelligentsia."[8] In

Chapter 1, he states, "Those who have studied contemporary spirituality find a common feature of it to be a sense that nature is sacred and that ethical responsibilities naturally follow such a realization."[9] Increasing numbers of people in industrialized cultures find favor with such "sacred nature" sentiments:

> Some of these people view the world as full of spiritual intelligences with whom one can be in relationship (an animistic perception), while others among them perceive the earth to be alive or even divine (a more pantheistic belief).[10]

Taylor then proceeds to divide dark green religions into four types:

- Spiritual Animism – immaterial, supernaturalistic aliveness of objects
- Naturalistic Animism – all-natural energetic 'aliveness' of objects
- Gaian Spirituality – supernaturalistic aliveness of universe or Earth as conscious meta-being
- Gaian Naturalism – Earth or universe as all-natural superorganism, a la Lovelock

Gaian Naturalism, specifically

> understands the biosphere (universe or cosmos) to be alive or conscious, or at least by metaphor and analogy to resemble organisms with their many interdependent parts. Moreover, this energetic, interdependent, living system is understood to be the fundamental thing to understand and venerate.[11]

Taylor continues his optimistic tone by quoting Jane Goodall, who calls for us to "reestablish our connection with the natural world and with the Spiritual power that is within us...then we can move…into the final stage of human evolution, spiritual evolution."[12] Goodall's belief in the power of "spiritual evolution" to move humanity beyond its own narrow interests and ego-centricity towards greater adaptability and complexity means that people will come to value Earth and its myriad lifeforms, not as resources to exploit, but as partners in the continuation of life itself, which naturally includes human prosperity. Evolution of the spirit seems to involve the emergence of a true environmental ethic extending valuation, care, and even love outwards to planetary dimensions. Such an ethic will open the door to considering that the wilderness and its inhabitants "have special value and deserve respect."[13]

Of course, "nature" as a prefix to almost any noun can seem regressive, attempting to pull humanity back to primitive stages of evolution. Groups like Earth First! frequently view the decline of civilization as a potentially positive event[14] because they don't believe industrial cultures can sufficiently transform to avoid irreparably damaging life on Earth. Some researchers see "earth religion" as "spiritually perceptive, humane, and ecologically beneficent,"[15] appreciating nature spirituality for its ability to expand human consciousness beyond the individual ego to global levels of awareness – and perhaps empathy – leading to changes in destructive behavior patterns, and these beneficent new behaviors can be encouraged as moral obligation or even sacred duty.[16]

He further senses that Dark Greens have a specific part to play in response to the climate crisis, especially through the emergence of a "terrapolitan earth religion"[17] promoted by various Earth summits, poets, indigenous spokespersons, scholars, and politicians such as Al Gore. These terrapolitans stress "ecological interdependence, an affective connection to the earth as home, and to nonhuman organisms as kin, and the overturning of anthropocentric hubris…because both biological and cultural diversity are highly valued as the fruits of evolution" leading to the emergence of a global, civic, earth religion.[18] Gaian Religion or Spirituality occupies an important niche in this process through promoting "feelings of belonging to place" which can lead to widespread transformations accommodating a global, rather than fragmented, limited, or provincial, worldview.[19] In turn, spirituality itself widens horizontally toward greater inclusion (and thus compassion) and deepens vertically toward greater experiential and intellectual understanding, further defining, for instance, the meaning of *God* and *Spirit*.

Beyond planet-worship, NeoPagans seek to revive selected ancient and medieval beliefs, rituals, and values as experienced and practiced by pre-Christian indigenous folk, and as applied to – or even stimulated by – the environmental crisis of the 21st century,[20] and which celebrates the fusion of Ecos and Spiritus as an already happily mated couple through nature-centric praxis and worldview. Many contemporary Pagans perceive a powerful presence in nature inherent in the living energies of forests, mountains, deserts, and oceans, which is also familiar to many in Native American traditions. This power-in-nature, when one is properly attuned to it, through ritual or other means, becomes accessible for a variety of purposes, for instance to heal or transform, a process often called *magick*.[21] However, unlike aboriginal tribal spiritualities, NeoPaganism has emerged in modernity, so it possesses awareness older groups may have only recently attained: the wholeness of the planet Earth. Their spirituality, then, can possess a genuine planetary consciousness and ethos.[22]

Beyond Nostalgia

Most religions derive their core beliefs and practices from a past of miraculous events and mystical avatars. Their rituals, holy days, taboos, and mysticism emerge from ancient wisdom viewed as no longer fully extant in the present, enchanting antiquity with mythic wonder and time-sensitive holiness. Some of their power thus derives from drawing this sacred past into the mundane present, bathing their adherents in the glow of that special, unrepeated moment or era when the religion began. The problem with this isn't that the past has no wisdom to offer, but that religions have consigned spirit to the repetition of institutionalized nostalgia, passively leaving the future of Earth in the hands of divine destiny or fate.

Similarly, dark greens and NeoPagans flourish on romanticized memories of the past and are often populated by idealistic reactionaries responding to the evolutionary progress of civilization, whom philosopher Ken Wilber calls 'retro-Romantics'.[23] Bron Taylor also cautions that Dark Green religions may "reject Enlightenment rationality in favor of a romantic, agrarian ideal"[24] which indulges regressive tendencies in those who reject aspects of modernity. In actuality, all religions, regardless of how romanticized, have constantly adapted to changing eras, more or less, and are subject to evolution, regardless of how infinite, eternal, and unchanging their theological claims. Perhaps ageless and perennial wisdom exists, but as soon as it interfaces with humanity, it becomes limited and mutable.

Further, nature religions and dark green philosophies are themselves products of modern civilization and its relative *pax terrana*, utilizing contemporary innovations such as modern medicine, global communication, hygiene, clothing, food, and digital devices to enhance and perpetuate their theologies, ironically driving internal combustion cars to ecotheology seminars and flying to climate change conferences. Only indigenous tribes, back-to-the-land communards, and Old Order Amish actually live technologically regressive lives, and even they enjoy the fruits of modernity to some extent. A few new religious movements, for instance The Church of All Worlds, have developed theologies of the future, but they remain rare and diminutive.[25] Such a religion would draw its ethics and vision from an idealized future where humanity has evolved beyond the need for violence, and has advanced in the areas of healing, interconnectivity, and world-centric morality to extraordinary degrees of efficiency and effectiveness, attempting, by their beliefs and behaviors, to draw that future into the present.

On the other hand, there are ecology-minded thinkers who accept a compromise position wherein nature and industrial civilization can co-exist, often through technological innovation. In a 2014 *Scientific American* article "Can Humans and Nature Coexist?" the author, Gayathri Vaidyanathan, discusses a new breed of conservationists willing to allow some species extinctions and who speak of "a future where nature and humans co-prosper" – with desalinization plants, industrial agriculture, and nuclear power plants included. "The fixes would allow humans to prosper in cities using fewer natural resources. Our civilizations would, in effect, be 'decoupled' – at least in limited form – from nature, and the wilds would creep back into abandoned countrysides."[26] According to the author, separating from nature, at least to some degree, will determine the extent of nature left to nonhumans over subsequent centuries. Such a withdrawal from nature can occur along with economic prosperity by concentrating into dense megalopolises, using fewer natural resources, and aided by increased efficiency in almost every sector of life. In other words, economics separates from resource consumption into a more-or-less closed system, what Ernest Callenbach in his novel *Ecotopia* called a "steady-state."

Such technologically friendly visions often form the basis of *bright green environmentalism,* the philosophy that seeks solutions through technical and civilizational processes; in other words, the belief that "the convergence of technological change and social innovation provides the most successful path to sustainable development."[27] Popularized by writer Alex Steffen, bright greens promote zero-carbon energy, dense urban settlements, total recycling, innovation, regulation, and personal responsibility to create radical changes in world systems such as politics and economics. The movement emphasizes proactive "tools, models, and ideas" rather than the problems and limitations to be overcome, and seeks to energize confidence for constructive solutions rather than repeating bleak prophesies of doom. The web site of Central Piedmont Community College contains a descriptive section on various types of Green Environmentalism:

> In its simplest form, bright green environmentalism is a belief that sustainable innovation is the best path to lasting prosperity, and that any vision of sustainability which does not offer prosperity and well-being will not succeed. It's the belief that for the future to be green, it must also be bright. Bright green environmentalism is a call to use innovation, design, urban revitalization, and entrepreneurial zeal to transform the systems that support our lives.[28]

In addition to such articles and ideologies, E. O. Wilson's 2016 book *Half Earth* suggests that humankind, through some herculean global effort, put aside into perpetuity at least half of the planet's landmass for untouched wilderness, so that evolutionary processes may continue on their life-sustaining course. Such a radical idea can only manifest with a radically different worldview wherein we treat Earth with a level of respect impossible for most of us in the early 21st century to imagine, much less bring to fruition. Again, this will require not simply better technology, but better *people*. Later, I will try to show that better people is exactly where we're headed, that evolution pushes us into a more sustainable future, and that environmental crises can be averted by literally building *up*.

Bio-Cultural Evolution

For the most part, I see nostalgia as useless or even harmful. The past should not be seen as an idyllic destination to which humanity should return or repetitively reference because evolution has brought us modern civilization and its relative peace and security. To state that life in the past was nasty, brutish, and short belies the true suffering and violence of previous eras. In Steven Pinker's *The Better Angels of Our Nature*[29] the author suggests in exhaustive detail that contemporary modernity can lay claim to being the safest and least violent period in human history, when centralized government, trade, and negotiation frequently replace homicide and warfare. These are all characteristics of what Pinker calls "The Civilizing Process."[30] His idea is to continue the meta-pattern of advancement, not regress to earlier and more comfortingly familiar forms that may well bring with them old habits of hardship, suffering, and sorrow.

Pinker traces the decline of violence through time and across civilizations, noting that in the state of nature, "survival machines callously exploit other survival machines" in brutal fashion[31] with the implication that as long as humans were 'natural' they tended to partake in the ferocious struggle for survival; however, our species appears hardwired for urbanization, with its tendencies toward cooperation, self-control, literacy, diversity, and accompanying reductions in vicious behavior. Along with Enlightenment rationality, individual sovereignty, centralized arbiters, global trade, feminism, and technological innovation, civilized life usually means departure from the warfare, revenge killings, and casual cruelties prevalent in previous eras.

Pinker divides this bio-cultural evolution[32] into "empathy-altruism" and "perspective-sympathy"[33] within a "non-random direction of history"[34] leading logically to social progress and revealing evolution's trajectory as directional change away from entropy towards greater complexity and adaptation. Humanity appears to be moving in developmental increments through progressive stages or levels of growth, specifically to greater conscious awareness roughly analogous in the global macro to lifespan maturation in the micro, expanding the circle of valuation to global levels.[35] Referring to Peter Singer's ideas about such expansion as an escalator leading inevitably upward, Pinker states: "A broader effect of the escalator of reason, albeit one with many stalls, reversals, and holdouts, is the movement away from tribalism, authority, and purity in moral systems and toward humanism, classical liberalism, autonomy and human rights"[36] in a value system "which privileges human flourishing as the ultimate good."[37]

Bio-cultural evolution, which is really collective individual evolution, leads to social progress, which for Pinker means a gradual decline in violence through an expanding circle of sympathy, an expansion that follows, and allows for the increase of, urbanization.

> Suppose that living in a more cosmopolitan society, one that puts us in contact with a diverse sample of other people and invites us to take their points of view, changes our emotional response to their well-being. Imagine taking this change to its logical conclusion: our own well-being and theirs have become so intermingled that we literally love our enemies and feel their pain. Our potential adversary's payoffs would simply be summed with our own (and vice versa), and pacifism would become overwhelmingly preferable to aggression.[38]

Although the author does not anticipate such events occurring any time soon, he does view it as a reasonable extrapolation of historical trends. In other words, it is a rational guess based on a meta-analysis of historical changes over thousands of years in which a pattern moves from lack of empathy to empathy and therefore from violence to stability and harmony, and that this is a natural function and result of evolution. The effect of time on cultures pulls them away from nature into artificiality, and yet we need nature to exist because we're still biological creatures.

Being 'natural' puts humanity into states prior to cosmopolitanism. For example, I would argue primordial humans had a parent-child relationship with their environment in which 'Mother Nature' both sustained and destroyed life in a self-perpetuating cycle, and we, her children, learned the whims of our Mother in order to flourish, the same as every other animal. Human history, however, does not end in this 'natural' state but continues through processes wherein humanity moves away from direct nature-dependence, becoming increasingly 'un-natural,' a progression which creates the 'artificial' environment most conducive to human survival and flourishing, unfortunately at the cost of non-human habitat. We act just as other animals act: for the benefit of our own species, and thus, I argue, our modifications of the planet are, in fact, utterly natural.

Several attempts have been made at systemization and graphic representation of human evolutionary development. Don Beck's *Spiral Dynamics*, for instance, offers a 3-D system of stages for human development stretching from the Instinctive stage 100,000 years ago, through Magical, Power, Traditional, Rational, Pluralistic, Holistic, and Holarchical stages, serving as one way to encode this maturation process.[39] Another example is Ken Wilber's "Egocentric, Ethnocentric, and Worldcentric" model, charting expanding circles of compassion, care, and consciousness "unfolding from body to mind to spirit" and divided into three domains: the physiosphere (matter), the biosphere (life), and the noosphere (mind).[40]

In the history of civilization, evolution drives circles of inclusion, agency, and equality to expand, increasing in size and scope over time, until in the early 21st Century it includes, for many, the whole world in an empathic matrix which may constitute the early stages of Teilhard de Chardin's orthogenic *Noosphere*, Earth's "thinking envelope" and leading to his "Omega Point" singularity.[41] Digital technologies aid this process by creating global networks of communication, transportation, and energy more or less unifying the planet and establishing historically unprecedented interconnectedness which, barring environmental collapse, promises greater interconnectivity in the future.

This natural result of evolution's powerful guiding force is more fully explored in Jeremy Rifkin's 2009 tome *The Empathic Civilization* as five stages of human consciousness: oral--mythological, script--theological, print--ideological, electronic--psychological, and empathic--biospheric. For Rifkin, the human journey has passed through phases of communications and conscious-awareness regimes, logically leading to our current civilizations and its concomitant requirements for greater empathic compassion.

> At the same time, the urbanization of human life, with its complex infrastructure and operations, has led to greater density of population, more differentiation and individuation, an ever more developed sense of selfhood, more exposure to diverse others, and an extension of the empathic bond.[42]

Along with evolutionary empathy, a pattern exists wherein complex human systems, such as civilizations, experience energy flow-through, which keeps them in a constant state of flux, resulting in either collapse or reorganization; in the latter, the new structure exhibits a higher order of complexity and integration than the former. As systems evolve and grow, they overlap, mingle, and diversify, increasing the ability of an individual to see their own struggles in others and expand empathic awareness.

For Rifkin, unlike Pinker, spirituality must be included in the process as integral to nurturing empathy; as he states, "Spirituality is a deeply personal journey of discovery in which embodied experience – as a general rule – becomes the guide to making connections, and empathy becomes the means to foster transcendence."[43] He also sees religion replaced by spirituality, which he calls "the very individual quest to find meaning in the broader cosmic scheme of things."[44] Combining evolution's course towards greater empathy, spirituality's transcendence and qualities of subjective meaning, and increased urbanization allow humanity to morph into new forms of social life, so that for the first time in history we begin thinking of the humanity as one extended family.

The evolutionary journey towards empathy results in a planetary 'near-climax' culture in steady-state symbiosis which breaks the entropy-empathy paradox and, through the internet and its progeny, transforms the world into a giant global public square and leads to a global 'brain' of which we are all an integral and simultaneously independent part. As new distributive and sustainable energy sources combine with the emerging biotic consciousness, humanity may "extend the empathic embrace while lowering the entropic bill. This would bring the human race to the cusp of biosphere conscious in a 'climax global economy' through stages mythological, theological, ideological, psychological, and dramaturgical stages of collective consciousness. At this point, he sees ethical behavior for the vast majority of people as a given.

The new bottom-up continentalization and globalization allow us to complete the task of connecting the human race and opens up the possibility of extending the empathic sensibility to our species as a whole, as well as to the many other species that make up the life of the planet.

Bio-cultural evolutionary ethics becomes personal: not simply an ethical prerogative but an essential moral imperative, and the experienced form of this global ethical morality emerges from Deep Empathy – the mystical and intellectual pursuit of an active relationship with Gaia through practices such as somatic therapy, meditation, intense prayer, nature-centered rituals, psychedelics, and other forms of planetary communion, with possibilities of real inter-connectivity and communication in the language of ecospiritual empathy, the probably hard-wired capacity to *know* (bio-gnosis) the feelings of the Other, even if that Other is the planet.

The Evolution of Consciousness

One of the gifts Charles Darwin gave the world was the simple idea that biological forms change over time. He offered the theory that the world is not static but dynamic, changing, *evolving*. Evolution implies that life modifies over time and that it modifies in specific ways designed to maximize survival. That is, life moves through time and becomes more complex and sophisticated so that living beings are able to adapt to changes in the Earth. Dinosaurs didn't survive, we presume, because they weren't able to adapt to the sudden climate shift that ended the Cretaceous period,[45] but small mammals did survive and adapt – and that's why mammals are with us today in such spectacular variation. The world seems made so that time acts as an agent of advancement along a specific line of development. For instance, humans are born as helpless babies, but most of us grow, experience, and learn, becoming beings that are more complex. Life itself has changed over eons from single-celled organisms billions of years ago to more complicated life forms like us. Complexity and adaptability are signs of evolution at work.

In other words, it can be argued that to evolve means that we become more complex (able to understand and do more) and sophisticated (possess more experience, knowledge). The human mind, emotions, and conscious self-awareness also evolve; they grow, advance, and mature in what appears to be a relatively constant direction: away from ignorance, immaturity, and unconscious behaviors towards wisdom, maturity, and self-awareness.

In the 1920s and 30s, French Jesuit priest, paleontologist, and visionary Pierre Teilhard de Chardin began applying Darwin's dynamic evolutionary theories to spirituality. First, he described the grand unfolding of the cosmos, from primordial origins and the advent of life and humankind to the development of the *noosphere* (the "thinking envelope" of consciousness). Just as the biosphere and atmosphere evolved to support life, so the noosphere is currently developing as an energetic layer of human thought covering Earth like a net with the potential to unite humanity as one family. In addition, Teilhard proposed his Law of Complexity-Consciousness, which relies on two principles:

- Through time there has been an evolutionary tendency for all matter to unite and become increasingly complex in nature
- With each increase in material complexity, there is a related rise in the consciousness of matter and a greater urge to unite[46]

In the 1950s, he envisioned the noosphere developing until all minds would be connected and all information instantly available to anyone on the planet. For this reason, he has been called the spiritual father of the internet. He also saw the noosphere preparing the way for the *soulosphere* where all hearts are psychically connected. In other words, Earth evolved humans, who are in turn integral to the creation of the noosphere, with implications that Earth itself is an organism just awakening to its own evolutionary potential. For Teilhard, Creation is being pulled along in a process called *orthogenesis*[47] towards a moment of global enlightenment that will end the chaos and turmoil of human history at a final step in evolution called the *omega point*,[48] beyond which lies a paradisiacal new world inspired by the Biblical New Jerusalem.

Not only does the physical world directionally evolve,

human consciousness does also, and because of the link between consciousness and spirit, spirituality seems to be evolving dynamically and directionally as well. When we heighten and deepen our consciousness, it affects the part of our spirits that expand on the vertical axis of the cross, with or without supernaturalism. Thus, we hitch our star to a greater whole that 'knows' more than we know and guides us to our highest good. Bio-cultural, conscious, and 'spiritual' evolution can be a source of hope, optimism, and energy to which we can hitch our visions. On this path, human cultural development continues, despite periodic setbacks and crises, in a wobbly path towards collective maturation, with its attendant compassionate engagement with ever-wider circles of inclusion, under evolutionary pressures apparently meant to maximize the survival potential for Homo sapiens. If we are to have faith, perhaps it should be in the natural processes of change and growth that we can perceive and utilize.

Chapter 2

Ecospiritual Visionaries

A 2008 article in *Kosmos* magazine entitled "Evolution Toward Global Cooperation" discusses the cumulative power of bio-cultural evolution in steering humanity towards its highest ideals.[1] The essay suggests global cooperation is a natural function of organic development, inevitably beguiling us away from tribal conflict towards planetary peace and sustainability. Spurred by global problems not solvable by any single nation, the author believes this worldview has the potential to "energize and motivate us to fulfill our evolutionary destiny of global cooperation."[2]

I believe visionary individuals and groups have labored throughout history, usually in relative obscurity, to urge and support humankind towards this cooperative future. A unique, often disregarded (or even persecuted) segment of a given population will coalesce into an alternative to the old mainstream majority worldview, either in the form of an individual (like prophets or social leaders) or as collective bodies (as in self-identified movements) consciously or unconsciously shifting socio-cultural paradigms. This hidden minority has gone by many names in the past, but all have been 'ahead' of their time and thus made contributions to the evolution of human consciousness by pulling us along, sometimes kicking and screaming, toward a positive destiny. Individual visionaries capture our imagination because they seem to anticipate later social or technical developments,[3] but it's the *groups* we'll concentrate on – those collective efforts that have begun to increase in number and influence as the 21st century unfolds.

Beatniks, Hippies, New Agers, Aquarian Conspirators, and Cultural Creatives are some of the names of these small but influential population segments subtly influencing humanity. These minorities can be seen at Green Party meetings, in Non-Governmental Organizations, supporting the United Nations, signing the Earth Charter,[4] teaching at progressive charter schools, marching for peace, shopping for natural products at farmers' markets, running organic farms and eco-friendly businesses, and in hundreds of other roles that seem unrelated but are really instances of the same effort to nourish a eutopian[5] future through peace, environmental, and social justice activism.

The following writers of the 20th and early 21st centuries identified these special groups, tracing the progress of emergent evolution by examining visionaries as a single, but usually unorganized, phenomenon. Presented in chronological order, each author peered at the emerging eco-spiritual and bio-cultural evolution community from a slightly different angle, illuminating it in unique ways, and each contributed to the burgeoning worldview and ethos by making apparent the interconnections of spirituality and Earth. These make up the cultural contexts for, and influences on, the Church of All Worlds. Spanning 40 years from the 1970s to the 2000s and focusing on North America, each book describes the ideals of millions of people all pushing or pulling in the same direction, evidently motivated by similar inspired visions.

Charles Reich – *The Greening of America*

As an American legal scholar and Yale professor, Dr. Reich observed the convulsions of the 1960s and sought to place them in their larger historical and socio-cultural context: recognizing radical events as tectonic shifts creating waves of change rippling through society. The first Earth Day in 1970 resulted from a slow awakening of holistic consciousness by the first generation of 'Terrans' raised on Star Trek, psychedelics, peace marches, yoga, and rock. An ethic of innovation advanced fresh perspectives and deep revolutions that were amplified, if not initiated, during the 60s.

Although the book was written in 1970, its sentiments are universally applicable. The roots of what the author calls the "American crisis" remain pertinent across generations and are of concern to all the authors in this section:

"Disorder, corruption, hypocrisy, war"

Lawlessness, whether violence, corporate greed, or political dishonesty, eats at the foundation of any republic, slowly eroding democracy, undermining social justice, and encouraging an atmosphere of evasion, self-deception, and indifference.

"Poverty, distorted priorities, and law-making by private power"

Drastic inequalities caused by systemic social arrangements result in skewed priorities wherein corporate CEOs earn millions while workers are denied basic healthcare. Oligarchic concentrations of power ensure little progress is made to address these inequalities.

"Uncontrolled technology and the destruction of the environment"

Perhaps no current issue has the far-reaching implications of ecological degradation and climate change. Although postmodern technology holds part of the answer, the will to implement clearly falters. Without a viable environment to support our endless debates, the debates themselves are moot.

"Decline of democracy and liberty; powerlessness"

Reich's first sentence proves timely: "The Constitution and Bill of Rights have been weakened, imperceptibly but steadily." I would only take issue with "imperceptibly" because the weakening has become blatant, with the consequences manifesting as imperial presidencies and a declining sense of public agency.

"The artificiality of work and culture"
Pop culture reigns iconic, accompanied by a profound lack of deeper meaning in life. Satisfying work, healthy play, service to others – all are affected by the shallow confines of commercialized herd mentality. Food remains over-processed, entertainment an opiate, and important issues trivialized while trivia assumes unearned significance.

"Absence of community"
Isolation and alienation create a semi-anesthetized populace plagued by emotional illness that compounds violence, loneliness, despair, and disregard for others. Relationships remain dogged by artificial gender expectations and the fruitless search for perfection, and the family is either mummified in some anachronistic nuclear form or severed by egoistic disputes.

"Loss of self"
Educational systems, job descriptions, and social restrictions continue to strip us of real personhood. True individual authenticity remains difficult to manifest as mass communication and unconscious assumptions splinter the personality and repress instinct, feeling, and spontaneity, further truncating wholeness, creativity, innovation, and activism.[6]

If these are the problems, what solution does Reich propose? The answer he offers is the *ascent of consciousness*. He first categorizes consciousness into three levels of advancement. Consciousness I, which he calls "loss of reality," begins with the freedom of the American frontier, liberating individual creativity and ambition from old social constraints, but ends with culpable innocence.

> Today [Consciousness I] still sees America as if it were a country of small towns and simple virtues. Invention, machinery, and production are the equivalent of progress; material success is the road to happiness; nature is beautiful but must be conquered and put to use. Competition is the law of nature and man; life is a harsh pursuit of individual self-interest.[7]

Consciousness I insists that everyone live in a less complex past and that success, defined mostly in materialistic (or religious) terms, comes through morality, hard work, and self-denial. It doesn't recognize that, for the most part, individuals have subsumed themselves to organizations, that social problems are not exclusively due to personal character, or that government may have a significant part in dealing with national issues. In other words, it's out of touch with the reality experienced by a significant majority of (especially urban) people.

Consciousness II, on the other hand, is the creator of the Corporate State. At its zenith, it deals a fatal blow to old class ranks and agrarian limitations. It successfully raises the individual to new heights of value, honoring plurality and articulating basic rights and freedoms. However, it also develops the 'organizational man'[8] through the industrial revolution and capitalist companies that have morphed into multinational corporate conglomerates.

> To [Consciousness II], what the reality of the times seemed to demand was the organization and coordination of activity; the arrangement of things in a rational hierarchy of authority and responsibility, the dedication of each individual to training, work, and goals beyond himself. This seemed a matter of utmost biological necessity.[9]

The machine mentality means that a person adapts himself to

the imperatives of the technological state, subsuming the self not to class hierarchies and tradition but to corporate caste-system employment, mass entertainment and conformity, and arbitrary governmental proscription. Life's meaning thus derives from the function performed for society and the satisfaction derived from a job and its compensations. This 'meaning gap' gets filled by material accumulation and conspicuous consumerism, continuing the corporate economic cycle. However, Consciousness II is also committed to social reform, which explains social security, civil rights legislation, identity politics, environmental regulations, and other programs – but again, this often reflects a herd mentality where the truly innovative reformer is vilified until a large enough percentage of the populace support their cause and it can slip into 'newest fad' status. Material prosperity is paramount, and almost everyone has more stuff than his or her parents do, but are we happier?

Consciousness III, the level that Reich suggests we are moving into and must assertively continue towards, addresses first the restoration of the self. Having been lost in social hierarchy and mercantile interests, our selfhoods must be reclaimed away from forces outside us. The true self must be liberated from the tension, fear, and rigidity encouraged by exterior sources such as media anxiety-mongering, purposeless governmental constraints, and corporate-driven consumerist obsessions. With the "self-destruction of the Machine," the author sees the third level asserting itself in moves toward personal authenticity, voluntary collective efforts for the common good, lifestyle simplification, careful and directed use of money and technology, environmental activism, sane law-making, organic livelihood, and a more holistic worldview.

New generational shifts tend to correct the extremes of the Corporate State. Inner self-knowledge guides each person to genuine lives and legitimate choices concerning work, association, activism, and play. Ever cautious of over-intellectualization,

Reich describes the foundation of Consciousness III as *liberation*.

> It comes into being the moment the individual frees himself from automatic acceptance of the imperatives of society and the false consciousness which society imposes. For example, the individual no longer accepts unthinkingly the personal goals proposed by society; a change of personal goals is one of the first and most basic elements of Consciousness III. The meaning of liberation is that the individual is free to build his own philosophy and values, his own lifestyle, and his own culture from a new beginning.[10]

Personal liberation, which was a major theme in the subsequent decade of the 1970s, provides the sturdy roots of ascension: the authentic self must be firmly established and loyally followed in all matters. Reich claims that this is not a selfish ego trip, but rather a "radical subjectivity designed to find genuine values in a world whose official values are false and distorted."

> It is not egocentricity but honesty, wholeness, genuineness in all things. It starts from the self because human life is found as individual units, not as corporations and institutions; its intent is to start from life.[11]

Every person's life matters and possesses value apart from its usefulness to the state or society, each individual is free to choose the form and content of her life, and each human enjoys the right to full agency even if she disavows competition, antagonism, or conformity. Personal boundaries are more fluid, easygoing, and communal. Diversity becomes a source of richness and celebration. Manipulation and coercion lose their allure, dishonesty declines, and artistic enjoyment flourishes.

Consciousness III invites full participation in the socio-political realm along with enthusiasm, joy, and hope applied to all interests. It's unimpressed with title, power, or authority, judging everyone and every act according to ethical standards of freedom, personal responsibility, and peacefulness. It's not afraid of alternative consciousness or expressing love in deeply meaningful ways. But most of all, it proposes radical reprioritizations that will transform society.

> We must no longer depend wholly upon political or legal activism, upon structural change, upon liberal or even radical assaults on existing power. Such methods, used exclusively, are certain to fail. The only plan that will succeed is one that will be greeted by most social activists with disbelief and disparagement, yet it is entirely realistic – the only means that is realistic, given the nature of the contemporary State: revolution by consciousness.[12]

First, Reich says, we must admit that decades of liberal and radical struggles have not saved us from a world of chaos, violence, and self-destruction. Although many strides have been made, we still find ourselves with serious social and environmental issues that have not been solved because the changes that have occurred have all been within certain accepted parameters of the existing system that never allows any real progress. The 'military-industrial complex,' corporate citizenship, two-party political system, and even the deeply held assumptions of civilization – all are transformable.

> Consciousness is capable of changing and of destroying the Corporate State, without violence, without seizure of political power, without overthrow of any existing group of people... The crucial fact to realize about all the powerful machinery of the Corporate State – its laws, structure, and political system – is that it possesses no mind. All that is needed to bring about change is to capture its controls – and they are held by

> nobody. It is not a case for revolution. It is a case for filling a void, for supplying a mind where none exists.[13]

In other words, by reclaiming our authentic personhood, we reevaluate our daily actions and decisions, changing them according to the needs of a new century. Along the way, we can inject into the present system these new memes and watch as the old structures that seemed impervious gradually transfigure. The new consciousness offers the heart, soul, and mind lacking in the old. All that's missing is the will, which may be provided thanks to a degrading environment and increasingly impotent social systems. It's not a generational thing, for we all have to live within the limitations of the natural world around us, but it *is* divided between those who get it and want to live and those who don't care or choose to remain alienated. None of the present institutions or structures can be sufficient for the task, but what *will* suffice cannot yet be fully imagined.

Finally, the new consciousness seeks nothing less than the "restoration of the non-material elements of humanity's existence, elements like the natural environment and spirituality that were passed by in the rush of material development."[14] The immanent and transcendent spirit, dismissed by secular humanists and imprisoned by religious exclusivists, forms the leaves of the tree, soaking up the sunshine and turning it into energy. Through a decidedly mytho-poetic worldview and profound mysticism, the greening of America finds its early seedlings in the basic laws on which Consciousness III community rests.

- Respect for each individual, for his uniqueness, and for his privacy
- Abstention from coercion or violence against any individual, abstention from killing or war
- Respect for the natural environment
- Respect for beauty in all its forms

- Honesty in all personal relations
- Equality of status between all individuals, so that no one is 'superior' or 'inferior'
- Genuine democracy in the making of decisions, freedom of expression, and conscience[15]

In addition, individuality is protected because, as the author writes, "the Consciousness III community is based on organic principles, not on identity."

> Nature is an organic community; its different elements and inhabitants do not resemble each other, they carry out very different functions and they rarely communicate, yet they all contribute to each other and depend upon each other.[16]

Corollary to this is the sentiment of "species solidarity" or the feeling of togetherness. Nature teaches us that interdependence is the fact of all life, and that empathic interconnection allows for prosperity of all living things. The relationship to Earth reappears continually in the dialogue and behaviors of visionaries because it lies at the root of many other issues being confronted. The war against nature correlates to our wars with each other and vice versa. We must mimic planetary life insofar as we "contribute to each other and depend upon each other."

Part of the spiritual element of Consciousness III involves the unflinching acknowledgement of love in our lives and in the universe. Difficult as it may be to define or fully comprehend, love lies at the heart-core of every other issue in human existence. But love is not only the feelings between two people; it lives in the community, the neo-tribal togetherness that modernity has devalued.

> Love is not given by one person to another as a sovereign act; love is discovered, it is generated, it is in the community and

not merely the product of each individual's will.[17]

Consciousness I and II attempt to filter reality through their lenses, causing beliefs and activities outside their embrace to appear weird, suspicious, or even dangerous. The point is that Consciousness III people form a distinct community, the vanguard of a new culture. This is the greening of America, and though some dismiss the excitement and hope of the 1960s and early 70s as youthful naiveté, the fact is this vision has survived and flourished, mostly under the radar of corporate media, growing and developing, unstoppable in its exuberant determination to lead humanity towards its brightest potential.

Marilyn Ferguson – *The Aquarian Conspiracy*

Manifested through the 1970s New Age movement,[18] the radical energy of the 60s develops into the deeper, nearly invisible community of "Aquarian conspirators" named for the 'Age of Aquarius,' an astrological period popularized in music, film, and counterculture lore. Ferguson, once editor of the *Brain/Mind Bulletin,* sees philosophical and behavioral patterns following similar lines of inquiry, and a vague sense of commonweal emerges based on shared values but scattered across disciplines and geography. The subtitle of her effort to explore the content and establish the perimeters of this movement is *"Personal and Social Transformation in the 1980s."* Looking at her present community as well as ahead to its future flowering, she sets out to track "the conspiracy" and ends up portraying a continuous phenomenon with a rich history. The book reads like another cannon-shot across the bow of what Reich called Consciousness I and II and opens again the gates to Consciousness III.

Ferguson observes a similar crisis in her decade as Reich did in his, with only a few differences, and her list of grievances remains just as pertinent, confirming how little real progress the old paradigms of liberalism, industrialism, and politics have made.

> Our crises show us the ways in which our institutions have betrayed nature. We have equated the good life with material consumption; we have dehumanized work and made it needlessly competitive, we are uneasy about our capacities for learning and teaching. Wildly expensive medical care has made little advance against chronic and catastrophic illness while becoming steadily more impersonal, more intrusive. Our government is complex and unresponsive; our social support system is breaking at every stress point.[19]

What is the answer to this recalcitrant crisis? Again, the visionary community, which seeks to heal the crisis and harmonize the future with our highest ideals, re-surfaces:

> A leaderless but powerful network is working to bring about radical change in the United States. Its members have broken with certain key elements of Western thought, and they may even have broken continuity with history.[20]

The new progressive collective finds itself even more deeply separated from the larger cultural context in which it subtly exists. It's also become more conscious of its own existence, especially as communication methods increase in scope and availability. Although pre-internet, the conspiracy begins to awaken and achieve self-awareness.

- It's not restricted by political affiliation, and often claims to be neither left nor right, but 'ahead'
- It seeks power only to disperse it.
- Its strategies are pragmatic (even scientific), but its voice is mystical

- It advocates no less than a new human agenda for civilization and beyond
- It is a new mind – the ascendance of a startling worldview that gathers into its framework breakthrough science and insights from earliest recorded thought[21]

Echoing Reich, Ferguson admits that historically "all efforts to remake society began by altering its outward form and organization" with the assumption that such alterations would produce harmony. However, whether capitalism or communism, democracy or dictatorship, nothing has worked. Only the deepest changes in the human psyche will serve. "The Aquarian Conspiracy is a different kind of revolution…it looks to the turnabout in consciousness of a critical number of individuals, enough to bring about a renewal of society."[22] A change in consciousness is again advocated as agent of real personal and cultural transformation.

Another way of naming this change is 'paradigm shift,' involving pre-existing but previously unknown principles that transcend, but don't necessarily replace, the old way of doing and seeing. It's an expansion of understanding, a widening and deepening of consciousness. A pattern repeats where one paradigm – feudalism, for instance – flourishes for a time, then gradually becomes outmoded as new ideas and techniques appear. Turbulence shutters through society as paradigms slowly shift, until a consensus allows the fresh perspective to dominate. Resistance usually arises as those heavily invested in the old ways attempt to thwart the new, but in the end, humanity's consciousness inevitably enlarges. We seem to be hardwired for it. Unlike the 60s, though, when most counterculture revolutionaries were easy to spot because of their clothes, hair, or rhetoric, Aquarian Conspirators are more hidden, forming networks, sharing insights and experiences, linking together in a project of hope.

Ferguson traces the history of this movement to medieval alchemists, Gnostics, cabalists, and hermetics, and to mystics like Meister Eckhart. Later, Blake, Emerson, Thoreau, and other Transcendentalists "rebelled against what seemed the dead, dry intellectualism of the day." They sought missing elements – the super-mind or 'Oversoul' – which exceeds ordinary thought. Continuing through the works of William James, Herman Hesse, H. G. Wells, Carl Jung, Alfred North Whitehead, and the seminal Pierre Teilhard de Chardin, the idea of an evolving and developing mind with its capacity for collective enlightenment gained adherents and historical depth. Other authors subsequently added their interpretations of the phenomenon: "Carl Rogers described the Emerging Man, Lewis Mumford the New Person...Jonas Salk said that humankind was moving into a new epoch,"[23] and Harvard Professor George Cabot Lodge notes,

> The United States is in the midst of a great transformation, comparable to the one that ended medievalism and shook its institutions to the ground...The old ideas and assumptions that once made our institutions legitimate are being eroded. They are slipping away in the face of a changing reality, being replaced by different ideas as yet ill-formed, contradictory, unsettling.[24]

Conspirators spread these "different ideas" across the country, planting new seeds for a "new reality." But they have, up to this point, been scientists and humanists. With the work of popular 70s writer Theodore Roszak, spirituality enters the picture more forcefully. He believes that "no politics could survive unless it did justice to the spiritual subversives, "the new society within the shell of the old." Ferguson thus begins the discussion of the often indescribable, awe-inspiring *experience*, which she describes as "transcendent, transpersonal, spiritual, altered, non-ordinary, or peak." These extraordinary experiences challenge normative cultural and perceptual reality, and when they are consciously articulated, people begin recognizing each other and creating an informal but mutually recognized whole.

The transformational process – that activity designed to stimulate the enlightenment experience – comes in multiple forms, including psychedelics, meditation, music, and of course, spiritual devotion. In the chapter "Spiritual Adventure: Connection to the Source," Ferguson reminds us that the transcendent goal remains unfulfilled until we connect with the higher, wider, deeper force that surrounds us, penetrates us, and holds forth a greater reality towards which to strive.

> A realm of exquisite order, intelligence, and creative potential begins to reveal itself. Meditation is now doing *us*. Reality breaks through into larger, richer spaces. Now it's not just a matter of seeing things differently but of seeing different things. Language fails, symbols fail. This territory is too unlike anything we have known...[25]

The "territory" can only be experienced, never fully described; so one aspiration of the Aquarian Conspiracy is relationship with the *Beyond* – the transcendent and transfiguring reality that can't be wholly known – an act regarded as revolutionary if it's outside the confines of established, organized religion. "Expanding consciousness is the riskiest enterprise on earth. We endanger the status quo. We endanger our comfort." The "transformation of the transformative process itself" begins with knowledge of things from the *inside*, a paradoxical wisdom born of stepping outside normal reality, touching an infinite and eternal presence, and returning to tell the tale. Such revolutionary mysticism often leads to commonweal with other mystics. "By radically altering one's values and perceptions of the world, mystical experience tends to create its own culture, one with wide membership and invisible borders."[26]

The search for meaning and transcendence from inner limitations can take the form of Western religion, but also of unorthodox, unconventional, and novel practices. Ferguson sees Conspirators moving away from Judaism and Christianity, wherein individuals shape themselves to fit the structure, and towards New Age spirituality, where individuals open themselves to the transcendent experience by whatever means succeeds. Some turn to Eastern philosophies and practices that more keenly pursue a direct connection to the transcendent, while others cultivate a personal practice by hybridizing several different systems together. The object is direct knowing of ultimate reality rather than mediated second-hand acquaintance with it. The spiritual adventure toward flow and wholeness means becoming (re)joined to the God within and accepting the non-linear and non-intellectualized truth that there is something more beyond the cosmos we think we know.

Ferguson concludes with thoughts on the "Whole-Earth Conspiracy" which, despite the failures of social programs, peace-making efforts, or political platforms, seems to bring each new generation just a bit closer to sustainability and spiritual maturity. The author doesn't suggest the Aquarian Conspiracy is the only way to proceed, however, reminding us that diversity and tolerance are hallmarks of the enlightened spirit.

> The Whole-Earth is a borderless country, a paradigm of humanity with room enough for outsiders and traditionalists, for all our ways of human knowing, for all the mysteries and all cultures.[27]

The Conspiracy is a global phenomenon, heedless of national boundaries or geographic remoteness. In the same way it ignores historical and cultural divisions, the Earth is being perceived as a whole, one planet on which we all travel through space and on which we depend for physical survival. Aquarians welcome opposing views, regarding dissimilarity as an opportunity for growth and the accumulation of experience an enrichment rather than an excuse for conflict or competition. The eyes open in awe, we look at the world around us, and everything seems new.

Unlike primal tribes whose cultures are relatively stable, Conspirators are restless, inquisitive, and dynamic, riding the stream of evolution like rafting a river. Sometimes there's white water and struggles against Jungian shadows to right the boat. Having survived a few rocky places, however, the river carries the raft towards constantly richer landscapes, with mystery and discovery around every bend. To sojourn to the new land, Aquarians must have faith in themselves, their fellow travelers, and in the buoyancy of the river itself. They look to each other with hope, authenticity, and empathy.

> And this may be the most important paradigm shift of all. *Individuals are learning to trust – and to communicate their change of mind.* Our most viable hope for a new world lies in asking whether a new world is possible. Our very question, our anxiety, says that we care. If we care, we can infer that others care, too.[28]

At its core, the Conspiracy concerns the heart and its capacity for compassion towards ourselves, others, and Earth. It also requires a conviction that progressive evolutionary cultural development is possible, even inevitable, and that Aquarian beliefs, values, and agendas support the developmental process. In some ways, this process mirrors the discoveries about the human brain and its capacity for growth and complexity. Ferguson proposes a connection between the individual mind and the larger collective that's globally emerging:

> The proliferating small groups and networks arising all over the world operate much like the coalitional networks

> in the human brain. Just as a few cells can set up a resonant effect in the brain, ordering the activity of the whole, these cooperating individuals can help create the coherence and order to crystallize a wider transformation.[29]

This suggests that Conspirators are part of a biological event in the human collective unconscious and that progressive movements are profoundly *natural* occurrences, hardwired into our species as developmental yearnings and instinctual self-preservation. If visionary minorities are products of evolution, then they function like atmospheric homeostasis, balancing out the extremes of human activity and pushing us towards maturity and happiness. Through transformational techniques and worldwide (inter)connection, the Aquarian Age slowly dawns for those ready to embrace its promises and responsibilities. These human agents of biological evolution have always been among us, a parallel society working in virtual secret to steer the world to the Promised Land:

> Over the centuries, those who envisioned a transformed society knew that relatively few shared their vision. Like Moses, they felt the breezes from a homeland they could see in the distance but not inhabit. Yet they urged others on to the possible future. Their dreams are our rich, unrealized history, the legacy that has always existed alongside our wars and folly.[30]

So, Ferguson offers the revelation that throughout history, along with all our failures and atrocities, a steadily growing number of people have envisioned and whenever possible enacted a biological imperative to influence the world towards higher consciousness and ethos. *The Aquarian Conspiracy* describes an emerging subculture exploring the future and its brilliant possibilities. Transformation moves from uncontrollable lightening to usable electricity, the nation-state morphs into planetary cooperative, consciousness widens, creativity deepens, and the awakening spreads to envelope the Earth.

William Irwin Thompson – *Pacific Shift*

Cultural historian and social philosopher Thompson examines a socio-cultural shift he perceives in North America, from what he calls the old *Atlantic* to emerging *Pacific* civilizations. Published in 1985, *Pacific Shift* theorizes that visionary movements alter the political, social, mythic, and psychological landscape. Shifts on this grand a scale, he believes, are reflected not in conscious awareness but at the level of myth-making and artistic interpretation. Like Ferguson, Thompson sees a long history of these tectonic realignments rippling through time, observable through interpretive painters, speculative writers, postmodern architects, avant-garde film-makers, and spiritualists.

> These imaginative individuals can recognize that transformations of history do not occur as events *in* history; they occur in myth. And so we should look to contemporary forms of mythology in art, philosophy, science fiction, and mysticism to see the recording of these meta-events that have been missed by the journalists of *Time* and *Die Zeit*.[31]

The shift moves on scales of such temporal and spatial magnitudes that only at the level of mythology and intuition can it be noticed and recorded – a minority of 'fringe-dwellers' labor at the edge of deep consciousness and meta-history, struggling to discern changes in patterns and the tremors of cultural transformation. Like Reich, Thompson advocates a "transformation of consciousness" as a prerequisite for and characteristic of the 'shifted' minority. The shift moves humanity from ego to *daimon*[32] – from the micro-view of personal gratification to a deeper, wider, macro-encompassing worldview. Humankind evolves outward, expanding its knowledge, experience, and wisdom in a biotic and spiritual process begun at Earth's genesis and hardwired into the universe. The history of this 'movement with many names' follows the contours of human growth, innovation, and advancement, continuing beyond modern industrialism, technology, and globalism, moving towards postmodernity and planetary consciousness.

For Thompson, the emerging world begins with ecology, the "home-word" enabling humanity to "return to Earth in a homeward direction and know it truly for the first time." With space travel comes photos of our planet, and we look back at our own home and can no longer deny its beauty, oneness, or fragile vulnerability. Having nowhere else to go, we must look inward and at each other, facing the truth of our demons and angels. Prisoners on Spaceship Earth and beset by the dark side of our nature, the near future at first appears grim.

> So there is no escaping it: religious warfare will continue, and the war against nature will continue. But religious warfare will continue to sicken humanity in disgust at the hysterical fanaticisms of zealots of all convictions, and the increasing poisoning of the earth will continue to sicken a generation for whom industrial civilization will not work...[33]

If the dire twins of violence and ecological destruction are the problems, what is Thompson's solution? The same one we have encountered: transformation of consciousness. The answer lies inexorably in the emergence of a new mind with the power to reconcile the illusion of opposites into an ethic of co-existence.

> In a polity that has the shape of opposites, an *enantiomorphic* polity, the prophetic wisdom of William Blake's 'In opposition is true friendship' will be finally understood politically and not just poetically. If one does have an appreciation of the

> phenomenology of opposites, in which we become what we hate, then a politics of compassion, as contrasted with a politics of violent conflict, begins to become a cultural possibility.[34]

Thompson maps the transformational "enantiomorphic"[35] territory by articulating a descriptive system, graphically resembling a mandala, in which apparent oppositions become energetically organizing polarities. These dualistic poles are described by Thompson through a system of correspondences.

- Two Modes of Existence: Chaos and Cosmos (dynamic change and fixed stability)
- Two Meditations on the Modes of Existence: Charisma and Routine (energy and receptivity)
- Four Faculties with Their Associated Tones of Consciousness: Daimon (Agape), Mind (Logos), Heart (Eros), and Body (Thanatos)
- Four Value Orientations: Conservative, Liberal, Radical, Reactionary

This system culminates in a graphic representation of human progression as moving cycles whose ultimate form is simultaneous and harmonious integration of all polarities. The author also traces the movement of the center of civilization (what he calls "cultural ecologies") from Riverine, to Mediterranean, to Atlantic, to the new Pacific. In the present ecology, Eastern mysticism meets Western science, and the "Pacific-Space" emergence brings with it specific values.

> As we move from a culture of competition, accumulation, and conflict in industrial civilization to cooperation, sharing, and co-evolution in a planetary ecology, we will be taking a step as important in our evolution as the movement

from animal to human.[37]

For Thompson, humanity gradually evolves from negative to positive behavior patterns and from provincial to planetary consciousness. The process occurs geographically and continues in the present as a steady but ongoing cumulative movement so profound that it's compared to the process of primates evolving into *homo*. The list contrasting the older cultural ecologies with the Pacific indicates the significance of the shift.

- From Print to Electronics
- From Ego defined by possessions to *Daimon* experienced as topological synchrony and diachronic performance
- From Civilization embodied in a world city to Planetary culture as participation in a moving process or network
- From Routinization through commerce and economics to Routinization through ecology and Gaian forms of 'planet management'
- From Creative disequilibrium and rapid change to Steady state and consolidation into form
- From Technological clutter and gigantic buildings and machines to Technological minimalism and miniaturization; technologies that mimic organic processes
- From Industrial nation-state to Enantiomorphic polity[38]

These changes reflect a movement from inorganic to organic, domination to cooperation, normative mechanization to individual values. The shift from industrial work, abstraction, and materialism to play, sensual consciousness, and an "unimaginable culture" represents the recognition of perennial wisdom adapted to, and adopted by, a new generation in their unique era personified by the Gaia mythos – the whole Earth concept preliminary to planetary consciousness. I believe Reich and Ferguson would agree the list of Thompson's Pacific shift is valid. The general contours of a 'shift in consciousness' are common in all the books of this section, a fact that suggests a certain level of synchronicity.

Thompson's new age will not be exactly academic or religious, regressive or revolutionary, but something wholly novel. There is a "dislocation of consciousness from civilization" towards a planetary consciousness within which democracy will give way to cooperative autonomy as more people internalize planet-wisdom and lose their taste for hierarchical governance and need for collective external restraint. The entrance to this new state of autonomy is an uneven affair arrived at by a small number of those placing their efforts and energies in this direction decades or even centuries before everyone else catches up. These pioneers are often considered charlatans or even lunatics during this interregnum.

The full manifestation of the political shift awaits a "political genius" on the order of Thomas Jefferson to emerge from the 21st century milieu who will assume the new style of cooperative leadership and "show how these ecological narratives are descriptive of a new kind of polity." Visions and sensibilities become social and political reality, and ideas of property-based commonwealth morph into realities of global-based commonweal. The basic rights of life, liberty, and happiness deepen in meaning and widen in scope to include environmental and social justice issues at the center of life itself. If industrial civilization produced the destructive power of pollution and nuclear weapons, something completely innovative will have to solve these problems, and the people entering this new land will have to be as fresh and original as the solutions. "The new planetary culture is not world-destroying materialism or world-denying mysticism," Thompson writes, but involves "loving stewardship of *this* earth." He concludes that "biological politics" is essentially different from politics derived from sociobiology or scientific socialism – meaning radically different than all the experiments of the past – be they communism, capitalism, theocracy, or any other program of centralized collectivization.

In *Pacific Shift*'s final chapter, "Gaia Politique," the author first submits that the living world cannot be replaced with, or even accurately described by, any human-made system. Nature is too complex for the reductive limitations of conceptualization. Second, the new edifice of civilization will be built not through thought alone, but by a synthesis: "a mystical spirituality incarnated in the context of aerospace and cybernetic technologies."[39] The future emerges as a mixture of mysticism and high tech. Intelligence remains important, but the intellect can instinctively reject what threatens the world as it's *known*. For some people, nothing actually exists outside what can be empirically confirmed, and if the realm of spirit lies beyond thought and observation, it will naturally be met with suspicion by those entrenched in a materialist worldview. It isn't that the mind should return to archaic forms of superstition, but it should leap forward – with humility for its limitations – through a Zen-like dropping away of body and mind (especially as concepts), allowing freedom for innovation, imagination, and spiritual fulfillment.

Gaia Politique is civilization with deep understanding of nature and an overriding commitment to peace and social justice, along with spirituality that is mystical, unifying, and planetary, born of the practice and devoted evolution of millions of people and groups. Thompson cautions that such depth of spirit is essential for the success of a compassionate and sustainable future. "Without these spiritual transformations of consciousness to balance the technological changes, the new planetary culture will indeed become a real Orwellian nightmare."[40] All these shifts are necessary in synchronous emergence to manifest the visions of a better, if never perfect, world, else the underlying unity degrade into just another normative standard enforced through violence until the bright visions die under the crushing weight of social conformity. The danger of planet-wide consciousness is that it can be manipulated and coerced into mob/herd mentality, a process painfully obvious throughout history.

Unlike the restless and impatient revolutions of the 1960s, however, the paradigm modifications described in *Pacific Shift* represent an organic process of evolution on the time scale of generations, with gradual advancement punctuated by occasional reversals, rather than an overnight insurrection. Thompson is cautiously optimistic about the potential for the evolution of consciousness and the place spirituality must play in its emergence.

> The revolution cannot come in time for us to quit our jobs or cancel our debts, and the end of the world cannot come in time to eliminate the mess we have made of history; nothing smaller than the earth is large enough to express this revelation and nothing smaller than this instant is vast enough to contain all the future that we need.[41]

As a New Age writer, Thompson finds solace in the grand scale of planetary transformation and the Zen moment containing eternity and infinity. Only these are substantial enough to provide the soil for the seeds of the future. Like the previous writers, spirituality provides an integral ingredient in the process of transformation, not in the form of competing religions, but as an ecology of spirit or "scientific spirituality"[42] which acknowledges the role of science (and thus the physical world) in spirit and the encompassing interconnection of all spiritual traditions in making up the whole. Religion will be transfigured by these new revelations, and the people who walk forward into this particular sunlight are the bioneer geologians of heaven on Earth, builders of the New Jerusalem through the alchemical group marriage of consciousness, divinity, and planetary embodiment.

William Irwin Thompson – *Beyond Religion*

Thompson co-founded the Lindisfarne Institute in Massachusetts to gather other travelers in a fellowship of exploration, and through his many books, he journeys into both the heart of our present era and into the soul of the future. To investigate his work is to plumb the depths of our historical moment and ride the waves of evolution outward into the unknown. I consider *Pacific Shift* a minor masterpiece of investigative scholarship into the seismic movement away from traditional Atlantic civilization (London and New York) to the Pacific Rim civilization (Los Angeles and Tokyo), which is as much a cultural and philosophical change as a geopolitical one.

One of Thompson's recent books is an 89-page dynamo titled *Beyond Religion*, with two subtitles: *The Cultural Evolution of the Sense of the Sacred* and *From Shamanism to Religion to Post-religious Spirituality*. It's the latter that got me thinking, even before I read a word, about what might evolve after religion. After all, religions are statistically declining, and the fastest growing category in the 2020 US Census was "spiritual but not religious," meaning "I'm a spiritual person without membership or participation in a particular religion." If this trend continues, the dominant territory will be "spirituality," and so describing this new land is of some interest.

"Spirituality" has traditionally been the domain of religions, and they've cornered the Spirit market for millennia, but as pluralism and freedom have opened up fresh possibilities and enticed us with new perspectives, religions as organized socio-cultural institutions have had to share space with upcoming forms of transcendence gathered by Thompson and others under the term "New Age," a category that combines re-discovered realms of the spirit such as Native American, NeoPagan, and Asian with more familiar Western esotericism. New Age spiritualities form part of the map Thompson explores.

Before he unfolds the map, however, he begins in Chapter

1 with a scathing assessment of the Catholic Church through memories of growing up in parochial schools and the subtle hints of pedophilic tendencies he observed in the priesthood. He suggests that the Church encourages this behavior by its very nature;[43] however, despite its failings, he thinks religion has had something important for humans: content to fill "the container of consciousness with a cosmology."[44] Whether you judge such cosmology, with its mythos and ethos, to be opiate or divine truth, the fact is that humans have been more obsessed with religious matters in the past than in the present, at least in the industrialized world. Certainly in Medieval Europe, the Church was a dominant force in society, with an exclusive hold on the minds and hearts of the populous, from peasant to king, through a combination of persuasion and coercion. In a way, we're still experiencing the hangover from the heady spiritual and temporal excesses that called for sectarian wars, sent "heretics" to the stake, caused the Protestant rebellion, and cast a pall over Christianity lasting, for many people, to this day. When our heads finally clear, what will the spiritual landscape look like?

Religion, by offering salvation but charging a person's soul for it, has been its own worst enemy, spreading dissention, self-righteous arrogance, and even violence across the globe. Yet, until recently, there was no real alternative worldview, and religion delivered on its promise of comfort and confidence to the masses whose lives were hellish anyway. The price seemed small for such a sense of certainty and wellbeing. It doesn't even matter the actual content, providing it satisfies primal needs of security, belonging, and direct or indirect transcendence. In other words, says Thompson, "Folks will believe in anything if it makes them feel better."[45] So, religion emerged out of our mutual need for (re)assurance and an antidote to the uncertainties of death. But now, for more and more of us, it is not enough.

If this seems harsh, and in many ways, it is, Thompson does not leave us without consciousness content for long. In Chapter

2, he charts religion's history from its roots in shamanism to its institutionalization as religion, and here he indulges in one of his core philosophies, with which I am by now familiar: the idea that human history unfolds through a series of developmental stages and cultural eras – long periods of time punctuated by (r)evolutionary shifts into 'higher' levels – that have a beginning, apex, and decline. This rhythmic, spiral nature of history nevertheless leads, through evolution, towards greater adaptability and complexity. Humans, in other words, advance with time as a species in the macro, just as they do individually in the micro.[46] With such an optimistic evolutionary model of history, typical of New Age thinkers, it's no wonder Thompson sees the best eventually occurring in nearly all human endeavors and affairs. And who's to say he's wrong?

Charles Cummings – *Eco-Spirituality*

One of the few books with *eco* and *spirit* in its title was written by Christian mystic and Trappist-Cistercian monk Charles Cummings, and displays a distinctly Catholic theological perspective on the subject, reflected in the introductory statement:

> This form of spirituality seeks and finds God in prayer, sacred scripture, and the sacraments, not only in loving service of the neighbor, but also in creation by reverencing life in all its diversity and non-living things in all their nobility as reflections of an all-wise and loving creator.[47]

These types of theological statements remind us that many religions contain within them seeds of potential ecospiritual values, and that cultivating those seeds may yet yield fruit. By equating creation with creator, the author strives to grant divine holiness, and therefore ultimate value, to nature. As he writes, "Non-living beings such as rivers and oceans, mountains and deserts, deserve their own measure of respect because they too reveal aspects of the divine. Each creature is a unique manifestation of the creator, a sacrament of the invisible God."[48]

Cummings' garden contains not just Biblical references, but also historical savvy; for instance, he writes that "The Cartesian-Newtonian paradigm has proved to be a path to ecological disaster; another paradigm is crucial for our survival in the environmental crisis we now confront."[49] Therefore, he critiques Enlightenment scientism as well as references supporting sacred text. Like several of our other writers, the author suggests an extension of the empathic circle:

> ...what is needed on the spiritual level is an expanded consciousness, a planetary consciousness. We need to stretch our consciousness from awareness of our personal or regional problems to include awareness of the planetary ecosystem on which we all depend.[50]

The author clearly expresses a modern planetary perspective along with his Biblical exegesis. If Christianity is to have anything relevant to say about environmental matters, it will be through the work of thinkers such as Cummings.

Devall and Sessions – *Deep Ecology*

The intimacy of Heaven and Earth is exactly what ecospirituality proposes, and the description of this synthesis begins with the articulation of value systems protecting the web of life as sacred. When Bill Devall and George Sessions wrote *Deep Ecology* in 1985, for example, their book added substantial philosophical grounding to the environmental movement because the authors recognize the place of spirituality in the larger effort to make peace with our physicality:

> For deep ecology, the study of our place in the Earth household

> includes the study of ourselves as part of the organic whole. Going beyond a narrowly materialist scientific understanding of reality, the spiritual and material aspects of reality fuse together…the search for deep ecological consciousness is the search for a more objective consciousness and state of being through an active deep questioning and meditative process and way of life.[51]

The two goals of deep ecology are "self-realization" which reaches beyond the isolated ego to a holistic, nature-inclusive state, and "bio-centric equality" which recognizes the rights of all beings and the value of all life. To achieve this wisdom, the spirit-consciousness must move beyond the self, transcending personal and cultural assumptions and boundaries. Humanity can thus become part of an "organic whole" and assume its place as member of the planetary family. "Ecological consciousness" allows humans to achieve global holism through an expansion of the size of our awareness, to the point where the planet and the individual consciousness are co-equal. Neither one subsumes the other, but both are partners towards the goal of accessing the deep wisdom and power of the planet itself – a relationship based on mutual respect and beneficence.

The three methods Devall and Sessions' advocate for reaching this "objective consciousness and state of being" are:

- active deep questioning
- the meditative process
- way of life

The first indicates that, as curious animals, humans have the ability and obligation to ask questions, not only about the world around but also about the culture in which we live. Deep questioning is about going to the heart of unconscious, unexamined, and unchallenged suppositions that form invisible boundaries and hidden taboos. Such constraints may have been useful in the past, but as humanity grows, the old boxes become too small and must be enlarged: adults are obviously too big for their baby clothes, and it would be ridiculous to try to wear them. So, too, evolution moves us towards greater consciousness, and the old ways become excessively binding, no longer appropriate for the new state of being. Questioning is the peaceful exploration and settlement of the new territory.

The second, "meditative process" suggests that even beyond the act of meditation itself, intuition, ongoing spiritual practice, and disciplined religious devotion are all part of transcending the self – growing beyond the present into the realization of new possibilities. Meditation means looking inward with an eye towards calming, centering, and grounding the 'monkey mind' that tends to jump endlessly around, worrying, considering, judging, and needlessly exhausting itself. Enlightenment is initiated by critically but compassionately admitting that there's room for improvement. The process itself is the journey to more peace, love, and enjoyment in one's life and the expression of those inner accomplishments in one's outward behavior. When we work for our own betterment, no matter how frustratingly involved or incomplete the task, we have already taken a step in our own, and thus our cultural, evolution.

The third, "way of life" relates to the step from knowing what we need to do to the act of actually doing it. The line between *theory-philosophy-knowing* and *application-activism-doing* can be difficult to cross; for example, a person may be a passionate life-long environmentalist but still drive a gasoline-powered car everywhere, fly airplanes, use toxic products, and eat pesticide-laden food – there remains a disconnect between what many of us *believe* and how most of us *consume* and *waste*. In the process of connecting the dots between local or global problems and our personal contributions to them, it's increasingly clear that our "way of life" needs serious examination and adjustment. We cannot merely talk about solutions; we must become part of them – active participants in the evolutionary advancement of our species. In hundreds of ways, from avoiding plastics to riding a bicycle, everyone makes a difference. Ecospiritual enlightenment is the mystical *eureka!* moment when one's awareness of deep connection with Earth and profound relationship with transcendent spirit crosses the line from reasoned thought, emotional depth, and empathic understanding, to dynamic action. Eco and Spirit combine to create an activist mode of enlightenment that bridges the threshold between what we know needs to be done and the act of changing our behavior in order to get it done.

Another way of viewing ecospirituality is in the development of empathic relationships between humanity and Earth. Thomas Berry (1914-2009), author, Catholic priest, and creator of the United Nations World Charter for Nature, writes eloquent visionary prose in conversation with the planet through a deep spiritual sensibility. He suggests that present circumstances demand a "new story" and an innovative cosmology, integrating experiential ecology and numinous eco-spirit.

> Empirical inquiry into the universe reveals that from its beginning in the galactic system to its Earthly expression in human consciousness the universe carries within itself a psychic-spiritual as well as physical-material dimension.[52]

Synthesis emerges from a commitment to both religious and scientific disciplines and to a courageous, often mystic experientialism, creating an integral vision of sequential transformations through the evolutionary urgency for self-transcendence. This is a new 'context of understanding,' an unprecedented Universe Story[53] that expands the context of reality and brings purpose to the active struggles for transcendent relationship and deep connection. If the physical universe carries within itself a "psychic-spiritual" dimension, then matter is suffused with spirit. In the middle ages, reality was often interpreted through a mythic Christian lens so that the 'music of the spheres' and angelic hosts abounded in the world. While not returning to that exact state, we can re-enchant the world of the future;[54] we can refocus our perceptions to include the psychic-spiritual. We can again find the common characteristics of an underlying unity between apparently unrelated elements in consciousness and the world.

> Within this context, all our human affairs – all professions, occupations, and activities – have their meaning precisely insofar as they enhance this emerging world of subjective intercommunion within the total range of reality. Within this context the scientific community and the religious community have a common basis.[55]

The divide between physical science and spiritual religion is false, a competitive conflict mitigated by a deep underlying universality.[56] With the expansion of consciousness, it often becomes clear that Spirit and Earth profoundly overlap and embrace each other. It begins with enlargement of the human psyche and the cultivation of global relationships, and ends with the realization of a trans-planetary consciousness and the fulfillment of the paradisiacal visions of a hundred religions. Most of all, the end of the shift cannot be described or known precisely because it is beyond what we can imagine; we don't yet have the colors on our pallet to paint the future – but we can begin the process of (re)imagining its general parameters.

Ray and Anderson – *The Cultural Creatives*

Sociologist Paul Ray and psychologist Sherry Anderson use various research studies involving more than 100,000 Americans over a 13-year period to reveal the fascinating story of the segment of the population they call the 'Cultural Creatives' (CCs). Published in 2000, *The Cultural Creatives: How 50 Million People are Changing the World* examines the visionary movement throughout the 1990s. Ray and Anderson strive to give form and face to what they consider a distinct and remarkable minority group, who are in reality the same type of people described by our prior authors in earlier decades, but more numerous and cumulatively influential. Optimistic in tone and evolutionary in scope, CCs are the direct decedents of Consciousness III pioneers, Aquarian Conspirators, Pacific Shifters, and Deep Ecologists. Sometimes they are the exact same people and sometimes new generations bearing similar energy.

The authors begin by envisioning a new country the size of France in the middle of North America – but basically invisible. This country is spread across the continent, appearing in every state, every community, and in various individuals without regard to socioeconomic, ethnic, religious, or regional background. It's invisible in the sense that the mainstream media does not recognize it, and its citizens are hardly known even to each other. They are called cultural creatives because "innovation by innovation, they are shaping a new kind of American culture for the twenty-first century."[57] The underlying values of this country include:

- serious ecological and planetary perspectives
- emphasis on relationships and women's point of view
- commitment to spirituality and psychological development
- disaffection with the large institutions of modern life, including both left and right in politics
- rejection of materialism and status display[58]

Ray and Anderson claim that since the 1960s, 26% of the adults in the US, currently about 50 million people, "have made a comprehensive shift in their worldview, values, and way of life – their *culture,* in short."[59] The authors consider this shift to be a major development in civilization, but the genesis of the movement was demure: in 1960 it's estimated that less than 5% of the populous would have fit the CC profile. Since then, their ascent has been rapid, spread dynamic, and effects substantive. Their influence is seen in calls for ecological sustainability, ethical business practices, holistic and organic food, alternative healing techniques, reduced material consumption, honest political service, and authentic relationships. The five CC areas most mentioned in the studies are environment, peace, social justice, personal fulfillment (without cost to others), and an altruistic sense of service. Inherent in these values is an awareness of the self as interdependent and interconnected with the global community and life in all its diversity. Perhaps as never before in history, this awareness fuels a social movement emerging biotically from within the human species. Ray and Anderson sum up the list of CC values as:

- authenticity
- engaged action and whole process learning
- idealism and activism
- globalism and ecology
- the importance of women
- altruism, self-actualization, and spirituality[60]

There's nothing new in this list, but the intensity and sheer numbers with which these values are pursued, the skill with which they're being developed, and the surprising 21st century forms they take indicate an unprecedented event in history. The notion of emergent and cumulative evolutionary progress lies at the center of the claim to exceptional heights and unexplored depths by visionaries in the present historical period.

CCs are the last of three categories the authors formulate to classify collective personality types and socio-political orientations. The first is the *Moderns*, who make up approximately half of the American population. Moderns constitute the dominant cultural category whose ideologies are reflected in the mainstream media such as *Time, Newsweek, The New York Times, The Wall Street Journal,* and CNN. Most Moderns are interested in, or at least use, technology (regardless of its environmental impact) and support the social, economic, and political status quo. They accept the commercialized urban-industrial world as normative, the assumptions of enlightenment rationality as self-evident, and science as holder of life's deepest answers. According to the authors, many Moderns also share an emphasis on:

- making and having money
- climbing the latter of material success
- being stylish and up-to-date
- having lots of choices
- supporting economic and technological progress
- rejecting the values and concerns of native, rural, and spiritually mystic people
- media entertainment
- big business and/or big government
- intellectual analysis as the best way to explain reality and solve problems[61]

Not all Moderns conform to all these characteristics but most accept the majority of them. Moderns basically run the US, which is why Stock Market reports are on every newscast, centralization rules, corporate logos are ubiquitous, machines exist in every home and office, one's job consumes most of the day, and material possessions litter the landscape of life and consciousness.

Unlike Moderns, *Traditionals*, at 25% of the US population, do not inhabit a dominant position in society, yet they are highly influential in the American mythic consciousness. Consisting of mostly small town and rural socio-political conservatives with a common set of values and customs, many have strong religious beliefs and are often Catholic or evangelical Protestant. What unites them is a worldview somewhat oriented towards past or traditional principles, ways of life, and personal identities. A partial list of the values defining Traditionals includes:

- patriarchy rules
- defined gender roles should be followed
- family, church, and community are very important
- familiar customs should be maintained
- sex must be proscribed
- military service is deeply honorable
- rural and small-town life is more virtuous than urban or suburban life
- preserving civil liberties is less important than supporting moral behavior
- freedom to bear arms is essential
- foreigners and foreign things are suspect[62]

Traditionals tend to ignore or resist aspects of modernity such as sex and violence in media, government agencies, big banks, intrusive corporations, and moral ambiguity. Generally, the authors found Traditionals are older, lower-income, and less educated than the average, and with each generation, their numbers decline.

Unlike these two groups, the lifestyle of Cultural Creatives includes an emphasis on books and radio, arts and culture, 'whole process' thinking, personal and social authenticity, focused spending, innovation, altruism, and spiritual growth. The promise of CCs, however, is delayed by a lack of self-identity as a coherent subculture. Like a theatre audience, CCs "look in the same direction…they read the same books and share the same values and come to similar conclusions – but rarely do they turn toward one another."[63] Ray and Anderson's book is an effort to create a sense of commonweal among the postmodern visionaries of the 21st century.

The process of becoming a CC is akin to awakening from a slumber of ignorance and patterned behavior. Initiated by spiritual practice, reading a book, hearing a lecture, or other event, one stirs from unexamined life choices and assumptions and begins an "inner departure" from childhood conditioning, initiating a course leading to "stepping out of the old culture's entrancement." Seeking and manifesting a life of open-heartedness, expanded relationships, sacred nature, inner experiential genuineness, and personal responsibility is not always easy within the Modern culture (or even within one's family), but the rewards reported by research subjects are transformational.

While Moderns represent the established mainstream majority and Traditionals tend to look backward, CCs usually lean forward, attempting to find a new story to replace what they consider the unsatisfactory or unsustainable stories of the other two groups. The CC story often begins with political and social movements such as civil and gay rights, women's liberation, environmental activism, youth rebellion, sexual freedom, peace advocacy, and other shifts in public awareness and tolerance. The story says that biological evolution drives human developmental evolution, which in turn leads to a maturation process wherein compassion, health, and love take precedent over ideology, selfishness, and self-destruction. Through subsequent decades and centuries, this hardwired process of maturing will continue until a critical mass of people reach a certain level of understanding, awareness, and wisdom, shifting the whole world in a change no less significant than the move from Medieval to Modern eras.

Among the most important shifts is the one toward awareness

of environmental issues. CCs are green, and environmentalism is an example of the historical shift from ignorance to awareness. Where once humans were generally unaware of how their behavior impacted the natural world and how it impacted human survival, now the knowledge of these impacts and interconnections is spreading.

> The environmental movement is the most successful of all the new social movements. It has succeeded in changing the central beliefs and desires of the population – not just in the United States or even the West, but in the entire world...In half a century, most people in the West have done an about-face in their beliefs about the natural world. We have stopped regarding it as a storehouse to plunder, or a resource to provide us with work and wealth, and we've begun to accept it as our home.[64]

Ecology is the science of the environment, and its ascent into human consciousness indicates how holistic thinking, expanded awareness, and altruism combine in CCs to solve problems and encourage evolutionary development. Many CCs are moving beyond theory into practice. "Having educated us through protests and information," some CCs are developing "new kinds of businesses, technologies, and cooperative ventures."[65] The future is not necessarily seen as a traumatic break from the past but as a shift to radically new directions. The Earth is often seen as an organism, even a conscious being, with which all life must cooperate in order to survive. The ecology movement challenges many assumptions of Moderns and Traditionals and represents a significant departure from ways and means long unchallenged.

Spirituality, rather than being stiffly defined as exclusive religions, is an integral part of the ecology movement because the spirit is seen as the agent of transformation, able to transcend old thinking and behavior patterns – the only element of our personhood with the power to lead us past pure intellectuality and into wider and deeper places of relationship with Earth, each other, and the divine (regardless of how its envisioned). Spirituality engenders a shift into a higher level of consciousness where more is understood and positive action facilitated. The authors ask, "How can we live today without knowing the state of our soul?" and "How can we suppose that our body is separate from our spirit, or that we exist apart from the great web of being?"[66] These are the questions of the cultural creative era, the ones that must be answered to move into a new age.

Ray and Anderson submit we are currently in a "between time" when the old paradigms remain present but are increasingly viewed as anachronistic and dysfunctional as new ideas and behaviors replace them. CCs, facing the paradox of this interim period and encountering old dualistic choices, seek a third way forward. "The creative response to today's Between is going to be one that bridges differences, that uproots the old statement of the problem with a new perspective."[67] Re-contextualizing issues from outside normative assumptions and accepted worldviews means crashing strongly established gates and upsetting some well-respected apple carts. But as Einstein once supposedly said, "We can't solve problems by using the same kind of thinking we used when we created them."

The map towards a creative future includes evolutionary change initiated by a minority of persons who have glimpsed beyond the current paradigm, contemplated the path onward, and consciously developed their minds and spirits to serve as guides. The cumulative leap that the minority encourages is a planetary rite of passage involving a series of stages that lead humanity past uncertainty, conflict, and chaos, into a space of renewed confidence and internal security to "open a knowing that cannot be taken away."

The certainty of this knowing is what 'grows' the neophyte

> and makes possible the third and final stage of the rite of passage: the return, bearing the gifts of wisdom and a deeper sense of responsibility to the people.[68]

This transformative map uses models passed down from generations of tribal wisdom-keepers that collectively ushers individuals through a series of steps away from their previous life and initiates them into an unfamiliar but broader new life. A novel consciousness accompanies the new life, and the authors see the wisdom needed for the current era involving weaving a fresh mythic story that allows for both ancient wisdom and creative innovation. CCs act as midwives to the new age, returning with "gifts of wisdom" and the ability to teach others the way. Like the Bodhisattva,[69] the pilgrims to the mountaintop return to their village with tales of adventure and fertile lands in the distance. They may not be able to live there themselves, but they can report on what they see and inspire others to journey on their own. The appearance of the Cultural Creatives, the authors suggest, represents a "promise that a creative vision of the future is growing. It's a resurgence of hope, of imagination, of willingness to act for the sake of a better civilization." And further, the work toward "reintegration of, and design for, a new culture can have great power in our collective imagination. What we want and what we choose can shape our future.[70]

Paul Hawken – *Blessed Unrest*

Environmentalist, entrepreneur, and journalist Paul Hawken subtitled his 2007 book *"How the Largest Social Movement in History is Restoring Grace, Justice, and Beauty to the World,"* and in its pages he investigates groups across the planet with varying projects and agendas that are bringing about what he believes are profound transformations in human society. It's an account of the people who are redefining "our relationship to the environment and to one another, healing the wounds of the earth with passion and determination."[71] The book emerges from the author's hundreds of lectures at which people from every walk of life approach him and share their personal or group work relating to environmentalism, peace, social justice, or indigenous wisdom. In time, the interconnections and dependencies between these groups became clear, along with their sheer number and scope – the author estimates there are over 100,000 such groups in the world, constituting the "largest social movement in history." As Hawken counted the vast number of organizations, he began to postulate that the movement he observed was somehow organic or even biologic. He writes that this movement has a distinct history, "what poet Gary Snyder calls *the great underground*, a current of humanity that dates back to the Paleolithic."[72] The work of Reich, Ferguson, Thompson, Ray, and Anderson can be considered 'surfacings' of this underground and examples of its periodic recognition.

Blessed Unrest begins with a general overview of the ubiquitous "movement," each group sprouting "like blades of grass after a rain" and spreading across the globe. Because of its decentralization, the movement cannot be divided, because of its egalitarianism, it tends to disperse concentrations of power, and because of improvements in information technology, its growth has been significant. Hawken regards the movement as humanity's response to crisis by persons with a particular set of values.

> Collectively, it expresses the needs of the majority of people on earth to sustain the environment, wage peace, democratize decision making and policy, reinvent public governance piece by piece from the bottom up, and improve their lives – women, children, and the poor.[73]

However, like Ray and Anderson, Hawken laments the movement's virtual invisibility, which he attributes to the fact that cultural developments often do not fit conventional categories and to the resulting difficulties defining cultural changes on the gradual scale of generations or even centuries. Neither does the movement have strong ideologies to clearly identify and delineate it from the background cultural milieu or to create conflict between competing ideas and their supporters. Instead of grand normative *isms*, regional processes, community needs, pragmatic solutions, and compassionate responses lead to radical democracy uncorrupted by corporations or modern nation-states.[74] The movement is vast, but because of corporate media myopia, its message, numbers, and underlying unity are lost to the public and the members of the movement themselves.

The basic questions of *Blessed Unrest* concern that group of people who, invisible or not, form the minority progressive vanguard.[75] Having attained a certain level of conscious awareness about the larger pictures of human and global interdependence, they act to deepen relationships between persons, groups, and Earth, and to heal wounds endured during the march of industrial civilization.

> This book asks whether a significant portion of humanity has found a new series of adaptive traits and stories more alluring than the ideological fundamentalisms that have caused us so much suffering.[76]

The "adaptive traits" characterize a change in behavioral patterns based on new knowledge and its dissemination through a population, and the "stories" indicate the changing of cultural mythos from the assumptions of modernity to the pragmatic necessities of what Brian Swimme and Thomas Berry call the *Ecozoic Era*.[77] Old cultural stories begin to lose their power before the next story can fully develop. The passion of visionaries for this fresh perspective is based on excitement for the project of developing the next culture founded on unique characteristics of the Ecozoic period.

Hawken divides his book into chapters dealing with individual histories and influences of the movement, beginning with "The Long Green," an examination of environmentalism. He argues, "The first generation – our own – to worry about global threats like nuclear proliferation and climate change is effectively ahistorical." In other words, ecological concerns are unprecedented in history, and unique global issues require a holistic and transnational perspective with a planet-wide consciousness. The author traces the history of the environmental branch of the movement from Emerson's *Nature* and Darwin's *On the Origin of Species* to Carson's *Silent Spring* and Brower's Earth Island Institute, including the writings of Aldo Leopold, Edward Abbey, James Lovelock, and Stewart Brand.

In the chapter "Immunity," Hawken speculates that not only may the Earth be a single living entity, but also humankind itself may form a collective organism integrated in mysterious and inexplicable ways.[78] The answer to current difficulties is the nurturance of the human collective consciousness, which has the power to initiate global innovations that individuals or small groups can't. The author further submits that such a massive mind acts as the planet's immune system, responding to toxins like political corruption, economic disease, and environmental degradation.[79]

> Just as the immune system recognizes self and non-self, the movement identifies what is humane and not humane. Just as the immune system is the line of internal defense that allows an organism to persist over time, sustainability is a strategy for humanity to continue to exist over time.[80]

Comparing the human species in its capacity to rectify and correct disease in its collective body to the individual body's complex system of protection gives a global perspective to the meaning of immune response. In similar fashion, the diverse network of organizations proliferating in the world today act to heal and maintain the planetary body, each group targeting specific pathogens to eliminate. Many people are now aware that the Earth is sick and that human history is rife with unnecessary human-made suffering. The process is slow and often discouraging as the same problems repeat over and over in a seemingly endless cycle of destruction. Most groups remain small with few resources, and it's not easy creating a system with no antecedent; however, as with our previous authors, Hawken is optimistic, seeing momentous organizational energy forming to meet the monstrous tasks.

Groups are divided into categories, such as Watchers, Friends, Defenders, Conservancies, Incubator NGOs, Networks, Street performers, Culture jammers, Social entrepreneurs, and Foodies.[81] Each has its niche, but all share values relating to easing suffering, protecting the environment, supporting innovation, creating sustainable enterprises, addressing a specific need, or offering a service. The question is whether these groups can work together. Being separate entities working on different areas with varied goals does mean unification is challenging, but the underlying values and ultimate purposes of each collective provides a framework for finding common ground. Hawken suggests that diversity is strength and unity follows recognition.

> If anything can offer us hope for the future it will be an assembly of humanity that is representative but not centralized, because no single ideology can ever heal the wounds of this world. This is the promise of the movement: that the margins link up, that we discover through our actions and shared concerns that we are a global family.[82]

The understanding that in our diversity we are whole represents a profound shift in consciousness, from isolated individuals to a unified community, millions of different human and organizational antibodies that can lock on to antigens, neutralize invaders, and simultaneously signal for help. Hawken lists some of the antigens being actively addressed:

- corrupt politics
- climate change
- corporate predation
- death of the oceans
- governmental indifference
- pandemic poverty
- industrial forestry and farming
- depletion of soil and water[83]

In the chapter "Restoration," the author finds solace in the fierce efforts of the movement and its diversity. Such redundancy encourages resilience so that damage can be done on social and ecological levels and the system as a whole will continue to flourish. The interaction between humans and Earth must be stabilized, however, lest a serious disequilibrium develop which must be repaired by ejecting the source of the problem (us). The movement stimulates equilibrium by being balanced itself without requiring overriding structures, central authorities, or dominance that limits flexibility or calcifies porous boundaries needed for interconnectivity, cooperation, and growth.

Hawken reminds us that spaceship Earth is powered by a mother ship, the Sun. In order to create real sustainability, humankind must learn to mimic the waste-recycling habits of nature so that, if possible, what was once pollution is reused. A trilogy of concepts – 'cradle to cradle,' 'waste equals food,' and 'staying within current solar income' – forms the basic tenets of the greening of industry and elimination of pollution and misuse.[84] In other words, we need to realize that future generations will have to pay the price for current trends of gluttony and waste, that all waste is actually the food for some other element in the system, and that the Sun provides all the energy we could possibly need if we simply harvest it. The technical means for achieving a stable state economy exists; only the collective will is missing. The will is founded on more than expertise, outrage, or even suffering – it needs a source of passion and transcendence wherein the daunting problems we face can be overcome. It needs spirituality.

> It has been said that we cannot save our planet unless humankind undergoes a widespread spiritual and religious awakening. In other words, fixes won't fix unless we fix our souls as well.[85]

From spiritual teachers like Jesus and the Buddha who emerged during the 'Axial Age'[86] come perennial values such as the Golden Rule, the sacredness of all life, and an active love for the world despite its imperfection. Hawken submits, "Compassion and love of others are at the heart of all religions, and at the heart of this movement."[87] It would seem that, like our other books, *Blessed Unrest* evinces a spiritual element to the community of faithful workers, whether they consciously regard themselves as spiritual or not. It takes a kind of faith to labor towards the unimaginable, to re-imagine the world in a way that fosters hope in things like growth without inequality, wealth without plunder, work without exploitation, and a future without fear.[88] Through the spirit of healing, forgiveness, and determination to be born again can we transcend the wounds of the past and step into the sunlight of a new future.

For Hawken, the movement has no defining moment, no charismatic leaders, no book to fully describe it, because it's "the breathing, sentient testament of the living world."[89] It constitutes an outgrowth of natural processes we see all around us. The movement is as organic as wildflowers and wind. In this way, the movement's participants are following the natural course of the Earth itself as agents of the planet. We're inseparably linked by a common destiny bound up with our ability to collectively turn the ship away from the rocks and into safe harbor. The author is optimistic that the dominant thinking of the movement will eventually influence every person, group, institution, and the whole planet's consciousness, and will "change a sufficient number of people so as to begin the reversal of centuries of frenzied self-destructive behavior."[90] Commerce, government, schools, churches, and cities will learn to re-image the world from the bottom up based on the principles of justice and ecology.

Barbara Marx Hubbard – *Conscious Evolution*

Hubbard is a noted futurist who has labored in the confluence of human consciousness and cultural evolution since the 1970s. Her 1998 book *Conscious Evolution: Awakening the Power of Our Social Potential* was updated in 2015 with a second revised edition. In the book, Ms. Hubbard's goal seems to be an examination of her beliefs about how humanity can, and presumably will, evolve along a trajectory leading from primitive violence and unrest towards peace and stability – a belief clearly shared by all of our previous visionaries. The cluster of ideas around conscious evolution relies on apparent historical trends indicating global movement away from cruelty towards empathic compassion.[91] Hubbard does not break new ground as much as update older ideas to early 21st century audiences, which is appropriate in a field where change remains one of the few constants.

Conscious Evolution begins with an eschatological statement of purpose referencing contemporary threats posed by nuclear weapons and climate change: "Conscious Evolution presents a plan that can bring humanity across the dangerous threshold of possible self-destruction to the point of the shift – when we realize we're going to make it, that we have the capacity to survive and grow."[92] This declaration expresses 1) the fear that humans will destroy themselves in a global level extinction event, or at least damage civilization beyond recognition, yet 2) optimism that a shift in consciousness is intrinsic to evolutionary processes producing far better results. An emotional duality thus permeates the work: warnings combine with solutions, and pessimism wars with hope. A kind of faith in evolution informs Hubbard's work: that, ultimately, biological forces pushing toward greater adaptability and complexity will shape a positive future. If disease ravages cities, we have the capacity to invent advanced medicine; if nuclear winter threatens ecological balance, we can discipline our revengeful instincts; and if climate threatens social stability, we will learn to shift economic systems and energy sources to sustainable forms.

Chapter 1, "The Awakening of Humanity," continues the Introduction's cautious hopefulness, with sudden evolutionary shifts joining gradual transformation as equal forces. The way humans comprehend evolution itself is one of those comparatively rapid shifts: from merely being acted upon, to awareness of the process, and finally to intentionally affecting the process. In this way, the author maintains, humans come to at least partially control their destiny.[93] "We are now changing our understanding of how nature evolves; we are moving from unconscious evolution through natural selection to conscious evolution by choice."[94] In other words, what was once done to us for our own good will be done by us in hopes of a greater good.

Ethics, by the author's implication, accompanies individual and cultural evolution. Time and experience result in increased empathy, outward from self and family to tribe, nation-state, and eventually planet. These expanding circles of compassion encompass greater diversity until Earth itself becomes kin, with all due rights.[95] As Hubbard puts it,

> This capability combined with other rapidly developing technologies, such as biotechnology, nanotechnology, and

artificial intelligence, if used in our current state of self-centered consciousness, could lead to the destruction of the human race. We must learn 'ethical evolution'...and we do not have hundreds of years in which to learn.[96]

Hubbard suggests that ethical evolution must complement technical advances lest we misuse our various synthetic creations to the detriment of ourselves and other life forms. This is the lesson at the core of the author's text: to avoid the consequences of allowing unconscious natural drives for power and security using modern technics to overcome our equally natural, but frequently underdeveloped, kindheartedness.

Using the term 'evolution' to cover both natural complexification and cognitive maturation means the two are inexorably linked, and in fact are products of the same process. The author states it this way: "We know that a plan of action or program is encoded in the genes of every living organism that guides it through gestation, birth, maturation, and death. Planet Earth is a living system." She further asks, "Is it not possible, then, that there is a prepatterned (but not a predetermined) pattern or tendency, an encoded design for planetary evolution just as there is for biological evolution?"[97] Noosphere and biosphere apparently function under the same set of arrangements and rules, and just as medicine and other artifices affect biological evolution, raising consciousness affects noospheric evolution. With this probability established, she then offers various methods that cause the desired effects, not to initiate revolutions, but to "cooperate more consciously to re-pattern our social systems and evolve ourselves."[98]

Although most of Hubbard's text follows its own pattern of secular empiricism, she occasionally uses the term *spirit* to describe some aspects of this re-patterning, but seems to have a relatively non-religious, non-supernatural definition, as when she uses phrases such as "being awakened" and "higher consciousness," or when she says that the inevitability of death was "challenged by the human spirit, which sought to go beyond humanoid limits."[99] Moving beyond the limits of our species becomes a spiritual task, an undertaking of global proportions guided by the human spirit, which allows for knowledge that the rational intellect cannot necessarily access, and so spirituality contains the seeds of further evolutionary leaps by suggesting a transcending "beyond" to which humans can aspire, and eventually reach.

For the author, this 'spirit' emerged in the seminal 1960s, ushering in unique ideas and lifestyles that still resonate into the 21st century. She identifies three crucial events of that era, which form the birth-awakening of the Social Potential movement:

- the Apollo space program (which gave us the first photograph of Earth)
- the first Earth Day (in which the consciousness of living on a finite planet reached new heights)
- the Feminist Movement (the "awakening of women *en masse* to a new identity, a new function, a new role in evolution")[100]

These events serve to expand human awareness from nation-state to planet, further encouraged by climate changes with no viable solution on less than a planetary scale.

Since the 1960s, humankind has apparently accelerated its modern civilizing progress, with both positive and negative results, and the process seems as though it's following a template, at least on this planet, with new ideations birthing new individuals and collective enterprises.

> Here we are, from the perspective of the new creation story, a planetary species just after birth, struggling to coordinate ourselves as a whole, fearing the destruction of our life-

> support systems, confused and afraid. Nonetheless, our planetary nervous system is linking us up through phones, faxes, global satellites, and the Internet."[101]

Notice the language being used: "new creation," "planetary species," "planetary nervous system," and "Internet." These terms are unprecedented in human history, reflecting and describing states of awareness unavailable to previous generations. Technology abets this shift in consciousness, along with natural spiritual transcendence, in a mutually-enhancing feedback loop. As social evolution intensifies (probably modified by climate crisis) and escalates the development and spread of human sentience, will a new world slowly (and sometimes painfully) emerge? Hubbard believes so, again, describing it in fresh and even whimsical terminology.

> Are we being prepared for a time in the not too distant future when we will have an actual, empathic experience of our oneness? Are we possibly at the threshold, as a newly emerging planetary organism, of our first *planetary smile,* a mass linkup of consciousness, now emerging in so many…?[102]

How often has anyone used "planetary smile" to describe what many religions have traditionally seen as the end of history – new heaven and new earth, nirvana, paradise? A smile generally denotes pleasure, joy, and other positive emotions, so in context, the author clearly believes "oneness" and "mass linkup" will be cause for celebration, with subtle religious undertones, especially relating to Buddhist practices of illumination and liberation.

In order for the smile to spread, those humans ready to do so must enhance the evolutionary order, and so formulate new meanings of existence. In the section "Five Lessons of Evolution," Hubbard lists the following apropos to this effort:

- Quantum Evolution – which means "a jump from one state to the next that cannot be achieved through incremental change alone"
- Crises precede transformation – problems stimulate innovative transformation
- Holism is inherent in reality – Earth and all life integrate into "one interactive, interfeeling body"
- Evolution creates beauty, and only the beautiful endures – "Every leaf, every animal, every body that endures is exquisite...the process of natural selection favors elegant, aesthetic design"
- Evolution raises consciousness and freedom – complexification leads to greater connection and compassion[103]

Each of these lessons "provides a response to the crisis of meaning we face in the post-modern world."[104] With the decline of religion as the dominant medium of spirituality and cultural ethos, civilized people must replace it with a new story, a fresh perspective, and innovative explanations for why we're here and what we're supposed to do with our lives. Humanity need no longer battle our physical bodies, each other, or invisible empires of theology and ideology in order to have a fulfilling life. We can reclaim deep humility and acknowledge that we actually know very little about reality. We can prosper and flourish in ways we cannot yet comprehend – as Hubbard concludes the chapter: "The stabilization of unitive consciousness combined with the extension of human habitats in space, [and] increased intelligence through our maturing global brain...will radically alter the human condition."[105] Just saying this seems wildly speculative, but the process of its achievement will require, like most things, a great deal of hard work and a bit of luck.

Worldviews often ossify as tribal or regional customs, traditions, and taboos, which repeat even when they have lost all purpose and meaning. Creating a new view of life, the self, and the world means transforming layers of historical belief systems so the next can ascend and dominate in its turn.

> What we are seeking is a worldview that will call forth our creative action and direct our immense powers toward life-oriented and evolutionary purposes. That guiding worldview is, I believe, conscious evolution. It holds that through our unprecedented scientific, social, and spiritual capacities we can evolve consciously and co-creatively with nature and the deeper patterns of creation (traditionally called God), thus enabling us to manifest a future commensurate with our unlimited species and planetary potential."[106]

What would it be like to have the Earth as our partner in forging a sustainable and profoundly beautiful world? To cooperate with the unstoppable energy of evolution so that we could harness its directionality and ride it like a surfer shredding an awesome wave. What we need, according to the author, is a new worldview, a way to interpret perceived reality in which we're immersed in evolutionary flow, tethered to the positive changes that aid us in prospering and flourishing. She calls this worldview conscious evolution, and thus through "unprecedented scientific, social, and spiritual capacities" we become "co-creators" along with nature of our destiny and that of the planet.

> Conscious evolution inspires in us a mysterious and humble awareness that we have been created by this awesome process of evolution and are now being transformed by it to take a more mature role as co-creators. In this view we do not stand apart from nature, but, rather, we are nature evolving.[107]

In some ways, then, biocultural evolution serves as a replacement for creator gods and religious fates; the numinous becomes the effervescence of time. The deep truth of how and why all life changes contextualize the march of history as a signal of the imbedded dynamics of the universe. Science, society, and spirituality cease their normative competition and, seen from a greater objective distance, meld into interactive characters in the same drama. Humility descends upon humankind as we note our limited, but important, part in the play stretching back to the formation of the Earth.

Hubbard calls these changes "quantum transformations" and "critical design innovations" of nature, but whereas natural forces may take millions of years, cultural evolution, "through language, symbols, arts, and music" accelerates the process of change to decades, and sometimes years. The cultural evolutionary theory appears grounded in recorded history, as previously mentioned, so that one can see the march of progress into modernity. This is not to claim that there aren't challenges to overcome, but indications are that they will be overcome. Optimism dominates the social potential movement, even as it remains nascent. The seeds of further growth seem obvious to its advocates: "Our fledgling worldview is still almost invisible, yet it is drawing to it brilliant minds in every field and function who hold the mysterious sense of hope for the future."[108]

The author explains her belief that "there is a natural pattern for the development of a planetary system, just as there is for a biological system" by outlining three methods of learning evolution: spiritual (deeper patterns of creation), social (proactive societal design), and scientific/technological ("the natural extension of nature's technologies, giving human nature the capacity to evolve evolution itself from unconscious to conscious").[109] These claims relate to 'growing up' from infancy to adulthood, from existing as a relatively powerless agent onto whom life is compelled to a relatively empowered agent who shapes life toward her own desires. Just as most healthy humans don't remain infantile, humankind cannot remain at infantile stages of consciousness.[110]

Conscious evolution seems to occur through the machinations of collective emotional, psychological, intellectual, and spiritual development, along paths already established by evolutionary forces, to which we unconsciously conform. How do we bring these forces fully into consciousness and guide them, as they in turn guide us, into greener pastures of love, peace, compassion, and gratitude?

> The social potential movement identifies peak experiences in our personal lives and cultivates individual wellness and transformation. The movement seeks out innovations now working in health, environment, communication, education, government, economics, technology, and other fields of human endeavor while designing new social systems that lead toward a regenerative and life-enhancing global society.[111]

Humans have bouts of violence and cruelty, but Hubbard suggests that these are not the true human being, and that together we can initiate a new age, which is a continuation of the processes that allowed us to progress as far as we have. Taking matters into our own hands, so to speak, and the willingness to take responsibility for the future requires finding and nourishing those ideas and innovators that are creating solutions leading to the world we want.

Despite its collective nature, the social potential movement begins with certain individual people who have ascended to advanced stages of consciousness, which the author calls "the cocreative person" whose awareness, sustainable lifestyle choices, and compassion form the foundation of the movement. As the numbers of these individuals increase, conscious evolution accelerates. "Only if we ourselves could evolve could our society transform"[112] means grassroots activism, personal actualization,[113] and private transfiguration. Holonically, the macro begins in the micro and builds outward toward the macro, just as biological evolution began with the simplest forms of life and developed complexity over time.

Chapter 11, "A Spirit-Motivated Plan for the 21st Century," elucidates Hubbard's strategies for making evolution conscious and social potential manifest. The process involves encouraging certain behaviors: "...we value any act, intention, or belief that expands our consciousness toward a more intuitive, spiritual, loving, whole-centered stage."[114] She describes an "Innovation Wheel" design as a visible matrix wherein ideas emerge and flow outward, joining and synthesizing with other related concepts in key area clusters:

- Governance and Law
- Education
- Economics, Business, and Philanthropy
- Health, Relationships, and Personal Growth
- Science and Technology
- Spirituality and Religion
- Environment and Habitat
- Culture, Media, and Communications[115]

The Innovation Wheel has at its center a constellation of "Golden Innovations" which help bring the innovation to fruition with their own set of effects, among them "moves society toward the goal of just, humane, regenerative, and choiceful future," embodies "higher consciousness, greater freedom, and more synergistic order," "has the potential for major social impact," has success that can be measured, and "is sustainable, replicable, and not dependent on one charismatic leader or other unique circumstances for its success."[116] The assumption is that humans are fundamentally rational, "based on faith in the goodness of human nature when we are placed in win-win social systems that bring out the best in us."[117] The circumstances that stimulate the finest in individuals and groups often relate to mutual care and sustenance, along with the inherent respect granted by such collective self-maintenance, which may be one reason democratic socialist nations, such as those in Scandinavia, stand out as so healthy, peaceful, and well-ordered.

In the effort to outline the process of evolutionary shifts, Hubbard describes what she calls The Four Ss: "Synergy" (experiencing group mind), "Synchronicity" (multiple meaningful 'coincidences'), "Syntony" (guiding intuition), and "Suprasex" (intimately joining with others).[118] The following Chapters discuss various means for disseminating the social potential movement, through media and especially education – as a proposed Master's Degree program of coursework, including: Cosmogenesis, The History of Conscious Evolution, Self-Evolution, The Planet in Transition, Design for a Positive Future, Fulfilling Our Vocations of Destiny, and Visions of a Cocreative Society.[119]

For Hubbard, the Great Awakening of humankind is an inevitable result of natural processes, and the Cocreative Society reveals its ultimate purpose as entering the Global Brain: "We now have become fully connected to the global intelligence system" with instantaneous access to all information and memory. As Homo sapiens become more advanced, what now seems like improbable dreams may well be commonplace. Such is the nature of the dynamic flow of time: "From one stage of evolution, the next stage tends to look like a miracle. How would a bird look to a single cell?"[120] The further we travel, the more 'past' is accumulated and the more god-like our abilities appear in comparison. Having come from single-cell organisms, the author says we should not be surprised about the wonders to come.

Finally, co-evolution creates the fertile ground for the maturation of the human family, from immature to advanced, just as children grow into adults. This process requires the passage of time, and probably some luck, so that, individually or collectively, settled behaviors of the mature replace childishness or adolescence. "The vast kindergarten of humankind formally served by the police, the welfare system, mental hospitals and prisons gradually grows up."[121] A fully-functioning adult may have challenges to overcome or accept, but they don't need significant external behavioral regulation because they've internalized common-sense, empathy, and compassion into actions that support and nourish self and others. "The problems we faced in the 20th century are not solved; they are dissolved, as the problems of a 2-year-old do not exist for a 20-year-old."[122] According to Hubbard, wars, conflicts, self-inflicted wounds, cruelty, apathy, and a host of other ailments will pass from consciousness like the powerlessness, fears, and tantrums of a child tend to dissipate with age.

Hubbard ends her book with a call to action and a list of resources and groups in which to collectivize that activism. She concludes:

> From the perspective of the social potential movement our goal for the 21st century should be a broad acceptance of the evolutionary agenda, supported by the worldview of conscious evolution and manifested through new social innovations and social systems that lead toward a positive and ever-evolving future.[123]

If Hubbard and others are correct, we may struggle against our evolutionary destiny, but it will be to no avail: we will evolve in inevitable ways that lead to our survival and complexification, and if true, such sentiments mark the pathway which we will be treading, with fits and starts, in the coming centuries – and such an optimistic worldview gives cause for working optimistically toward those coming challenges and ultimate triumphs.

Michael Dowd – *Thank God for Evolution*

Subtitled "How the Marriage of Science and Religion Will Transform Your Life and Our World" Dowd attempts to cover his subject while tying it together with a cord of Christian environmentalism. Marrying science and religion might well result in a new synthesis, like Einstein combining electro-magnetism and gravity to produce Relativity, and such a synthesis promises, if achieved accurately, to produce a higher-level and more encompassing theory. Through the combining of ideas, individual, social, cultural, global, and religious evolution takes place.

The co-evolution of science and religion requires a grand unifying integration of these two methods of perceiving and interpreting reality: the external/objective realm of empirical evidence and the internal/subjective realm of experiential consciousness. Both methods often vie with each other in a zero-sum competition; however, if history is any indication, there exists an over-arching system with co-contributing aspects fusing into a single unit – a dynamic polarity rather than antagonistic dichotomy. This is Dowd's initial project, reflected in chapter titles such as "Evolution is Not Meaningless Blind Chance," "The Nested Emergent Nature of Divine Creativity" and "Growing an Evolutionary Faith." Even though I'm skeptical of Intelligent Design, his arguments eventually transcend the simplistic formula of ending infinite regression by postulating an invisible, infinite, and eternal deity.

Laying the groundwork, Dowd states a foundational premise: that time pushes life through stages of increasing complexity and adaptability, just as Teilhard de Chardin and others have suggested. Early on he states that "genetic guidance" allows for the accumulation, retention, and distribution of knowledge across history and geography, leading to technical innovations easing the labor-burdens and physical limitations of Homo sapiens. He writes explicitly that the Internet is a continuation of this long inventive process that has altered civilized persons permanently.

> The World Wide Web has made possible collaborations no longer stifled by geographic distances and political boundaries. Throughout this evolution of human communities and networks, an inner transformation has also been taking place. At each stage, our circles of care, compassion, and commitment have grown and our list of enemies have diminished. Our next step will be to organize and govern ourselves globally, and to enjoy a mutually enhancing relationship with the larger body of Life of which we are a part.[124]

As we've already seen in previous authors, there exists a visionary element to descriptions of changes and growth our ancestors initiated millennia ago, battling nature's programming to build civilizations with more kindness and empathy. Dowd seems to be suggesting that the very essence of evolution isn't just to make us complex or adaptive, but more 'good.' The arc of history bends toward the emergence of better people, able to live, play, and work together with unprecedented cooperation and peace.

With a better model of humanoid, we can branch out from small, provincial understandings and attitudes to larger sets of allegiances centered on shared global identities. That is, we began with birth-clans, regarding non-relatives as possibly dangerous strangers; then groups of clans learned the benefits of togetherness and made tribes, which one day became kingdoms, which eventually became nation-states. The logical trajectory seems to lead to planet-wide identification and unity, an expansion that may be slowed, but not stopped. In the future, the circle of compassion will probably embrace non-human animals and all of nature on a planetary scale. Many people are already thinking this way, and the Earth flag outside my house identifies my allegiance to the whole world.

Evolution processes time into matter that develops along fairly predictable patterns from simple to complicated, at least in the observable universe. In *Thank God for Evolution*, biological and cultural progress seems undeniable, working within a specific matrix: "...as evolution proceeds, more complex organisms and systems tend to show up and that each stage of evolution transcends and includes (incorporates and builds upon) earlier stages."[125] We'll see this idea again when we look at Ken Wilber's work. He even mentions Hubbard's Conscious Evolution, so he's aware of contemporary ideas.

Although the author is a practicing Christian, his view of spirituality extends beyond one religion. He establishes a naturalistic definition of what he calls "evolutionary spirituality" which involves spirit's integration into the whole of life.

> Yes, the practical is spiritual. Spirituality is not merely about prayer or meditation, mystical experiences, or, indeed, anything ethereal. It is about cultivating right relationships at every scale of reality, whether we are religious or not.[126]

He doesn't reject the possibility of supernatural studies, but tends to ground spiritual things in the daily life of the material world. In this way, he hopes to bring spirit and science closer together by acknowledging where they overlap, to establish common ground in which they may meet and mingle, discovering, like our reconciling couple Ecos and Spiritus, their shared values and interests. But what is a "right relationship"? Buddhists hold such rightness in high regard since it's part of Siddhartha's basic teachings. The Eight Fold Path is one of the Four Noble Truths, the very foundation of the religion, and lists eight right beliefs and activities that lead to enlightenment and liberation.

We can certainly say a relationship that's "right" will be 'good':

satisfying and enhancing to both parties, making everyone involved deeper in wisdom, at peace with self and others. And it must scale to different aspects of life and consciousness – from livelihood and parenting to beliefs and daily activities. In other words, spirituality becomes a parallel perceptive lens alongside science that enhances the latter while asking and answering philosophical-interior/subjective questions science usually doesn't ask and can't generally answer.

Dowd further suggests that science and spirit emerge from a "Great Story" which is "the sacred story of everyone and everything. It springs from a grand narrative of an evolving universe of emergent complexity and breathtaking creativity."[127] This cosmology colours people's vision of reality with the spectrum of a particular tribal tale accepted by the individual as their own. Collective storytelling causes not just national, racial, and religious identities; it can also persuade otherwise decent folk to fight in wars, kill 'enemies,' and discriminate against anyone outside the group. Organizations can do much good, but crowds can also perpetrate much evil. The difference comes from their values, goals, and methods, and these characteristics usually fall under the purview of psychology and religion rather than science, with the exception of Sam Harris and his promising explorations of the scientific perimeters of well-being, which can establish morality and ethics based on measurable physical wellness and psychological health.[128]

In the chapter "Evolution and the Revival of the Human Spirit," we get to the author's primary task of synthesizing Ecos (science) and Spiritus (transcendence). Calling himself and his wife "evolutionary evangelists," he first contextualizes his worldview using William James' question about the fundamental nature of the universe: is it benign or indifferent? Outside of human imaginative projection, does the cosmos have benevolence towards us, or are our lives meant merely to propagate the species? So one thing we're talking about is how we perceive the world; that is, the mythic, cosmological lens through which we view our surroundings. Atheists, for instance, see a world without intrinsic meaning or purpose except that which is given to it by humans (and perhaps other animals). Religions trend in the other direction, weighing the world down with excessive meaning where everything counts on some celestial scoreboard.

To ask these questions suggests that the cosmos, or at least the world, exists in some form that has presence or being, such as the furthest expressions of Gaia theory. A non-dualistic worldview finds humans as one part of something larger and more whole, that our perceptions of that whole are limited and incomplete, and that when it is complete, we'll see what's hiding from us. Dowd believes we might find the universe trust-worthy, with predictable changes that lead, for the most part, to the greatest good.

> The Universe can be counted on over time – it can be trusted, deeply trusted – to move in the direction of more diversity, more complexity, more awareness, more transformation and growth, faster and faster, *and* more intimacy…we can depend on the Universe to feistily hold on to its learnings, its creative breakthroughs, its evolutionary advances. To use relational language, it is fiercely loyal.[129]

Are these sentiments falsely anthropomorphizing the Universe? Again, it depends on one's worldview, one's story about what it means to be alive. The spiritual view is holistic rather than reductionist, and reality as we know it works together to create and sustain life, so it has a greater purpose which intimately involves humanity. Since evolutionary processes appear to result at its leading edge consciousness and the ability to ponder philosophical and theological questions, we might be forgiven for assuming that this ability is the result of, and by extension the purpose of, evolutions millennial movements. If we're to avoid the teleological rabbit hole, God should be avoided under the objections that deity-explanations are simply too simplistic, the product of lazy thinking. Then what is driving the evolutionary bus? Dowd uses several terms interchangeably to try and name the dynamic processes of life: "...we must begin by trusting the Universe, fostering faith in God, *making life right*. These are three ways of saying essentially the same thing."[130]

Combining science and spirit means taking the viewpoint that, despite its tribulations, the Universe (or deity if you prefer) forms consciousness from matter, and that regardless of external/objective arguments that not everyone sees it this way, for many in their internal/subjective experiences, belief in a greater benevolent reality, whether cloaked in religious terminology or not, can heal and make whole the wounded individual person. Since Dowd observes good coming from faith-in-the-larger-Whole, he submits that the Whole itself must ultimately be good. He calls this "holy faith in evolution" that will "usher the world's religions into their greatness in the 21st century."[131] I'm skeptical that religions as collective institutions can survive indefinitely (at least in their current forms), but the belief in a religious renaissance – where supposedly the violent and intolerant parts will fall away, leaving only the peaceful and intelligent parts – does have a certain appeal, since collective efforts toward transformation are often more effective than solitary ones.

The final chapters of the book offer an envisioning of the world for the next 250 years, assuming the ideas in the book are adopted universally. For instance, Chapter 17 is titled "Beyond Sustainability: An Inspiring Vision" which begins by listing coming challenges, including:

- Climate change
- Continuing loss of biodiversity due to human causes
- Impact of growing human population on food, energy,

pollution, habitats
- Gap between the rich and poor, haves and have-nots
- Peak oil
- Geopolitical conflicts, including NBC (nuclear, biological, chemical) or GNR (genetic, nanotechnology, robotic) error or terror
- Biocomputers becoming more intelligent than human beings
- Aligning self-interest with the well-being of the whole[132]

Some of these are really fears of the new or unknown rather than potential catastrophes, but all offer humankind opportunities for integral building and surpassing levels of development. Dowd remains optimistic about our ability to overcome these problems, based partly on a realistic assessment of history, which shows an obvious pattern of problem resolution. His hopefulness is further revealed in the next section "Long-term and Short-term Positive Trends" wherein he details the ends to current issues:

- Bad news, chaos, and breakdowns catalyzing creativity and transformation
- Technology further enabling and empowering human connectedness
- Circles of care, compassion, concern, and commitment widening
- Cooperation and interdependence expanding at multiple levels
- Feedback (inner and outer) becoming more available, accurate, and helpful
- World's religions integrating evolution and ecology[133]

These trends arc toward the expansion those values and qualities advocated in both Dowd's work as the natural result of evolution, but accelerated with the addition of a spiritual outlook emphasizing the positive features of humanity. Finally, the author lists "Likely Good News in the Next 250 Years" including

- Human population stabilizing and then declining
- Clean renewable energy sources replacing toxic, nonrenewable energy sources
- The 'Sixth Great Mass Extinction" ending
- Biomimicry design revolution in law, medicine, governance, economics, religion, and education
- All significant pollution problems solves
- Global self-interest, personal self-interest, and corporate self-interest aligned
- The birth of what Joel de Rosnay has called the 'cybiont': humanity, technology, and nature as one symbiotic, synergistic organism
- Global democratic/biocratic revolution, holistic governance
- World-wide religious revival[134]

Each of these possibilities reflects human innovation, but because humans are part of the Universe, they actually suggest the innovation and creativity of the Universe itself, giving the term agency, or at least reality in the discussion of visionary ecospiritual evolution.

Chapter Conclusions

The visionary authors in this section share a sense of developing grace and an optimistic approach to serious problems, and they see a leading edge of reformers, imagineers, bioneers, and geologians focusing attention on solutions that they hope will lead to a bright and beautiful future. These people have become aware of, and have awakened to, specific needs that require active but compassionate response. They aren't leaders of a movement in the historical sense; they're simply reacting to various imperatives by the means available to them. The cumulative landscape of these individual and small group actions, however, is emerging as a global phenomenon.

The authors we examined advocate an expansion of consciousness based on the premise that humans are capable of enlarging their minds and expanding their hearts to contain more diversity, accept more variety, love more people, serve with more devotion, develop more maturity, widen in sophistication, deepen in wisdom, and ascend to higher levels of being. The capacity for transcendence, for extending beyond apparent limitations, is a characteristic of the human species, but belief in the ongoing reality and dynamic efficacy of transcendence is a hallmark of visionaries, with substantial elements of environmental awareness combined with spirituality, so eco-awareness appears to be an inherent ingredient of this community as it moves itself – and all humanity – into the 21st century.

What solved previous problems won't suffice for present ones. Fresh perspectives and unprecedented activism are called for at almost every level of engagement, from local to worldwide and from individual to species. Each author in this section brought a worldview and ethos that shed light on a slightly different facet of these movements. For Reich, it was made of people who reached Consciousness III, getting free of artificial social constraints and unchallenged cultural assumptions in a revolution of consciousness. For Ferguson, it was made of Aquarian Conspirators, those who adopted a new paradigm through increased awareness. For Thompson, it consisted of those who made the shift to the Pacific cultural ecology and achieved a spiritual awakening leading to higher, deeper, and more advanced levels of awareness and livelihood. For Ray and Anderson, it was made from millions of culturally creative people who moved toward a new territory of values and a new way of living. For Hawken, it was made of groups and individuals collectively addressing immanent environmental, social justice, and spiritual needs of the present and future. For Hubbard it was humans consciously choosing their evolutionary course. And for Dowd, it was about synthesizing religious faith and the science of evolution. Despite the nuanced differences in how the movement was considered by these authors, they all address common issues.

Environment, Ecology, Earth Wisdom

Every author we examined acknowledges that the state of the planet's natural ecosystems is under siege and that without healing the wounds wrought by excessive industrialism and consumption, physical life is in danger and the survival of *Homo sapiens* uncertain. Other philosophical debates and worldly concerns are moot if this issue is not effectively addressed. Visionaries understand these realities and take measures to adjust thought and living patterns to conform to the needs of Earth in supporting all life.

Spirituality

Each book at minimum recognized the influence of the spirit in shifting paradigms. Sometimes called 'consciousness,' spirituality is the passionate energizing force behind the ability of the individual to move from unconsciousness to enlightenment and from realization to action. The spirit's transcendent qualities makes it ideal for overcoming seemingly intractable challenges by seeking and appealing to the unknown truths beyond apparent present limitations. Spirituality becomes a process of the human psyche in conjunction with nature and the divine or ultimate reality.

Ecospirituality

Most of the authors synthesized ecology and spirituality into a new consciousness able to recognize their covert unity and overt importance to the future. Without respect for the planet, suffering continues; without respect for the spirit, progress is impossible. Together, these understandings plant the seeds of real global transformation through a paradigm harnessing the innate spiritual yearning for wholeness and transcendence and applying the empirical knowledge of Earth as a finite entity. The unifying characteristics of fragile physicality and infinite spirit serve to bring humanity together as a family with common needs and similar goals.

Planetary Consciousness

Several books offered a vision of both individual freedom and collective consciousness that is not merely large group or transnational, but global. Utilizing spirit towards empathic (inter)connection with each other and Earth as a living organism serves the greater yearning towards a melding of humanity with Gaia in a single sharing as a single being. Without losing one's own individuality, the ability to *know* at will what others are feeling and dialog with a planetary consciousness means we can understand what is needed on a terrestrial level and respond for the good of the whole as well as the self.

Evolutionary Movement

In order to accomplish all the above, a sense of moving from where we *are* to where we're *going* is necessary. That is, life is incomplete, dynamic, growing, constantly heading towards realizing its best potential in a procession away from self-destruction and suffering to self-preservation and joy. Change is inevitable, but maturation is voluntary, based on the efforts of people who instinctively or consciously labor on behalf of humanity and our home planet. Intrinsic but latent abilities allowing these shifts await the processes of time to manifest.

Unity in Diversity

One repeating theme of these grand movements was the recognition that diversity is not threatening or dangerous but joyful and desirable. So much suffering has resulted from the simple inability to respect difference and honor multiplicity, which produces true health in any organism. When opposites are seen as complementary and equally valid polarities instead of competing dualities, conscious acceptance of variety can form a foundation of unity against the agents of forced conformity, division, and entropy.

Peace and Social Justice

No environmental paradise is sufficient if it serves as a field for constant warfare, nor is the transformation complete without radical equity and freedom for all living beings. Peace is more than non-violence; it's a state of existence – a mental, emotional, and spiritual reality. Inner peace breeds external non-violence, and both promote just treatment of the *other*, that which diverges from one's self or community. The democratic project remains incomplete as long as bigotry or prejudice exists. Peace and justice support each other, and visionaries, knowing this, support peace and justice.

Compassion

Underlying all progressive values and principles is compassionate behavior. No matter what the justification, cruelty, destruction, or brutality in any form immediately indicate immaturity and even mental or emotional illness. Many religions seek to cultivate and disseminate compassion, and evidence suggests that it's the end result of successful spiritual practice. Kindness, consideration, integrity – these are the products of spiritual maturity. All the authors in this section emerged from the founding ethic of mercy and love, and all search for the path to enlightened kindness.

Visibility

Another constant theme of the reviewed books is the lack of their community's visibility to the mainstream (modern) media.

The mirror that reflects culture bears few images of or for the pioneers, who are sometimes regarded as disreputable fringe extremists rather than harbingers of things to come. For this reason, visionaries do not see themselves as a unified community. Only with the advent of internet communication are diverse and varied worlds reflected in these authors coming to glimpse each other and know they are working in similar directions.

The Incomprehensible Future

All these authors point through the mist of time to landscapes barely discernable in the distance, tracing the faint outlines of a future unknown and mostly unknowable, to eras that will bear only slight resemblance to our own. That we cannot know what is to come or how the seeds planted today will bear fruit is both frustrating and exciting: the explorer filling in the blank edges of the map, forging into new territory with courage and curiosity. The misty outlines of the future seem bright with promise to our collection of writers and dreamers, and why not labor in love to birth that brightness sooner rather than later?

The names given to visionaries in any given era is not as important as the fact that in every era they've been present in history, guiding humankind away from our worst natures into the brilliance of our innate promise. Eutopian visions abound precisely because of the sense that they are ultimately possible, perhaps even inevitable. Visionaries are the leading edge of the vast process of planetary development, and I believe their values will birth a new stage in human maturity. The optimistic global evolutionary worldview and the enfolding cosmic spirituality that makes it possible is the source of life's meaning and purpose. None of us *have* to struggle to make more of our selves or our species; we do it because we are led on paths of illumination, guided by voices of hope, and graced by angels of love.

Chapter 3

The Church of All Worlds

This section is about a modern NeoPagan organization called The Church of All Worlds. CAW was inspired by a science fiction novel, founded by a practicing wizard, and formed from conscious bio-cultural evolution, ecospirituality, and utopian visions of the future. Not only does CAW offer a fresh religious and philosophical worldview, it's also socially progressive and morally innovative, viewing the planet as a being and seeking to live in accordance with the ethos of Tomorrowland.

I was introduced to CAW in 1990 when a friend who knew my interests in religion and nature gave me a copy of the Church's influential journal *Green Egg*. Even before I opened it, I knew by the cover that I had found one of my spiritual homes. My perspective on CAW emerges from personal experiences through gatherings, rituals, 'sacred bullshit sessions,' magical work, and a sense of community engendered by the people attracted to this demure 'grok flock.'

However, my academic training and background also inform that perspective. As a professor, I examine religions and spiritual traditions with the objectivity of analytics and detached inquiry. For instance, I employ a healthy skepticism about supernatural claims and am semi-agnostic concerning invisible realms or beings. In light of modern scientific paradigms, I prefer to base my beliefs and practices on historically and empirically verifiable fact rather than faith. This is not to say that experiences aren't powerful and transformative, but I tend to separate personal understandings and interpretations from universal pragmatic knowledge of the observed cosmos.

CAW didn't emerge fully formed like Athena from Zeus' head. The authors we've studied, as well as several other historical and ideological influences, contribute to the Church's present contours and characterize its innermost workings as a spiritual group. The following represent the most important inspirations at the core of the Church's beliefs, practices, and values.

Hippies

CAW began as a benevolent conspiracy between Tim Zell and Lance Christie when they were college students in the early 1960s. The GI Bill helped democratize universities, and new notions and viewpoints flooded academia. In this milieu, Tim and Lance read Robert Heinlein's science fiction classic *Stranger in a Strange Land,* which filled their fertile minds with such novel and unprecedented possibilities that they each founded a group based on the book: CAW and Atl. While the latter was a secular devotional to Abraham Maslow's Actualization, the former became a religious organization, eventually identifying primarily as NeoPagan.

By mid-1960s, something unconventional was happening among a relatively small number of young people. A movement emerged from the beats, hipsters, and bohemians of the 1950s, fueled by the Kennedy assassination, writers like Kerouac and Kesey, Cannabis, LSD, the birth control pill, rock music, civil rights movement, feminism, and the aforementioned expanded educational opportunities. The rarified result proved to be the Hippies: romantic, regressive, communitarian, and hedonistic – the perfect antidote to the 1950s command and control excesses. Like CAW, Hippies were influential, one might even say mythological, beyond their actual numbers. They represented freedom, spontaneity, pleasure, and critique of the social order.

Two books are helpful in understanding them: Timothy Miller's *The Hippies and American Values* (2003) which explores the ethics of dope, sex, rock, community, and cultural opposition, and Barry Mile's coffee table extravaganza *Hippie* (2004), which is divided by year:

65: London to San Francisco, Hippie roots in poetry, fashion, and music
66: Psychedelia, LSD, the politics of ecstasy, Pink Floyd, the Dead, Vietnam, the Bus, Acid Tests
67: Sgt. Pepper, the Summer of Love, Monterey Pop, Love & Haight
68: Anti-war protests, Paris, Street Fighting Man, Chicago, the Black Panthers, Cream
69: Berkeley Riots, the Weathermen, Woodstock, Altamont, Charles Manson, Timothy Leary, Communes
70: The Age of Aquarius, Main Street Hippie, Earth Day, Trials in the UK and US, Alice Cooper
71: Jimi, Janice, and Jim gone forever, Heavy Metal thunder, Nudity, The Legacy

For those who know about the late 18th century and early 19th century English and later American Romantics – from Wordsworth to Whitman – some hippy values may seem reminiscent, and indeed I think they were expressions of what might be called Perennial Romanticism, a repeating impulse which periodically arises into social consciousness in response to some disruptive civilizational innovation. The English Romantics responded to Industrialization by harkening back to the green fields, forests, and villages of Medieval Britain, and the hippies responded to commercialization and technocracy by harkening back to simpler days of communal pioneer, rural, and small-town America.

Further, hippies ushered in contemporary interest in alternative consciousness, whether the liberation of cannabis, art, music, and psychological insights of LSD, the empathy enhancement of MDMA, or the shamanic journeying of peyote or ayahuasca. The power of these substances to grant deep visioning and healing seems significant enough to warrant serious study, which is exactly why my doctoral alma mater, the California Institute of Integral Studies, has a program of psychedelic research.

Being a hippy usually meant a conscious dedication to personal freedom (while not harming others), spontaneity, fun, and even joy. Life itself deserved to be lived fully and ecstatically, without constricting social taboos. Most hippies saw pleasure and happiness as their birthright, one surrendered by many people whose sadness reflected in institutional drudgery, boring work, conflict, war, and physical dis-ease. Thus arose the 'live for today,' 'do your own thing,' and 'if it feels good, do it' ethos that frequently bordered on hedonism. Child-like wonder at reality meant that hippies strived to see the world with fresh eyes, and often responded to life's ups and downs with playfulness and awe.

Finally, hippies sought to manifest imagination, creativity, and vibrancy, out of a sense of innocence or to mimic the psychedelic experiences. Color, flow, innovative designs, tie-dye clothing, light shows, and whimsical art and literature marked this characteristic. I remember my own black light posters that glowed with eeriness but also beauty, as if my room had moved into another dimension, and I with it.

New Agers

Another countercultural realm from which CAW drew inspiration and thealogy is the New Age movement. Mostly a literary and spiritual phenomenon, writers such as David Spangler and William Irwin Thompson produced eclectic and genteel volumes synthesizing ancient, Hindu, Buddhist, and postmodern ideations extolling the virtues of diversity, wellness, ecological awareness, and individuated spirituality. As traditional American religions continued to decline in number and influence, the gap filled with an amalgamation of elements. New Age seekers meditated, practiced yoga, followed a guru, found their true inner selves, and pursued mellowness and bliss. They also bought Shirley MacLaine books, read *The Celestine Prophecy*, watched videos like *What the Bleep Do We Know?*, hung chakra tapestries, ate natural food, and dug the mellow vibrations of ambient music in the presence of rose quartz crystals.

Nevill Drury's richly illustrated *The New Age: Searching for the Spiritual Self* (2004), outlines the major areas of interest:

Wisdom from the East, Wisdom from the West
Pioneers of the Psyche
Towards the Transpersonal
Esalen, Gestalt, and Encounter
The Psychedelic Years
Maps for Inner Space
The Holistic Perspective
Mystics and Metaphysicians
Spirit, Myth and Cosmos
Science and Spirituality
The Challenge of Death
The Future of the New Age

During this time, CAW was reaching its apex of celebrity and impact, occasionally even making national news. *Green Egg*, the Church's official journal, was the standard for Pagan magazines, and its articles reverberated throughout the English-speaking Pagan world. NeoPaganism was the fringe of, but solidly within, the New Age milieu for much of the era. In the 1980s, several important books were penned, especially Margot Adler's *Drawing Down the Moon* (which devoted a chapter to CAW).

The New Age concerned personalized, individually created spirituality – the seeker took what they resonated with, and ignored the rest. Conforming to set dogmas in order to sync with others became anathema. In this search for meaning, some traditions, such as Native American, were shamelessly appropriated; for the most part, however, New Agers sincerely sought genuine spiritual insight in their post-Christianized and increasingly secular culture. They attempted to procure ancient wisdom and refine it to modern standards, and this generally included NeoPagan groups like CAW. In 1970, the first Earth Day began a further journey into environmental awareness, and popularized the reality that the planet serves as our spaceship, limited in what it can absorb and provide – a shift in awareness still being disseminated and processed.

Sub-Cultural Visionaries

Subcultural Visionaries were partly explored, as we already described, in *The Cultural Creatives*. Remember, the authors suggested that up to a quarter of the US and UK populations fall into the CC classification; the other two categories being Traditionals and Moderns. The text follows a similar path as our previous books, but updated for the twenty-first century:

The Three Americas
Challenging the Codes
Turning Green
Waking Up
A Great Current of Change
Maps for the Journey
Into the Between
Caterpillar, Chrysalis, Butterfly
Inventing a New Culture
The Ten Thousand Mirrors

Note how these chapters reflect subtle shifts in consciousness, progressing through increased awareness of the growing numbers of Maslow's self-actualized people and their increasing effects on society. Insofar as CAW has always championed the outsider – geeks, witches, black sheep – who are not in total sync with their peers, the Church has investigated and promoted the leading edge of history, the avant-garde at the precipice of social innovation. CAW appreciates oddball storylines like Star Trek, Harry Potter, X-Men, Doctor Who, Lord of the Rings, the Addams Family, and many others. Just knowing that one is part of a large sector of the population diffuses alienation and begins the process of mutual recognition and collective activism. The book's blurb is telling:

> The Cultural Creatives care deeply about ecology and saving the planet, about relationships, peace, and social justice, about self-actualization, spirituality, and self-expression… but because they've been so invisible, they are astonished to find out how many others share both their values and their way of life. Once they realize their numbers, their impact on America promises to be enormous, shaping a new agenda for the twenty-first century.[1]

CCs live in hope that instead of a fall from civilization's grace, humanity can transform and transition to a new epoch of sustainable prosperity and empathic peace, so that children grow in peace and enlarge their worldview to encompass the planet and all its diversity in a bear hug of love. CAW might as well be the official religion of this emergence.

Sub-Cultural Visionaries work on the fringes of society, creating new mythologies, technologies, and worldviews forged in the heat of the moment in time at the leading edge of evolution. They're not usually honored during their lifetimes, with a few practical exceptions, because they're ahead of their time, out of sync with their peers. Since the Internet, they can at least bond with others of their own kind, in many cases forming networks with more influence than previously possible. In many ways, the different drum has triumphed and come to dominate certain sectors of society, especially as tech replaces physical prowess or leadership charisma with technical knowledge and digital chops.

Earth Spirituality

Ecology suggests that, while there is value in separating and examining parts, there's also much gained from identifying and analyzing the Whole. Systems theory and other techniques seek out larger patterns of interconnection, interrelationship, and integration, painting wide-angle pictures of the complexity of life and consciousness. A non-reductionist worldview allows for synthesizing oppositions and reconciling polarities with yin-yang mojo. When we combine Ecology and Spirituality, which is part of the larger effort to amalgamate science and spirit, we achieve a larger Holon.[2]

Ecospirituality allows for concepts with moral weight, such as the *sustainability imperative*, which places ethical constraints on damaging the planetary commons, and *Gaia*, which creates a potent worldview wherein Earth becomes a living meta-being, perhaps sentient or even intelligent, of which humankind is one (albeit important) part. Nature religions like CAW acknowledge the primacy of the environment that nourishes life while speculating about physical transcendence based on postmodern transcendentalism.

Nature Religions regard the natural environment, and often the entire planet, as sacred and worthy of veneration. Non-nature religions have for so long concerned themselves exclusively with otherworldliness and the afterlife that they have rarely had anything important to say about the Earth that nurtures us. A notable exception is Matthew Fox's *Creation Spirituality* and *The Coming of the Cosmic Christ*, books that helped get him ejected from the Catholic Church and into his own brilliant research on medieval Christian mystics of love and naturalism like

Hildegard of Bingen, Meister Eckhart, and Julian of Norwich, writers of what he calls 'original blessing.'

As noted previously, Eco and spirit also come together effectively in University of Florida professor Bron Taylor's *Dark Green Religion: Nature Spirituality and the Planetary Future*, with chapters like "Radical Environmentalism" and "Terrapolitan Earth Religion." His work displays deep understanding of the ways ecological concerns and sacredness intersect in society and produce commitments to defending Mother Earth against degradation. Oberon Zell moved these ideas further along to Gaea, personification of the Earth Mother Goddess figure, the meta-intelligence from which all other intelligence emerges.

Taylor's Terrapolitan Earth Religion arises as a "global, civic, environmentalist world religion" and "green culture" loyal to the planet as a whole, requiring a substantial expansion of empathy outwards until successfully embracing the entire world. NeoPaganism, by sacralizing nature and finding spiritual focus within its bounty, fits into Taylor's schema and manifests a direct religious structure onto it. Although I think some Pagan supernaturalism, if taken literally, deteriorates quickly into superstition, NeoPaganism offers a tangible form of the Terrapolitan Earth Religion, and CAW serves as one viable expression of its ideals.

Body Positivity

Because Heinlein's *Stranger in a Strange Land* (*SISL*) described free sexuality and casual nudity, CAW usually supports polyamory[3] and nude gatherings as liberating activities. During the 1990s, for instance, the Pagan gatherings I attended were at a naturist resort; I enjoyed going clothing-free, and casually appreciated the varied bodies around me. I regard this acceptance of our natural selves as the healthiest and most mature attitude, and because CAWers honor everyone's bodies, they tend to judge others or themselves less, knowing that diversity is nature's way of keeping things interesting. Marriage or handfasting, on the other hand, concerns joining, sharing, and mating, and if children are born, CAWers tend to teach them to love their own bodies and respect others' as well. In fact, CAW 'families' may be conventional-nuclear, extended, non-biological, or polyamorous. All benevolent forms of love are acceptable, and they're likely to question the often-invisible cultural assumptions about families, love, sex, and other basic behaviors.

There is reason to believe that the ideologically conservative Puritans still influence us today, with laws concerning "pornography," sexual mores, and gender identity. Body hatred and shame have lessened; the question is what would society be like if they'd never existed? How many of us would never have had to hide parts of ourselves for fear of legal reprisals and social ostracism? CAW explores these paths not taken, these ideas suppressed by prejudice, and externally prohibited yet harmless practices.

Futurism

Perhaps no aspect of the Church is more important than its futurist orientation. As noted in the first section, most religions derive their core beliefs and practices from a past of miraculous events and mystical avatars. Their rituals, holy days, taboos, and mysticism come from ritually repeating past actions, avatar teachings, texts, or stories, over and over, modified only as impelled by evolution. The past need not be ignored, but neither should it be the object of nostalgic obsession. The cult of Tradition has held sway over culture and its religions long enough; humanity has little time for such indulgences.

CAW dances to a different jam band: they don't wrestle the past forward into the present as much as invoke the future back into the present, seeing in the progress of humankind an optimism based on the workings of evolution and on adopting future values now. CAW's mythology, mostly science fiction, begins with *SISL*, through *Star Trek*, and on to continuing technological innovations like artificial intelligence, transhumanism, space colonization, and sustainable vertical cities called *arcologies*. However, external innovation does not complete the story. The key term remain *evolution*: not just biological and technical, but also emotional, psychological, socio-cultural, and spiritual.

Several texts can help, beginning with the aforementioned *Drawing Down the Moon* chapter titled "A Religion from the Future – The Church of All Worlds." In it, author Margot Adler begins by exploring science fiction as "the new mythology of our age," orienting the Church towards future potentiality rather than received tradition. She writes: "The ultimate potential of Gaea [is] the telepathic unity of consciousness of the [planetary] nervous system, between all human beings, and, ultimately, between all living creatures...a total telepathic union." With visions like this, CAW has positioned itself as a unique voice within the spiritual and evolutionary milieu of Western Civilization.

Ultimately, *Star Trek* charts much of CAW's mythic envisioning, enfolding both technological advancement and psycho-emotive maturation. The continuing *ST* saga has enthralled me since childhood, when I eagerly dominated the TV on Friday nights for the original series. The characters and moral dilemmas of the 23rd century Federation didn't simply mirror the issues of the time, but boldly speculated that humankind would overcome its own worst instincts and build a peaceful world, and that technology would aid us in that adventure. Many of the gadgets and social advances on the show have since come to pass, and I think it has an impressive record of foreseeing innovations we now take for granted. Thus, science fiction serves as mythology, not for recounting past events or figures, but for exploring and manifesting the uncharted lands of tomorrow.

NeoPaganism

Of all nature religions and earth spiritualities, it can be argued that the darkest, greenest, and ultimately most essential is Paganism. This cluster of loosely organized traditions claims as core to its theology beliefs and practice inspired by the sacredness of nature and the planet. Like the First Nations of North America, for instance, it often contains strong animistic elements in which all life possesses a soul, spirit, or consciousness, or at minimum intrinsic rights and value. The 'Wolf People' or 'Bird Tribe' share the world with humans, interact with us, and have mythic personalities or stories of their own. To cross the boundaries between ecology and spirituality requires faith in the underlying unity they share; to blend the two in an alchemical marriage. Producing the sacred child means joining an expedition into relatively unknown territories: if we take ecospirituality and combine it with the postmodern visionary community, we arrive at a remarkable constellation of green spiritual groups made of people whose worship and devotion encompasses divinity and nature and whose orientation is ecospiritual and evolutionary. These are the *NeoPagans*. Before we meet them, let's review some definitions.

Paganism may be defined as the general term for those religious or spiritual traditions, usually outside the world's large established religions,[4] that are either polytheistic, tribal, naturocentric, goddess honoring, or some combination thereof. *Pagan* derives from the Latin *pagani,* meaning "rural dweller." The term is used here to indicate all nature religions or Earth spiritualities, of which *NeoPaganism* is one subcategory. Other subcategories include Celtic reconstructionists, Heathens, and various world indigenous, aboriginal, tribal, and nativist traditions.

NeoPaganism describes a community of contemporary religious and spiritual traditions and cluster of distinct movements that owe some or all of their theology and/or praxis to the restoration of ancient traditions but whose organizational forms and practices originate from Gerald Gardner's *Wicca*[5] beginning in early 1950s Britain. NeoPaganism is a subset of Paganism combining the perceived pre-Christian origins of Paganism with the innovative creativity of a new religious movement. Pagans live and worship in every culture in the world, but NeoPagans arise out of Europe and North America and originate in the 20th century. Although the two terms can be (and often are) used interchangeably, our major focus is on NeoPaganism as interpreted through CAW.

Wicca is a 'denomination' within NeoPaganism established by Gerald Gardner in mid-1950s England,[6] and is one of the oldest and largest extant NeoPagan groups. Gardner claimed that Wicca was a revival of surviving Witchcraft traditions, but evidence for this remains controversial. Most Wiccans worship the Horned God (Pan or Herne) and the Triple Goddess (Maiden, Mother, Crone), and claim to be the renaissance of pre-Christian European Witchcraft traditions.

Gaea is the specialized name coined by Oberon Zell for the divine Earth Mother Goddess embodied as an intelligent planetary meta-being.[7] Gaea is believed to be an entity of immense complexity and awareness. The name derives from *Gaia,* the ancient Greek goddess personifying the Earth (the Roman *Terra*) and, as we noted, as utilized by Lovelock and Margulis in their "Gaia Hypothesis."[8] The spelling of Gaea is specific to CAW, and has not yet found substantial favor outside NeoPagan groups.

Witchcraft, as specifically used in this book, denotes the indigenous shamanic traditions of pre-Christian Europe and their modern expression among Pagan magick[9] workers. Witches are usually regarded as the more practical and psychic end of

Paganism – they choose to be trained and cultivate innate talents and abilities believed to be inherent in specific persons, a training that allows increased intuitive and (super)natural powers to be utilized in the cause of positively changing reality.

A Brief History of NeoPaganism

Primal Paganism

When Marcelino Sanz de Sautuola was led by his young daughter into the caves at Altamira, Spain in 1879 to witness the beautiful Paleolithic wall paintings dancing in his torchlight, the discovery changed how many people viewed primal (or "prehistoric") humans – the club-wielding brute was replaced by a people with a vibrant and creative culture, the foundation of our culture.

When many contemporary Pagans peer into this misty past, to the time when human ancestors were painting animals on cave walls, they see a projected version of their own mythic past. The archeological and anthropological evidence of this time take vibrant shape in the Pagan imagination and expand into a purely speculative and self-serving history. Verifiable historical facts are not always as important as their theological and mythopoetic[10] interpretations in the present; Altamira and other primal sites that provide glimpses into the lives of our forebears serve as beginnings of this NeoPagan mythological story, and over two decades of study, I've observed that many NeoPagans trace their cultural and religious heritage to these primal times.[11]

The study of primal or "pre-historic" cultures concerns archeological and anthropological evidence of early human settlements from Paleolithic to Neolithic, including examples of surviving implements, objects, henges, and earthworks, as well as speculations derived from them – especially as these early cultures give historical background to current Pagan practices and mythology. Since most primal peoples were 'pagan,' at least within the self-created NeoPagan historical myth, their study contextualizes contemporary Paganism within a wider religious community and history.

Marija Gimbutas (1921-1994)[12] initiated contemporary archeological research into the historical validity of a pan-European Goddess religion. Her work in Bronze Age periods led her to specific linguistic and mythological interpretations, including the notion that varied goddess symbols indicated a universal worship of the Great Mother. In order for this universal cult worship to be fact, however, goddess veneration would have either spread through contact or emerged simultaneously across a large area. Her work has been consistently criticized by scholars since its introduction in the 1970s, and such response has validity, especially concerning her speculative interpretations of selected evidence; however, negative reactions by scholars may also be inflamed by the feminist implications of widespread worship of a feminine deity. Either way, Gimbutas' theories were enthusiastically embraced by many NeoPagans for supporting the contention that the Goddess was honored by primal and ancient peoples of Old Europe.

Folk Religion

Several important elements in early 'folk' religions stem from the practice of *animism* and *pantheism*. Animism, as described by Taylor, concerns the belief that supposedly "inanimate" objects like rocks and rivers are actually alive and might even be living beings with their own (albeit radically different) consciousness.[13] For example, some First Nations peoples refer to the "stone people" or "river people" just as they do "buffalo people" or "bird people," as if each were a separate tribe.[14] Pantheism, as defined here, is the notion that deity is only immanent in the physical world, expressed wholly through nature.[15] Divinity is therefore synonymous with and limited by the observable universe. These two elements together allow for a relationship with deity or spirits *through* nature, one of the basic tenets of folk religion.

Having mythically, and perhaps culturally, connected themselves to pre-Christian folk religions of the European countryside, many NeoPagans seek a cogent heritage and philosophical lineage emerging from a universal human impulse at the core of their beliefs and practices. Thus, folk practices become integral to the perceived history of Paganism and lend legitimacy to certain contemporary practices.

Along with the purported folk religions that coalesced in pre-history as Paganism, there is also distinct folk wisdom that informs NeoPagan traditions. Storytelling, herbal medicine, midwifery, organic farming, natural interrelationships, divination, and ecospirituality are all seen as hearkening to a mythic period of dependence on the Earth and on a small tribe of others for survival. Through the centuries, according to this interpretation, rural people amassed a compendium of knowledge, understanding, and wisdom that is part of the heritage of humankind.

The Pyres of Medieval Europe

Historians generally accept that with the emergence of agriculture and writing, a major branch of civilization spread from Mesopotamia westward across Europe and eventually developed empire-building cultures. One of these, the ancient Romans, dubbed the country folk *pagani* ("rural dwellers") with the unflattering overtone of *bumpkin* or *hick*, and by the time Christianity began its expansion, contempt for Pagans in the countryside was joined by outright social and theological hostility.[16] Part of the Pagan mythos is that survival soon required discretion and eventually secrecy, and thus few records were written; instead, the Pagan legacy remained oral for centuries.[17]

During the 'High Middle Ages,' especially the climatically mild twelfth and thirteenth centuries, many aspects of old rural Paganism took on new forms: minstrels, troubadours, popular fairy tales, Morris dancers, proto-theater troupes, and even village vicars paid homage to the old ways that were deeply connected to nature spirituality. Because of a series of historical events and trends (including the Black Plague and the Protestant Revolt), the suspicion of devil-worship and "witchcraft" deteriorated into full-blown panic, sweeping in waves across the continent.[18] Pagans name the tragic results of this hysteria 'the burning times,'[19] and evidence suggests most victims of the Inquisitional flames or hanging rope were not even self-identified Witches or Pagans per se.[20] Power struggles and major socio-political shifts challenged the medieval worldview and eventually resulted in the Renaissance, scientific revolution, Enlightenment, and emergence of modernity.

Early 20th Century

At the end of the nineteenth century, Charles Leland (1824-1903),[21] an American who settled in London, wrote *Aradia, or The Gospel of the Witches*.[22] Leland exercised considerable influence over the nascent Pagan reconstructionist movement with his description of a functioning community of "Italian *strega* or sorceresses" which "has been practiced for many generations."[23] His book persuaded some that there were surviving Pagans in the form of underground Witch covens who had been in hiding from the Burning Times or before, and that the lack of information about them had negative consequences.

> This ignorance was greatly aided by the wizards themselves, in making a profound secret of all their traditions, urged thereto by fear of the priests. In fact, the latter all unconsciously actually contributed immensely to the preservation of such lore, since the charm of the forbidden is very great, and witchcraft, like the truffle, grows best and has its raciest flavour when most deeply hidden.[24]

Leland's book creates a goddess who descends to Earth to teach the peasants witchcraft and aid their struggle against feudalism and Christianity. Leland's "witches" were from agricultural villages and therefore lived rural or village lives. Today, the Craft constitutes a synthesis of indigenous wisdom and spell-working skills, but its origins are generally agrarian. At the dawn of the twentieth century, the ground was seeded with ideas that would, fifty years later, blossom into NeoPaganism – a chapter of *Aradia* was even adapted by Wiccan priestess Doreen Valiente into *The Charge of the Goddess,*[25] a seminal recitation document in Wicca and most contemporary NeoPaganism.

During the twentieth century, several other popular writers and some scholars were involved in re-discovering the agricultural roots of Paganism in a sympathetic manner. Typical of this phenomenon is Jessie Weston's *From Ritual to Romance,* which ostensibly covers the Arthurian legends but also connects earlier Pagan elements with later Christian ones. In the Dedication page, the author mentions Frazer's *Golden Bough,* the Bayreuth Festival of 1911, J. E. Harris' *Themis* and its perusal of "vegetation rites," and R. S. Mead's assistance in completing "the chain of evolution from Pagan Mystery to Christian Ceremonial."[26] Sources such as this provide further evidence of the slow re-emergence of both pastoral Paganism in popular consciousness and of the community structure of later NeoPaganism, including festival gatherings, magickal workings, Earth rituals, and the "mysteries" of Witchcraft.

Another author who helped popularize this historical mythos and exercised considerable influence on the course of NeoPaganism was Margaret Murray (1863-1963), the anthropologist who wrote *The Witch-cult in Western Europe.*[27] Murray's dubiously researched and often discredited work nonetheless holds considerable weight in the NeoPagan movement – if nothing else, she helped expose the isolated pockets of Paganism that probably survived from pre-modernity, scattered across Europe. Evidence in Christian architecture and local ceremonies suggests that older knowledge and wisdom was integrated into Christian life and researchers such as Carlo Ginzburg have discovered records of hereditary magicians during the Inquisitions;[28] in the main, however, contemporary manifestations of NeoPaganism may be traced to Witch covens that formed because of Murray's work: concepts such as the Esbats (full moons), the Wheel of the Year, and the Horned God all derive from Murray's writings. Since, as already noted, many NeoPagans don't always differentiate myth from historical fact, Murray remains a core personality in the formation and present form of the movement.

Industrialization, warfare, and the resulting physical and psychological displacement typically encourage pastoral, romantic, back-to-nature, and ecological movements, partly explaining the rise of NeoPaganism between the world wars. Particularly, however, it was in the 1950s, after the repeal of the last Witchcraft Act in England,[29] that Gerald Gardner wrote *Witchcraft Today*[30] and *The Meaning of Witchcraft*[31] that almost single-handedly opened the floodgates of NeoPaganism. Combining ritual nudity and the occult with influences from surviving covens, Ordo Templi Orientis,[32] and Rosicrucian Order, Gardner created a seminal form of NeoPaganism called *Wicca* that is of interest here for its pre-Christian, rural European roots: Wiccans worship an Earth Goddess, celebrate the eight seasonal Sabbats and thirteen full moon Esbats of the year, hold religious services outdoors in nature whenever possible, practice herbal healing, and honor a plethora of polytheistic gods, goddesses, elementals, and other spiritual beings embedded in nature, along with the five natural elements embodied as Elementals.[33]

The 1960s

Rachel Carson's 1962 *Silent Spring*, with its active exploration of the consequences to planetary biosystems of modern industrial agriculture, did much to inaugurate the contemporary environmental movement. Increasingly sophisticated in analysis and worldview, environmentalism and ecology spawned groups from the Sierra Club to Earth First! Included in these were the sacred nature advocates who adopted old pagan worldviews, either synthesizing a spiritual system of eco-ethics or adopting a religious praxis, the latter influential in the formation of NeoPaganism's strong ecospiritual element.[34]

As previously noted, it could be argued that the decade of beatniks, hippies, flower children, and the Age of Aquarius represents an example of the periodic resurgence of Romantic Bohemianism;[35] the popular imagination appears to oscillate between "conservative" and "liberal." Conservative periods seek to maintain past cultural accumulations while liberal phases actively seek growth, progressive social development, and emergent human evolution. This theory of cyclical waves alternating *chaos* and *cosmos*[36] helps explain why "The Sixties" remains such a dynamic and influential mythos decades later: it was the latest re-surfacing of the minority progressive impulse. If this is the case, the products of the energy of the Sixties – among them communards, early environmental activists, and NeoPagans – remain transformational to this day.

Celebrated in music and legend, the back-to-the-land movement (a subgroup of the hippy movement) remains significant in proportion to its actual size, and communards occupy a historically nuanced niche in the European and American imagination.[37] Their vision of the simple life based on interconnection, mutual sustenance, cooperative enterprise, organic worldview, countercultural initiatives, deep freedom, peace, and love produced many functioning and radically alternative communities. All of these innovative ideas and activities were revived, modified, or initiated in the 1960s in a milieu of social experimentation and cultural upheaval.

The history of NeoPaganism consists of some empirical

fact and considerable creative mythos that in its totality is considered by many Pagans to be real and true, providing the background and backbone of the Pagan self-image. From the first (hypothetical) shamans through the evolution of folk religion, the mists of time obscure (but also provide the necessary ingredients for) the mythology of Paganism, much like the clouds of Mount Olympus cultivated the fertile imaginations of the ancient Greeks. In time, the Romantics, Bohemians, Beats, and Hippies again gave voice to the creative impulses of the mytho-poetic mind, offering counter-points to mechanization, industrialism, corporate mercantilism, and other features of modernity.

British NeoPaganism

As noted, Wicca began in 1950s England, after the repeal of the last medieval Witchcraft Act, so it has distinctly European roots. Graham Harvey's 1990 book *Contemporary Paganism* gives an excellent review from a British perspective. For instance, some covens claim to be continuous from the medieval period, but Harvey's interest is in modern forms these groups have taken. Beginning with the eight seasonal Sabbats, he notes that most Pagans, as nature religions, do not so starkly divide between what Mircea Eliade called *sacred* and *profane* realities.

> The dichotomies of sacred and profane or religious and secular are of little value here because they imply far more than the idea that some things are more significant than others. They set up a barrier between ordinary or 'mundane' activities and ceremonial, symbolic, or 'religious' which is not significant in nature-celebrating or life-affirming traditions.[38]

Groups or individuals that self-identify as Pagan tend to see all benevolent human activities and all of nature (benevolent or not) to be sacred, part of the larger reality of holiness. Therefore, "dirty" things, both literally such as soil and fungi, and figuratively such as sexuality and profanity, get included in the realm of "spiritual," which can be disturbing to those committed to the dichotomies. "That which is 'worldly' is not necessarily indicative of lack of significance, importance, or sacredness. What is significant for Pagans is the attempt to discern that which affirms Life and that which negates it."[39] For most Pagans maintain a sense of relaxed engagement with the full range of life's experiences. "If people seek an escape from the world into 'spirituality' or 'heaven' or 'enlightenment' they are clearly told that the divine and the human exist in this world of food, drink, sex, humour, sadness, desire, constriction and ecstasy."[40]

Some Pagans practice theistically, with a sense of spirituality separate from but overlapping physical/material reality, but others practice non-supernaturally, relying on psychological and ecological sources for transformational energy – which, they claim, is quite powerful by itself. Magick reveals itself to the latter group as a powerful tool for changing consciousness, and thus the psycho-social environment of the practitioner. Harvey defines magick as "a coherent way of understanding the world in which something within each person – the will – can be used to effect change or affect others beyond the self" with "the will" defined as "an intellectual, emotive, and imaginative focus" of consciousness."[41]

Other highlights of Harvey's work include "eco-magic," scared sexuality and gender, shamanism and psychedelic sacraments, and rites of passage. He even touches on CAW, in a section on the influences of literature on Pagan groups, citing Heinlein's part in the Church's origins.

What was gained from these writers – apart from the general romance and heroism of an alternative vision or even lifestyle – was the importance of a libertarian blend of individualism and communitarianism, and of personal responsibility, life-affirmation and especially of intuitive and empathetic knowledge for which the term 'grok' was coined."[42]

It is indeed difficult to underestimate the influence of *SISL* on the formation and continued values of CAW, even in Britain.

American NeoPaganism

Major contemporary writers include Margot Adler (1946-2014) whose work is highly respected both inside and outside the tradition. Adler's thorough, sympathetic, and comprehensive treatment of the movement, marked by the psychotherapeutic influences of her grandfather[43] and her personal skills as a National Public Radio journalist, stands among the most utilized sources for information on the subject, especially regarding the 1970s and 1980s. She begins her first chapter by noting the emergence of a "diverse and decentralized religious movement… that remains comparatively unnoticed, and when recognized, is generally misunderstood."[44] This movement displays remarkable diversity yet holds certain beliefs and practices in common.

> Most Neo-Pagans sense an aliveness and 'presence' in nature. They are usually polytheists or animists or pantheists, or two or three of these things at once. They share the goal of living in harmony with nature and they tend to view humanity's 'advancement' and separation from nature as the prime source of alienation. They see *ritual* as a tool to end that alienation. Most Neo-Pagans look to the old pre-Christian nature religions of Europe, the ecstatic religions, and the mystery traditions as a source of inspiration and nourishment. They gravitate to ancient symbols and ancient myths...adding to them…other writers of science fiction and fantasy, as well as some of the teachings and practices of the remaining aboriginal peoples.[45]

Margot Adler devotes an entire chapter of *Drawing Down the Moon* to CAW, a group she calls "a religion from the future." She offers some of her personal experiences with the Church (including a nude mailing party), followed by an exploration of science fiction as religious literature and a brief history of the Church ending in the mid-1980s. She then visits Oberon's "Theagenesis" philosophies emphasizing their evolutionary theory as progressive rather than open-ended and noting that the full potential of Gaea is "the telepathic unity of consciousness between all parts of the nervous system, between all human beings, and ultimately between all living creatures."[46] This unity retains individual choice or sense of self but results in a "new level of awareness and emergent wholeness."[47] She also discusses the 'neo-tribal' aspect of CAW emerging from concepts of extended family, describing the Church as "based on custom and tradition rather than on dogma and belief, grounded in what one *did* rather than in what one *believed*." (Neo)Tribal traditions tend to stress "social and personal interaction" and have anarchistic governing systems maintained by "conventions and discussion leading to consensus."[48] Most members, according to Adler's research, feel themselves to be strangers in a strange land, aliens in a culture not of their making, struggling to maintain their vision in a sometimes hostile world.

If Adler represents the intellectual and academic approach to studying NeoPaganism, Starhawk (1951-)[49] represents the more intuitive, feminist, and activist approach. As a Pagan theorist, popular author, and advocate of ecofeminism, Starhawk is highly influential within the movement, serving as a spokesperson for Witchcraft to the non-Pagan community. Her assertive approach emerges from her commitment to manifesting Pagan values in the larger society, and her book *The Spiral Dance* presents an activist manifesto for modern Goddess religion.

> On every full moon, rituals...take place on hilltops, beaches, in open fields, and in ordinary houses...women and men from many backgrounds come together to celebrate the mysteries of the Triple Goddess of birth, love, and death, and of her

Consort, the Hunter, who is Lord of the Dance of life.[50]

Her descriptions of Pagan phenomena such as the coven, God and Goddess, magickal symbols, the *cone of power*, and *wheel of the year*, give flesh to the theoretical bones and heart to the study and practice of NeoPaganism.

Starhawk's influence has to do with the rich contours of her vigorous life. *Spiral Dance* is a vibrant work, filled with a wealth of rites, rituals, and celebrations developed over years of practice with her various groups, mainly Reclaiming,[51] that are connected philosophically to the values and worldview of the NeoPagan community. For instance, the *cone of power* is a way to use the 'stirring' energy of circling around a central point to magickally focus intention and desire toward a positive goal, with chants like "Wipe the slate clean/Dream a new dream!" and "We're taking back the night/The night is ours!" that raise power for individual projects like self-transformation and collective projects like facing crime and overcoming its grip through action. Starhawk's other books also reflect her commitment to sharing the distinct vision of NeoPaganism with the world.

Ethnography of The Church of All Worlds

CAW was founded in the tumultuous 1960s and has flourished, with occasional turbulence, into the twenty-first century. Inspired by *SISL* and lead by Oberon Zell, the Church of All Worlds (CAW) represents the continuing human endeavor to reach for a radiant future amid the circle of life and immanence of spiritual transcendence. As a uniquely American NeoPagan church with international scope, CAW pioneered the ecospiritual worldview and restored lost wisdom from the past while obsessing about how to beautify the future. I believe it represents no less than a template for how humanity might, and probably will, craft the coming century into an enduring legacy of peace, prosperity, compassion, and love – perennial values that live in the heart like seedlings in the dark soil of evolutionary destiny and abiding hope.

We begin with a few definitions:

- The ***Church of All Worlds*** is a NeoPagan religion founded in 1967 emphasizing Earth as Gaea and science fiction-inspired futurism. See website: www.caw.org.
- ***Oberon Zell*** began the Church in the early 1960s aided by his friend Lance Christie while in college. Oberon has been active in the NeoPagan movement since that time and is currently also headmaster of the Grey School of Wizardry (an online learning institution) and artistic creator of the "Millennia Gaea" sculpture offered through Mythic Images, the company he runs.
- ***Theagenesis*** is defined as meaning 'beginning of the Goddess' coined in a 1971 essay by Oberon Zell proposing that the planet Earth is a conscious, intelligent meta-being historically called The Earth Mother Goddess or, more contemporarily, Gaea. Synonymous with Oberon's "Gaia Thesis," Theagenesis came about, according to its author, after a vision in 1970. It was presented as a sermon to CAW that same year, and subsequently published as the main article in *Green Egg*, the journal of CAW.[52]
- For the purposes of this section, ***Magick*** is defined as the ability to change one's consciousness and perceptions, and therefore the (subjective) world, at will, with the understanding that when subjective perception alters, objective reality changes for the individual. Additionally, magick may involve specialized rituals focused towards a specifically positive result, meant to connect the individual or group with non- or semi-corporeal energies believed to reside in nature. A common NeoPagan saying is that "magick is like prayer, but more work." The term is usually spelled with a *k* to differentiate it from

performance or stage magic, which relies on trickery rather than the mind's capacity for transformation or (super)natural forces.

- ***Panentheism*** is the concept that a personal, creative deity is both wholly immanent in the physical universe and utterly transcendent in spiritual realms. Spirit (by any and all names, including *God/dess*) *is* all things, is *in* all things, and is *more* than all things simultaneously, allowing the divine to be both living planet (Gaea) and the infinite mystical reality at the core of spirituality. Panentheism differs from *pantheism* in that the former allows for an indwelling divine presence rather than a godhead that is exclusively abstract or entirely synonymous with the physical-material realm, and posits divinity as the eternal animating force behind and within the universe.
- ***Polyamory*** means 'many loves,' and is the practice of having more than one committed, intimate, and often sexual partner with the full consent of everyone involved, sometimes creating blended families. Polyamory can also refer to a general lifestyle orientation allied with multiple-partner relationships. Also called 'responsible non-monogamy,' the practice is not precisely polygamy (one person with multiple spouses) but rather a late twentieth century designation reasserting choice and free will outside current normative social standards for marriage.

CAW as a New Religious Movement (NRM)

The term *new religious movement* originated in post-World War II Japan as *shin shukyo* or 'new religion,' replacing *cult* in general academic usage. Cataloging new Japanese religions stimulated interest in domestic examples of emerging and alternative groups. In 1965, a new immigration bill allowed an influx of Asians to the United States who brought with them recently created religions and older traditions such as Krishna devotion; these new arrivals were welcomed by a generation of American seekers weary of the often stifling and entrenched status quo.

NRMs generally refer to religions originating after 1945 as unprecedented creative synthesis or as a foreign tradition new to the United States.[53] CAW claims to be an example of both, since it contains several unique modern religious creations[54] and claims to partake in the (mythic) pre-Christian history of Paganism. Incorporated in 1967, the Church exemplifies NeoPaganism in the United States and stands as a recognized but under-examined NRM.

The premier investigator of CAW as an NRM is J. Gordon Melton (1942-)[55] who counts the Church "among the largest and most influential of all Neo-Pagan religious groups during the 1970s."[56] Melton acknowledges that CAW "was the first of the Neo-Pagan Earth Religions to obtain full federal recognition" as a tax-exempt non-profit organization[57] and notes that the Church is pantheist "which focuses on immanent rather than transcendent divinity."

> Pantheists hold as divine the living spirit of nature. Thus, the CAW recognizes Mother Earth, the Horned God, and other spirits of animistic totemism as the Divine pantheon. In this manner, the Church of All Worlds became an early forerunner of the Deep Ecology movement.[58]

In a 2007 article, Melton revisited the concept of new religious studies, especially their significance to contemporary scholarship. Noting the subtle post-millennial shift from *New Age* to *Next Age* orientations, he submits that NRMs remain "alienated both socially and culturally from a particular culture's dominant religious milieu." In addition, there are both NRMs whose leader/founders have died and whose pace of change has slowed and NRMs whose leader/founders still live and whose changes with maturation, if any, present opportunities for further scholarly work.[59]

CAW's Ecospirituality

As previously discussed, *ecospirituality* implies a hybridization of environmental ethics and religious studies. The "Romantic-pastoral" path of NeoPaganism and (neo) tribal traditions (i.e., nature and Earth as sacred) are explored in writings on Earth spiritualities, planetary consciousness, folk religion, rural magickal traditions, and activist groups such as Greenpeace and Earth First! CAW both sympathizes with and incorporates these passions, drawing philosophies from some authors and from others justification for proactive efforts such as tree planting and healing ritual magick.

The alchemical marriage between science and religion is one of the unique characteristics of CAW, whose theology includes both empirically observed and metaphysically experienced validations. By locating humankind within a vast process common to all life, an underlying truth of both disciplines is revealed and the stance of ecospirituality results in optimism about the future because, in the end, Earth knows how to cultivate and maintain life. With a kind of confirmed faith in the offspring of science and spirit, we approach CAW's hopeful confidence that humanity will continue to participate in the grand liturgy of the universe with sanguinity.

In addition to NeoPagan writers and organizers in the United States, British researcher Ronald Hutton (1954-) writes in *The Triumph of the Moon* that CAW emerged as "an organization of radical mystics" who "established the identity of modern paganism as a response to a planet in crisis."

> Its spiritual core lay in the concept of the earth a single, divine, living organism. The mission of pagans, according to this concept, was to save 'her' by transformation of the values

> of Western society.[60]

Hutton is correct when he suggests that CAW is mainly populated by "radical mystics" insofar as their outlook, beliefs, and some practices are considered radical from more established perspectives, and because most members pursue direct, rather than mediated, experiences of divinity.

According to Hutton, not only does CAW see the planet as a "single, divine, living organism," but the Church also sees that the living planet, despite its divinity, is not immortal or indestructible – it's rather "in crisis" just as an individual might experience crisis in his or her life. Earth as Gaea, therefore, is presented as an expansive meta-being who, like ancient Greek pantheon, is fallible and can suffer. In order to save Her, CAW has as part of its mission the "transformation of the values of Western society" uniting social justice and environmental activism. The Church is not only a repository for a certain restorative theology but also a flashpoint for spiritual activism.

Hutton connects several ideas central to CAWs Gaean concepts, including contemporary scientific theories concerning James Lovelock's planetary organism and the impact of space travel.

> It's very likely that this view of the earth, although rooted in some ancient ideas and images, and very obviously derived from the modern notion of female divinity as inherently related to the natural world, was given final impetus by the first photographs of the planet from space, in the 1960s.[61]

CAW is a (post)modern religion directly inspired by modern images of the planet as a solitary 'spaceship' set in the darkness of the cosmos. Such images foster an awareness of the delicacy and vulnerability of the planet as a whole, without visible national borders. Human ideological or nationalistic conflicts are therefore understood as shallow artificial creations of the human imagination adjustable through shifts in consciousness. In a sense, CAW's optimistic idealism emerges partially from the modern sense of being one world, one species on a limited sphere of life. CAW is the beneficiary of the unprecedented technical proficiency that allowed photos to be taken from space, a feat unavailable during the formative periods of other religions; this difference makes CAW a unique religious phenomenon, essentially dissimilar to the large monotheistic religions.

Although CAW embraces science, it's not beholden to the constraints of objectively verifiable methods. Room exists for the mysterious, intuitive, and fanciful. Dreams weave in and out of the Church's structure and theology like a tapestry made of wildly contrasting but ultimately complementary colors. Spirituality, by some definitions, is ephemeral and disembodied, but in CAW physical and spiritual realities alchemically combine into a religious synthesis that includes the myth of primal Paganism, interpretations of folk religion, the trauma of mass burnings, early twentieth century pastoral revivalism, 1960s experimentalism, Goddess spirituality, and postmodern ecospirituality.

Founding, History, and Purpose

The Soviet Union's 1957 launch of the first orbiting satellite motivated the United States government to begin offering grants and scholarships, especially in science and mathematics, to a segment of the population who had rarely gone to college before: the working class. Finding themselves in college, these students brought a different, less entrenched and less privileged perspective to academia. At graduation, not all of them aspired to enter the military-industrial complex; some who did not go to work for government, industry, or corporations found themselves with considerable education but no prospects, or indeed interest, in signing up for the Cold War. The stage was set for the "tune in, turn on, drop out" generation. Many of these young people turned their educations to radically new idea(l)s and ideologies, challenging the status quo and re-imagining almost every aspect of American life – including religion. Questions were raised about the seemingly intractable boundaries of religious orthodoxy, theology, cosmology, divinity, and spirituality.

Tim Zell (Oberon Zell) and Lance Christie, two students at Westminster College in Fulton, Missouri, met at a fraternity party in September 1961. They were middle-class American males with a common love of science fiction and philosophy and a penchant for romantic idealism – two poster boys for the post-Sputnik era. Despite their mainstream lives, however, they felt alienated from the majority of their peers and from the culture at large, so that when they read Heinlein's *Stranger in a Strange Land* (*SISL*) in 1962, they immediately resonated with its message of alternative lifestyles (including polyamory and sacred sexuality[62]) lived out by an enlightened literati. CAW was later based on the fictional "Church of All Worlds" in *SISL*, a series of temples housing groups of devotees to the charismatic character Valentine Michael Smith and his messianic message of responsible free love, personal transformation, and the language of deep empathy ('grokking').

Tim and Lance sensed their minority status in terms of beliefs, worldview, ethos, and personal practices, but they clearly emerged from the mid-twentieth century modern American milieu that also stimulated civil rights, women's equality, and other political identity and freedom movements. In their context of material comfort and democratic freedom, exploration of lifestyle alternatives and radical boundaries was possible. Tim flourished in this setting and, as a clinical psychology major, sought not only to understand social constraints on behavior but also to actively challenge them. Tim was both inspired by, and eventually became a contributor to, the romantic-progressive effusion of energy typifying the decade.

Tim and Lance first created a Maslovian self-actualization[63] group called Atl.[64] While Lance continued Atl in a more humanistic and psychic direction, Tim discovered the new Wiccan religious movement brought over from Britain, and he later coined the term *neo-pagan* to describe its broadest outlines. When CAW began the incorporation process to register as a religious organization in the late 1960s, the State of Missouri initially rejected its application because the Church had no clear concept of a (monotheistic) God. This rejection, eventually overturned, shows how narrow the definition of *religion* could be at that time, CAW and other NeoPagan groups flourished.

During the 1970s, CAW became one of the most important NeoPagan groups in the United States, especially through its journal *Green Egg* that provided the growing community a forum for communication and sharing. However, when Oberon and his long-time partner Morning Glory settled onto a rural Northern California homestead, began raising unicorns,[65] and basically withdrew to a rustic communal existence more or less disconnected from society, CAW lost its founding leaders and its centralized headquarters, continuing as a collection of scattered and independent branches.

By the 1980s, Oberon and Morning Glory emerged from seclusion, Green Egg was revived, and what became known as CAW II flourished. Throughout the 1980s and 1990s, *Green Egg* grew in length, sophistication, and stature and CAW experienced a period of development. However, by the mid-1990s, the organization of the Church began experiencing a divisive split between those who emphasized CAW as a non-profit entity and those who saw it as a visionary spiritual family. Unable to reconcile these two realities, the Board of Directors, which at the time was the major authority in the Church, became dominated by members with a more corporate and profit-making trajectory. In all fairness, visionaries aren't always the best financial planners and there were some improprieties reported, but the ultimate result was the Board voted in 2004 to terminate CAW as a legal entity rather than deal with the mounting difficulties. From what I observed during this period, the Board veered onto a more corporate path, lost the guiding vision, and because of personal and financial complexities, decided to remove Oberon from his position as 'Primate' (guiding leader) and dissolve the Church. *Green Egg* ceased publication, many Nests disbanded, and many members, frustrated with legal wrangling and personal disputes within the leadership, left. This internal strife is remembered by Morning Glory as being "embroiled in the middle of a horrific schism that tore the Church apart and ended up with a small group on the inside and everybody else being kicked out.[66] The schism resembled a bitter family quarrel, disappointing and alienating to almost everyone involved.

By 2005 the Board members who had disbanded CAW II had either left the Church or were deceased, so Oberon and Morning Glory decided to re-incorporate CAW in California and re-establish its original vision. Known as CAW III and under the leadership of Oberon, Morning Glory, and a few members who had not favored dissolution and could be coaxed to return, the Church re-dedicated to its founding ideals. In 2006, the new Board, consisting of Oberon (President), Morning Glory (Vice President), long-time member Jack Cain (Treasurer), and six other participants decided to officially censure those involved in the 2004 Board termination decision and send letters of apology to those members wronged by past actions. Later that year, I visited the new headquarters, which at the time was located in Cotati, California, and with boxes of Church material still piled in several rooms, conducted two interviews Oberon and Morning Glory. The Clergy Council was working to re-form CAW and re-structure those institutional weaknesses that precipitated such agonizing problems.

The Church is currently prospering in its latest incarnation, with Oberon as Primate and a committed inner circle as Board of Directors; however, Morning Glory died in 2014 and the Church's headquarters moved from Cotati to Santa Cruz, California, including a small shop and meeting space called The Academy of Arcana.

As to its purpose, the Church of All Worlds sees itself as a sometimes loosely, sometimes intensely affiliated group of individuals striving to live out and disseminate their specific vision, and to gather in commonweal their intellectual and spiritual resources toward their visionary goals. As stated in the CAW Membership Handbook, "The Church of all Worlds is an organization founded to promote – with proper respect for diversity – a particular world vision."[67] According to CAW literature, its mission is to:

> Evolve a network of information, mythology, and experience to awaken the divine within and to provide a context and stimulus for reawakening Gaea and reuniting Her children through tribal community dedicated to responsible stewardship and the evolution of consciousness.[68]

What first strikes many readers is the level and type of vocabulary in this statement. Terms such as "reawakening Gaea" and "evolution of consciousness" take for granted a certain philosophical orientation and level of education that are, in fact, typical of CAW members. The mission is grand if not grandiose, and yet for most members is within the realm of practical possibility.

To "evolve a network of information, mythology, and experience" accepts that humans evolve from simple to complex states, and that one may actively "evolve" networks of people, collectively promoting increased complexity and therefore adaptability. CAW embraces evolution, not necessarily in the classic social Darwinian sense but in the broader applications of Franz Boas and his followers.[69] Most CAW members believe that cultural evolution exists but it doesn't lead from 'primitive' to 'civilized' states, nor is it the privilege of one group; rather, cultural evolution is part of a general movement of humankind growing from 'immature' to 'mature.' This view implies that both healthy human development and cultural development move from ignorant and undisciplined to knowledgeable and self-controlled. Indigenous tribes, for instance, aren't respected based on civilizational standards but on how well and peacefully they live with the land and each other. Many CAW members see themselves embedded in a dynamic cosmos influenced by social, biotic, and 'theotic' realities hardwired to recapitulate the experience of an idealized individual, from innocence, ignorance, and childishness to wisdom, knowledge, and compassion.

Evolving a "network of information" suggests that through the progressive matrix of cultural and cosmic evolution, information about spiritual alternatives offered by NeoPaganism becomes an element in bringing about transformation and that *information* is an agent in the process. For CAW, the 'information age' is not just about data or background static but is part of the very stuff of human (and possibly global) evolution – the more information, the swifter the developmental transformations. Returning to the lifespan analogy, as a child gains and processes information, he or she becomes more knowledgeable about the world and so becomes better able to live in it; therefore, information fuels growth and maturation – individually and globally.

In terms of hardware application, the information age concerns the development of communication webs, such as the Internet, that create a primitive version of Teilhard de Chardin's noosphere or "thinking envelope"[70] based on biomimetic technologies and organic models of information processing and exchange.[71] Exponentially expansive, such technical innovations appear capable of creating a single 'grid' of intra-species awareness constituting the growing intelligence of Gaea. CAW generally views the noosphere as part of the process of Gaea's growth through human evolutionary development. As humanity matures, Gaea, as a living being, also expands in complexity. The Goddess oversees this maturation because She and Gaea are partially synonymous while Divinity remains panentheistically *more* than Gaea.[72]

Evolving a "network of mythology" indicates the weaving of stories is of equal importance to information. If data represent discreet objective knowledge, myth represents holistic subjective experience through collective memory and archetypal symbolism. Oral tradition, written literature, and unconscious assumptions constitute stories that we tell each other and ourselves, and which connect us to the Whole. The story of humanity's rise from primitive to civilized state is one such story told by civilization, which naturally places itself at the pinnacle of evolutionary progress. The manifestation of CAW's visions requires adopting a story reflecting, supporting, and encouraging the ecospiritual vision:[73] CAW myths, for example, encompass expressions of a positive future, approval of eroticism and sexuality, advocacy of peace and social justice, efficacy of positive magick, and the sacredness and seniority of Earth.

Evolving a "network of experience" speaks to the subjectively empirical curiosity of CAW based on its familiarity with theoretical and (ethically) applied science and technology and its history with science fiction. To *know* something means accepting it as fact *after* personally experiencing it: the Earth is finally round when it's observed as round, and LSD is good or bad based not on public opinion or political fashion but on experimentation and confirmation. Specifically, new and spiritually important experiences tend to attract the attention of CAW members. Consciousness-altering substances stimulate experimentation and analysis, as do alternative sexual and familial arrangements, intense ecstatic rituals,[74] and celebratory play.

Other methods of stimulating alternative consciousness include shamanic drumming, dancing, singing, various forms of magick-working, physically challenging activities such as hiking or vision quests, and the establishment of deep empathic connection to other people through various psychological and magickal means. These pursuits appear to be stimulated by (a) an interest in pre-modern sensual and psychic experientialism and (b) a desire to create inter-relationships in the face of hyper-individualism. Not only do individuals pursue various experiences, but they also share them with others of like mind and heart so that the collective can contemplate and cherish the experiences to their fullest.

All three of these networks might fit any secular New Age movement, but the purposes of "evolving" in CAW emerge as spiritual and religious: first to "awaken the divine within" indicating a sense of interior self-divinity either as divine 'spark' or presence of deity (or both); and second to thereby reawaken Gaea as a conscious meta-being in the pursuit of enhancing the inter-relationship between planet and humankind. The second goal implies dynamic reciprocity, mutual benefit, and consciousness on both sides of the equation; while modern scientism views Earth as fundamentally inanimate, the planet-people communion challenges this worldview.

By developing networks of information, myth, and experience, either within CAW or in other contexts, Church members believe they can rouse the Earth Mother Goddess through paths of inner spirit shared among a commonweal in an increasingly sophisticated, complex, and expansive matrix, indicating a special, but not exclusive, human relationship to the divine. What CAW and other NeoPagan groups do is add a third element to the human-divine connection: they place the Earth either in a holy trinity or as a mediating agent to the divine. For instance, for some members Gaea is the only Deity while for others She dwells amidst a pantheon; She can also be seen as an intermediary or intercessor between humanity and God/dess. Informational, mythological, and experiential networks develop through tribe, stewardship, and consciousness. More specifically, CAW involves 'neo-tribalism,'[75] the adaptation of certain characteristics of the historical tribe-unit while eliminating the undesirable aspects to create a postmodern form.[76] Neo-tribalism, as envisioned by CAW, promotes the re-establishment of voluntarily close, mutually interdependent, and self-sustaining groups of cooperating people who, while retaining individual rights and freedoms, choose to live and work in a collective context.

CAW also seeks to develop sophisticated stewardship models of behavior as an assumed prerequisite for a fully ethical life. Like the similar 'environmental stewardship' in Green Christianity, which seeks a Biblical basis for protecting Earth as good stewards of the Creator,[77] naturally-green NeoPagans often advocate activism and lifestyle choice as a spiritual duty towards sacred nature. In CAW, stewardship is an assumed prerequisite for an ethical life as well as a fundamental Church tenet. A steward acts to administer something as an agent for another party, and CAW views humans as responsible for protecting the Earth into perpetuity as the heritage of future generations. According to many NeoPagans, only utter presumption and arrogance would lull people into falsely believing that humanity reigns supreme among a natural matrix of life so complex it remains poorly understood. NeoPagan stewards hold Earth as a birthright from God/dess, a precious gift to be honored and appreciated; in this way, the Church believes the relationship between the trinity of human, Earth, and deity opens to fresh interpretation and meaning.

The "evolution of consciousness" assumes that humans have a distinct "consciousness" consisting of thought, emotion, environmental response, sentience, and awareness of self and others – an awareness that can, like the physical body, grow, expand, and mature. Many CAW members posit that consciousness exists at the juncture of transcendent spirit and immanent matter as a spiritual reality that is deposited into and co-joined with physicality and which continues, in one form or another, after discorporation[78] from the body. Consciousness, therefore, is regarded as different from 'being conscious' – the latter serves as metaphor for the former in that being 'asleep' or 'unconscious' applies to those who possess an underdeveloped or poorly evolved consciousness. In CAW, an important effort centers around becoming more awake, aware, in tune, and empathically connected with the self, others, the planet, and divinity. The practices of NeoPagans serve this goal and CAW in particular has created a system whereby belief in the evolution of consciousness manifests.[79]

According to Oberon and Morning Glory, the *purpose* of CAW is:

> To restore a sense of feeling of unity among the people in the world and a sense that we are all children of the same Mother, and to promote the awakening of Gaea, the awakening of humanity, the awakening of spirit…and integration of all these things that have been alienated and disassociated…the purpose is to bring together.[80]

To "restore" feelings of unity indicates that they have been lost, usually because certain aspects of modern industrial civilization have effectively alienated humanity from nature. One of the central tasks of CAW is to heal this estrangement and reconcile all parties to the benefit of each; this healing is accomplished through reunion or reunification stimulated by the re-establishment of an idealistic tribal community of equality, mutual support, and altruistic values.[81]

In certain ways, being a new religious movement means being un-circumscribed by history or tradition; CAW maintains a change-with-the-times ethos partly emerging out of its science fiction roots and partly from its adventurous values. CAW is inclusive rather than exclusive, embracing and welcoming rather than restrictive or jealous. Oberon appreciates the name *Church of All Worlds* as being inclusive and interfaith. He believes CAW altars should include menorahs and crèches because "our history and origins allows us to embrace the magick of creating what works for us."[82] Unlike many religions that make exclusive claims on their adherent's spiritual loyalty, CAW accepts a multiplicity of truths and includes in its worship the images, symbols, and energies of other traditions as legitimate expressions of the divine. The Church not only absorbs the past and transplants it into the present; it values the act of creating the present, weaving magickal webs of imagination and innovation along common CAW principles and ethics. Instead of members' conforming to ancient textual standards, the Church regularly remakes itself in the image of its leadership, membership, and (within limits) contextualizing socio-cultural zeitgeist. Oberon doesn't believe CAW must claim ancient origins or wisdom and therefore remain rooted in the errors of the past or "stuck with really ghastly stuff embedded in their scriptures. We can say 'Yes, we like this part; we don't like that part.'"[83]

Without mistaking a casual attitude with contempt for continuity, most CAW members take a highly creative attitude toward religion, judging each belief and practice according to what they claim is an inner ethical sense. The loci of spiritual confirmation and legitimacy aren't in a claimed miraculous past or external text but are immanent and immediate in the intuitive centers of the members themselves and in the perceived vibrant energies of nature. Since there's no Bible or Koran to dictate the parameters of the tradition, CAW bases its theology and praxis on the accumulated characteristics of its membership acting in contemporary time while not confining its truth to individual whim. The Church attempts to steady itself with the grounding weight of pre-modern nature traditions; CAW seeks to restore certain values, ethics, and healing practices that many believe sustained the spiritual lives of humans for millennia and which are seen as needed to rebalance the postmodern world.

However, CAW doesn't concern itself only with *human* life and consciousness but also with nonhuman cohabitants. The Church attempts to actualize planetary consciousness, but not just for people. Birds, butterflies, bison and all animals, along with trees, grass, fungus, earthworms, and the multitude of life are part of the consciousness process.[84] Clearly, Maslow's self-actualization progression[85] remains central to CAW's identity and vision, but the actualization of the entire planet, including all living phenomena and the planet itself, gets added. Most CAW members consider all animals to be a sacred part of Earth Mother Goddess – Gaea – and therefore consequential beings in their own right. The Church as a green religion believes in the mission to bring actualization, awareness, and consciousness to all creatures.[86]

An important aspect of CAW's purpose concerns the repetition of language related to waking up, awakening, or coming out of sleep. Indeed, most CAW members share a sense that humankind has been in a slumber of ignorance and unassailed assumptions that are now being challenged by those outside the assumptions – namely Pagans. Just as the Goths harried ancient Rome, CAW often sees its task as opposing the dangerous excesses of civilized life. To secure a sustainable and prosperous future, human awakening results from "reawakening Gaia" – by re-establishing the lost relationship with Her through acknowledgement and/or worship. For CAW, waking up (to) the sacredness of the Earth requires spirituality, a critical human element that conceives what lies beyond humankind's reckoning. Morning Glory postulates that Gaea Herself sleeps, at least in relation to humans, and needs reawakening so that the relationship can re-establish in the present. This mother and child reunion will not repeat the initial human-Earth experience but rather reflect human maturation in a more equitable form.

On a different level, the oneness felt in the past and during peak experiences in the present will remain constant, granting glimpses into that holistic and transcendent state which erases all contention.

The basic CAW credo attempts to harmonize disparate ideas and realities, in both self and cosmos. The belief is that the smallest flower or grain of sand holographically encapsulates universal truths and spiritual significances; for instance, as more than mere biological entities, trees also stand as (a) part of the complex and interconnected biospheric web; (b) living metaphors representing the Tree of Life, stability, and strength; and (c) individual beings with unique animistic spirits. Such sentiments reveal a sense of radical interconnection, interdependency, and relationship that recognizes a wider scope of agency. Earth, nature, other gods, other groups, and other individuals all receive equal recognition as (in)valuable expressions of the divine.

However, an elitist attitude also exists here – CAW sees itself as ahead of (rather than 'above') everyone else, in a position of guiding others to a higher, deeper, and broader reality resulting in happiness, sustainability, and peace. CAW's purpose, then, involves "reawakening Gaia and reuniting Her children" including the following acts: re-stimulating the consciousness of the planet; re-establishing the lost relationship between humanity and a sacralized Earth, and renewing the covenant between physical and divine. The covenant is maintained through evolving intellectual, mythological, and experiential networks, neo-tribal communitarianism, stewardship models of ecological responsibility, and the development of the innate human consciousness. Optimism flourishes in such ideations, along with a religious passion tempered by dedication to modern pluralism and postmodern ecospiritual morality. CAW's not-so-hidden agenda, besides its overt world-changing radicalism, is to experience and spread joy and ecstasy. Relentlessly optimistic about the future and mystical in its relationship to the planet,

CAW consistently attempts to sow these attributes into the general culture. One of their mottos is "We brainwash people into thinking for themselves. Whether or not it succeeds remains to be seen.

Size and Scope

Researchers invariably encounter problems when they seek to assess the size of the NeoPagan movement: practitioners aren't forthcoming, records aren't kept, unknown solitaries abound, and a laissez-faire attitude permeates the subject. Contemporary Pagans possess a keen awareness of their minority socio-cultural position, which engenders a sense of caution – an understandable attitude since in some areas of North America suspicion of and even hostility toward Witches and other NeoPagans remains significant. All this pose challenges to this research in terms of attempting to ascertain the number of practitioners.

CAW apparently keeps more records and collects more data on membership than most NeoPagan groups; however, my experience indicates that because members generally dislike authority and distrust any attempt at control through identification and surveillance techniques, there's a significant difference between the number of registered members and the total number of non-registered practitioners, with the latter being almost impossible to determine accurately. Therefore, the total number of CAW adherents remains unknown, especially after the chaos of temporary institutional discorporation in the early 2000s. Most membership data were lost during this time, and since reincarnating in 2005, CAW has been rebuilding its membership database.

Oberon, who is currently in charge of CAW records, admits that knowing the size of CAW is a problem. The people "who have aligned over the years and who consider themselves in their heart of hearts to be true CAW people, number around a couple of thousand."[87] So the closest estimate the Church's leadership offers is approximately 2000, with the number of regularly practicing adherents about half that. Although dues-paying membership data are currently unavailable, the total is probably under one hundred. Given the reluctance of many CAW adherents to join organizations, registered membership is not required to be part of CAW. Oberon justifies this by asking about the number of people who consider themselves Christian but don't have membership in a church – they follow the teachings of Jesus and therefore they are Christians. Clearly, he considers CAW to be a category of NeoPaganism in addition to a non-profit corporation.

CAW embraces persons of varied background and personality, including almost every conceivable category, although the Church appeals mostly to Caucasians of European ancestry. Theoretically, it welcomes the world in all its diversity, human and nonhuman, into its informal membership and sees Earth – and other potentially inhabited planets – as the pool of its future adherents. Xenophilia – the love of the strange, different, and new – is decidedly a core value of the Church.

Composition

From my years of observation, the average age in CAW is approximately 30. First-generation founding members have declined in number over the years but still hold respected and active positions of memory, wisdom, and authority in the Church. Oberon is aging and members of the second generation are in their forties and fifties, poised to be the next group of leaders. Younger people remain a minority, drawn mostly from CAW or NeoPagan families; having grown up in the tradition, these youthful members take for granted many of the Church's more unconventional beliefs and practices. My son, for instance, regards nudity as routine and the sacredness of Earth as self-evident; he and many other gen x and y members view anime,[88] manga,[89] computer and Internet gaming, and the *Lord of the*

Rings or *Harry Potter* series as postmodern expressions of ancient themes and mythic principles. These younger members bring fresh ideas and perspectives into CAW, but whether or not they will continue to support and fill clergy positions has yet to be determined.

Both sexes are nearly equally represented, with a slight female majority. Although feminism remains central to CAW's identity, newer members tend to look beyond male-female dichotomies and issues to gay, lesbian, bisexual, and transgendered concerns, perhaps because feminist ideas are already securely ensconced in the Church and so assume a lesser role in discussions. A few critics outside CAW posit that because of its ethic of sexual freedom, women tend to be sex objects, but I've neither witnessed nor heard confirmation of such accusations from female members. Quite the opposite: women tend to hold power equal to or slightly greater than male members consistent with the Goddess's authoritative position in the Church's theology.

There don't appear to be any racial issues in the Church, so it may be assumed that no overt racial prejudice exists and that all persons are welcome without regard to origin or ancestry. In fact, people of color seem especially valued since they embody diversity. There are few minorities in CAW, however, and I've yet to personally meet a member of African or Native American descent. This may be due partly to the Church's association with NeoPaganism, which clearly has a European legacy. Ancestry seems more influential in NeoPagan groups than in other religions since one's bloodline is often honored and one's genetic memory plays an important role;[90] for these reasons, most CAW members are of European heritage and trace their roots to ancient and medieval Europe rather than Africa, Asia, the Middle East, or other locations with equally rich Pagan traditions.

There's substantial diversity in the socio-economic status of CAW's membership – from moderately wealthy to genteelly impoverished. Some members work at low-wage jobs while others have significant monetary resources. Some are students with set or no real incomes, but with family or community resources that support them. Actual income may be low on average because many members pursue artistic or other creative passions and their first priority is not the accumulation of significant wealth. I'm unaware of any super-rich or involuntarily indigent members and would describe almost all I've met as middle class.

Stratification

One of the central tenets of CAW is equality between all persons and groups – for instance, most members are committed to rooting out conscious and unconscious gender, racial, religious, political, and cultural prejudices. Authority in the Church is based on knowledge, wisdom, dedication, and skill, and the governing structure is currently being modified to encourage even more equity. The Board of Directors and Clergy Council were once two distinct entities, but recently an effort has been initiated to combine the political necessities of incorporated status with the spiritual prerogatives of the clergy. Even though an authoritative hierarchy governs and delimits the Church, the institutional commitment to diversity within that structure offers members considerable latitude in terms of participation, worship, practice, and influence.

Clergy members: Oberon Zell (Priest, ordained 1967) is the designated 'Primate' (the ceremonial head of CAW); since the renaissance of the mid-2000s, Oberon has assumed a more central role in guiding the Church along its original course. Morning Glory Zell (Priestess, ordained 1974) who died in 2014, was recognized as Oberon's counterpart; she exceled at planning and executing many of the Church's elaborate rites and rituals. Alder MoonOak (Priest, 2016), pastor of the Church of All Worlds, Florida located in Gainesville. Marylyn Motherbear (Priestess, 1999) is a long-time member (from the 1970s) who is currently involved in several external projects but is considered a CAW Priestess. The clergy are responsible for establishing the 'spirit' of the Church, upholding its bylaws and corporate status, and leading Church functions such as member advancement and various rituals.

Integration

In order to understand how open CAW is compared to many of its NeoPagan brethren, one must remember that NeoPagans generally pride themselves on being spontaneous and non-organized. Covens and other groups are decentralized and the whole Pagan movement so amorphous that it has yet to make a significant appearance in the public (media) or academic (scholarly) consciousness. In addition, the medieval persecution of "witches" convinces many NeoPagans that anonymity remains the safest strategy: most groups neither keep membership records nor stand in high profile in their communities, and many gather in secret with an emphasis on closed meetings that require initiation and familiarity to attend. In contrast, CAW keeps membership data, has a formal system of member progression, and maintains a high civic presence wherever there's a membership of sufficient size. The Church flourishes on engagement with the larger society; therefore, CAW is structured as an institute as well as a church – the former being part think tank and part educational organization.

CAW members tend to integrate into the larger society rather than remain isolated from it; there's little sense of outright hostility toward the cultural context in which the Church resides. Members usually have ordinary jobs, albeit with an emphasis on the arts and high tech, and many have standard marriages and family structures. Some are active in their communities, serving as Coast Guard reservists, charity volunteers, civic committee members, and local activists. They have conventional hobbies, schedules, and recreational or travel agendas. In other words, CAW members generally choose to be included in the surrounding society. In my opinion, any discontinuity experienced by members comes from the reaction of society towards them, such as negative attention to those members who choose alternative lifestyles, family arrangements, or consciousness-raising techniques, especially when those lifestyles become public.

Therefore, although CAW differs theologically and philosophically from much of the majority culture in the United States, there's not a strong separatist or isolationist element, the focus is on gradual evolutionary transformation of the majority culture rather than its actual downfall. There is, however, considerable discontent about, and dissention from, specific social and political systems as they operate in the United States. Politically, CAW members are usually Democratic, Green, or Independent, while a few reject political systems altogether, calling themselves compassionate anarchists or 'autonomists' who prefer a vision of the world in which government is no longer necessary because most people have internalized an ethos of peaceful co-existence and cooperation. The most extreme example of non-integration might be those few members who homestead more or less off-grid in rural intentional communities similar to but more sophisticated than hippy communes.

Conversion and Proselytization

Most NeoPagans insist they are born Pagan rather than convert to Paganism. They report a sense of being different from others, beginning in childhood and continuing until their discovery of the Pagan community. While *conversion* suggests an active acceptance of one tradition after the rejection of another, often prompted by external persuasion, most CAW members simply encounter in the Church a group of people reflecting who they already are. The feeling is usually described as the relief of "coming home" or "finding my people" rather than as a drastic transitional epiphany. The official policy of CAW is that one can be a member of the Church *and* any other religion simultaneously, so no conflict of faith is perceived and no conversion necessary.

On the other hand, CAW can engender a type of conversion experience, such as turning away from violence, dishonesty, or socially and environmentally destructive lifestyles. As in the religious conversion experience, the Church serves as catalyst for transformational occurrences; as a personal example, CAW brought together my passion for environmental protection and spiritual growth in ways I hadn't imagined possible. The Church's historical roots but futurist vision 'converted' *me* within a minute of reading my first *Green Egg*, an experience shared by many other members. For example, Oberon had a similar 'conversion' when he and Lance read *SISL*, and for Morning Glory, it was meeting Oberon and hearing about CAW. For member Eric Hebert, the experience of conversion from Judaism to NeoPaganism began years before he stepped into a bookstore, saw just the *cover* of *Green Egg*, and knew he had found his way home.

Related to the conversion-discovery dichotomy is the fact that most NeoPagans, and thus CAW members, don't attempt to persuade others to join their religion. Since most members believe they are born with certain Pagan characteristics, attempting to attract people who don't have those characteristics is nonsensical – one must energetically resonate with a spiritual path or it will not be enriching or useful. Public events such as tree-plantings and open Sabbat rituals occasionally provide some outside attention, but many members recall what they regard as the uncomfortable proselytizing in their childhood churches or from door-to-door groups such as the Mormons or Jehovah's Witnesses. It's especially unlikely that Pagans would successfully attract others by presenting their socially unorthodox beliefs to random strangers; generally CAW is discovered and investigated by individuals who then contact the Church, not the reverse.

Commitment

Initially, CAW demands little from its members: at the first level of participation, only interest is required. Later, the choice to join the Church by filling out a membership form and sending it to CAW Central in California along with modest annual dues may be made. Further involvement is strictly voluntary and neither encouraged nor discouraged. On the other hand, to participate fully in CAW requires considerable commitment to its worldview and ethos. The passion evoked in its membership suggests deep loyalty to CAW's ideals and practices, and the constant flux in membership statistics indicates substantial freedom of movement across religious and spiritual lines. The impulse to experimentation and constant growth means some people gain what they will from their CAW experience and then move on – a reality fully accepted by the Church leadership. It's generally considered part of CAW's task to affect positively as many seekers as possible on their various life paths without keeping them forever.

Some research suggests that NRMs traditionally have high turnover rates,[91] and this certainly holds true for CAW. Of the 2,000 members that Oberon and Morning Glory reported as marginal adherents to the Church or its doctrines, less than twenty are currently actively working to rebuild CAW. Because NeoPaganism is such a new phenomenon and because CAW's beliefs and practices are unorthodox, their appeal is not universal, and the Church itself currently lacks the institutional stability to form a larger member base.

Education

My observations suggest that a significant majority of members have at least two years of college. In 1995, Green Egg sent out a survey to all its subscribers (mostly members) and inquired about their educational levels (Table 1). The results from the 283 respondents confirm the importance of higher learning in the

Church: 47% reported graduating from college with a minimum of two years coursework. Although this was an informal survey, I submit that it accurately reflects the high educational levels of CAW members.

Membership in CAW beyond initiatory levels encourages either higher education or innate intelligence in order to satisfy the reading and essay-writing requirements. For instance, one of the requirements to enter Circle Two is to read three books: *Stranger in a Strange Land, Drawing Down the Moon,* and *The Spiral Dance*. In order to advance to Circle Three, one must write a short essay (1-2 pages) "describing your understanding of this Church, and how you see yourself fitting in."[92] And for entrance to Circle Four, one submits a longer essay (6-12 double-spaced typed pages) comparing three religions, "the one you were raised in, one you have investigated on your own (besides NeoPaganism) and NeoPaganism."[93] Essays are read and judged by clergy members who determine if the essay demonstrates acceptable depth and exhibits a reasonable level knowledge of the subject matter.

Chapter 4

CAW'S Beliefs

CAW's practices manifest from a set of unconventional beliefs, not only about the nature of divinity as polytheistic and panentheistic, but also concerning what many members see as unsustainable assumptions of modern civilization: industrialization, reliance on fossil fuels, centralized organizations and distribution of goods, nuclear family structure, and so on. These beliefs often lead to action, both in the private realm of lifestyle choices and the public realm of involvement in community activism. However, CAW generally defines 'belief' not as assuming the reality of what can't be confirmed but as a 'faith' in what can be empirically or experientially confirmed as real. Beliefs are therefore regarded with skepticism until either objective or subjective verification occurs.

The Goddess

A major element of NeoPaganism is its commitment to the feminine divine, especially as embodied by the Goddess. Those who write about this form of deity as well as those in the general field of women's spirituality, study the unique properties and implications of female-centered religion and spiritual metaphor. Such work is often motivated by an attempt to provide distinction from, and sometimes antidote to, the negative aspects of 'patriarchal' cultural dominance. Worship of the Goddess is a powerful form of feminist critique, raising to the level of divine certain characteristic behaviors and concepts often associated with feminine energy and feminized nature.

These spiritual values find articulation through contemporary writers such as Charlene Spretnak (1946-),[1] whose vision of Goddess spirituality takes the form of embracing the personal body and honoring the Earth body. Beginning with dualistic sexual reproduction and the establishment of sex polarities, Spretnak critiques "patriarchal socialization" with its disembodied world-view and deconstructive postmodernism. The renaissance of Goddess worship represents a challenge to patriarchal-dominant culture and creates alternatives to the values and arrangements of that culture.

> The central understanding in contemporary Goddess spirituality is that the divine…is laced throughout the cosmic manifestations in and around us. The divine is immanent, not concentrated in some distant seat of power, a transcendent sky-god…it's possible to apprehend divine transcendence as the sacred whole, or the infinite complexity of the universe.[2]

Along with Riane Eisler,[3] Rosemary Radford Reuther,[4] Carol Christ,[5] and Lucia Birnbaum,[6] Starhawk appears again for her development of a Goddess spirituality influenced by, and influential within, the NeoPagan community. *Spiral Dance* is subtitled "A Rebirth of the Ancient Religion of the Great Goddess" and in this work Starhawk lays out the fundamental historical Goddess myth central to NeoPaganism:

> Once again in today's world, we recognize the Goddess – ancient and primeval; the first of deities; patroness of the Stone Age hunt and the first sowers of seeds; under whose guidance the herds were tamed, the healing herbs first discovered; in whose image the first works of art were created; for whom the standing stones were raised; who was the inspiration of song and poetry.[7]

The story of an ancient Goddess lineage reaching back to primal folk religions and beyond reveals a bid for legitimacy based on seniority: feminine deity is seen as the original, most ancient, and most venerated. In NeoPaganism, the exchange of ideas like these reaches the level of sanctity, to the point where it could be assigned as one of the central tenets of the movement. NeoPagans stand within the larger Goddess spirituality movement and participates in its re-establishment in the United States and Europe.

Theagenesis

In my experience, the Pagan worldview often encompasses vast stretches of gradual evolutionary change, and its epistemology inclines toward knowledge through embodied planetary consciousness and natural spirals of time. To most Pagans, Earth itself constitutes divine revelation, and Earth religions such as CAW perceive a deep relationship with the natural world, which contains the seeds of global transformation. Because modern industrialism and human population levels seem to have created potentially serious environmental issues, part of the postmodern NeoPagan project seeks resolutions to these issues through ecospirituality.

For CAW as well as other NeoPagan groups, science and especially ecology provides half of the basis for Earth spirituality because it takes seriously the complex interconnectivity of nature, including humans. By viewing the world in holistic terms, ecology helps legitimize the Earth as a subject of respect and protective activism. In Oberon's case, ecology also provides the spark for his Gaia Thesis, in which Earth is regarded not just as a living organism but also a conscious, intelligent meta-being and ultimately as Gaea, the name given to this embodied Earth Mother Goddess.

In his article "Theagenesis: the Rebirth of the Goddess,"[8] Oberon presents his mostly original *Gaea Thesis* (which predates Lovelock's "Gaia Hypothesis"[9] by two years). He describes part of the widespread NeoPagan mythos when writing about ancient tribal people, who he regards as Pagans, as holding common beliefs and practices, including:

> veneration of an Earth-Mother Goddess, animism and pantheism, identification with a sacred region, seasonal celebrations, love-respect, awe and veneration for Nature and Her mysteries, sensuality and sexuality in worship; magick and myth, and a sense of humanity being a microcosm corresponding to the macrocosm of all Nature.[10]

Contained in this quote are several common assumptions, namely that NeoPaganism reflects primal understandings of the world and that this ancient tribal worldview included this list of characteristics.

CAW partakes in the NeoPagan story of its ancient religious past in order to suggest historical continuity and a pre-Christian lineage co-extant with the early stirrings of human consciousness; this story locates Paganism deep in the core of our species and implies a central position in subsequent human affairs. According to one school of the NeoPagan mythos, humankind possessed – and still can possess – a primordial inter-relationship with nature. Whether or not ancient people imagined an "Earth-Mother Goddess" per se, they probably tended to be animistic and perhaps even pantheistic. It seems probable that they would have identified with their bioregion since knowledge of edible plants, changing seasons, and animal migrations would have been imperative for survival. Oberon's remaining features such as "love-respect" and "sensuality and sexuality" are assuredly later developments. Such beliefs emerge from and bolster the NeoPagan image of rural traditions of the original *Pagani,* with additions from more recent Romantic and progressive upsurges.

By using the theories and discoveries of modern science and combining them with Pagan theology, Oberon attempts to create a synthesis. For example, he writes that no matter how often cells divide and subdivide "the same cellular material, the same life, passes into the daughter, granddaughter, and great-grand-daughter, forever," resulting in the aggregate total of new cells comprising "one single living organism!"[11] From this foundation of established scientific fact, Oberon expands to incorporate additional details from Lovelock's subsequent works as well as Duval and Sessions' *deep ecology*.[12] He submits that Gaea is a single living organism and 'Her' parts cannot be removed, replaced, or rearranged without consequence. Just as in the human body the brain and nervous system is the last organ to develop, so in Gaea the last biome to develop is the Noosphere, composed of Earth's aggregate population of *Homo sapiens*.[13]

This is more than mere anthropomorphizing; evidence allows for the possibility of a planetary organism. Gaea theory, however, goes further, exploring the spiritual aspects and implications of this proposed planetary being. The maturation of a planetary biosphere requires the evolution of total telepathic union among the "cells" of its Noosphere. When such an intelligent species ultimately develops telepathy to the extent that it shares a single global consciousness, a planetary mind awakens in the "brain" of the Biosphere.[14] Oberon concludes that there exists, and has existed, a name for this embodied divinity with a million-year history of success prior to civilizational monotheism: Gaea, or the Goddess. He claims that this (re)discovery of the connection of the ancient Goddess with Earth as a being is as important as Copernicus' discovery of the heliocentric solar system.[15]

Thus, the core of CAW's ecospiritual vision is a named meta-being at the very center of Western pre-Christian culture with the face and body of the Goddess. A feminine deity makes some sense because of the birthing, nursing, and nurturing capacity of women; presently, only females may physically bring life into the world. Although they usually do it with the quickening power of the masculine, the Goddess is independently powerful with the protective strength of a mother. In this way, CAW attempts to engage Western Civilization in a dialogue about its own historical context, especially its masculine God, analyzing it through an alternative feminist worldview.

Theagenesis deals mytho-poetically with nature (albeit through the lens of modern theoretical science) and combines it with spirituality (albeit through the lens of sacred nature), creating the synthesis of ecospirituality. Oberon's work may be more sophisticated than a country swain's harvest dance, but it carries on the tradition of attributing spiritual commonweal[16] to Earth and of divinizing nature. An argument is made in CAW that some Pagans have the ability to perceive the nature-spirit interface just as others are competent at visualizing quantum mechanics or sculpture. If science offers unique insights into the physical-sensory realm, there seems to be no reason but cultural bias to believe that mystics can't possess unique perceptions into non-empirical reality.

Beyond the fact that all humans rely on Earth for physical sustenance, most CAW members attach a moral and ethical prerogative to ecospiritual living based on the sacred concept of Gaea. That is, if the planet is a sacred being, it ought to be protected and honored as divine. Therefore, one aspect of the Church is the alchemical synthesis of mytho-poetic history, Gaia theory, ecospirituality, ritual praxis, North American native wisdom, and modern social pluralism – together these inform Western postmodern Paganism and create the fertile ground for CAW's beliefs and practices.

Polytheism and Panentheism

Most practitioners of the Church of All Worlds Tradition believe that Divinity takes many forms, and they worship whatever form is meaningful to the individual. The Myths and Mysteries of many Deities provide deep sources of ignition and wisdom for practitioners of the Church of All Worlds Tradition.[17]

The immediate theological difference between NeoPagan and Abrahamic faiths consists of the former's polytheistic worldview: most NeoPagans honor a plethora of deities, from a multiplicity of Earth beings to the God and Goddess.[18] They tend to envision considerable variety and complexity at the spiritual level and to form relationships to a host of divine beings representing different aspects of life and physical reality. For instance, the forest deities – Pan, Herne, or Cernunnos – possess a different energy and archetypal function than a goddess of hearth and childbirth such as Brigid. Spiritual beings inhabit diverse spheres of influence and engagement under specialized relationships and are intimate and familiar in ways an abstract Godhead usually is not. Some Pagans reject the concept of one God altogether, but most admit that the spiritual realm abounds with infinite possibilities, including the possibility of a single, unified deity with different interpretations and expressions. CAW in particular, being a church of "all worlds," partakes in the abundance of Earth energies and translates that variety into many gods and beings who cohabitate with humans. The 'one spiritual size fits all' concept is deemphasized in favor of individual-based perceptions tailored to personal needs and character. For instance, although pantheistic members might find divinity wholly within the physical cosmos, more spiritually-inclined members find solace in metaphysical truths and discoveries that suggest greater and more profound perceptive abilities inherent in humankind as well as a metaphysical universe beyond perceived physicality.

Polytheism indicates more than a theological position, however; it suggests a broader worldview typical of NeoPagans.

Many Pagans will tell you that polytheism is an *attitude* and

> a *perspective* that affect more than what we consider to be religion. They might well say that the constant calls for unity, integration, and homogenization in the Western world derive from our long-standing ideology of monotheism, which remains the majority tradition in the West. They might well add that monotheism is a political and psychological ideology as well as a religious one, and that the old economic lesson that one-crop economies generally fare poorly also applies to the spiritual realm.[19]

Polytheism, as many NeoPagans practice it, exists within a complex sociological and political context that's meant to challenge cultural assumptions about reality and truth and offer an alternative worldview affecting religious, ecological, and social interaction. CAW sees monotheism as representing not just a religious position, but a social, cultural, and political one as well. Unity, integration, and homogenization in such forms as the American 'melting pot,' public and Sunday school indoctrination, and concepts such as 'one nation under God' would likely be held in contempt by many members or viewed with considerable misgiving. Any attempt at forced conventionality sends waves of disapproval and resistance through the members with whom I'm familiar. Therefore, it would be fair to call CAW a *polyistic* religion, theologically and socio-politically.

Polytheism challenges not only the monotheistic worldview, but also normative standardization in morality, politics, education, and relationships. For most NeoPagans, monotheism represents not just the idea of one God but also one specific envisioning of God as an omnipotent male deity self-identifying with a particular religious tradition. *Poly* people commit to inclusive diversity and to religious polyamory as a relationship and familial model. The *theism* part of polytheism acknowledges that the ultimate concept of reality takes on a metaphysical tone that's focused on a deity or deities and on the divine in the world. As we've noted, panentheism, the term coined by German philosopher Karl Friedrich Christian Krause in the 1820s, locates divinity both within the observable physical universe and beyond the universe in realms of spirit.[20] For some CAW members, there's no reality outside God/dess but simultaneously there's a discreet deity (or deities) that can be perceived and experienced in a limited way by humanity. In other words, the divine is seen as radically immanent and omnipresent because divinity is infinite and eternal, extant in ways not fully accessible to imperfect human concepts or imagination. As author and Episcopal Priest Matthew Fox writes, *panentheism* is "healthy mysticism" rather than a theism that positions the divine 'out there' or even 'in here' in a dualistic manner separating creation from divinity.

> Panentheism means 'all things in God and God in all things.' This is the way mystics envision the relationship of world, self, and God…[it] melts the dualism of inside and outside – like fish in water and the water in the fish, creation is in God and God is in creation."[21]

Using Fox's interpretation, CAW is a mystical church that embraces a non-dual theology: divinity and nature are basically indistinguishable, which is why the Church views Earth as a divine entity, the intimate Goddess who has given the gifts of intuition and magick so that a personal relationship may be cultivated and an empathic (inter)connection developed through ritual and worship. Fox's Christological panentheism is sympathetically received in CAW, which in my experience tends to regard wisdom regardless of its source.

David Skrbina compares panentheism with pan-psychism using the analogy of a sponge: "Just as water can saturate the sponge without being the sponge, so too God is said to saturate all things while being transcendent and unchanging. "An alternative explanation is that "God is the soul of the cosmos, a world-soul, and the physical universe is His body."[22] Although Skrbina concentrates on the 'mind' of God present within all things, he admits that if that universal mind is a deity, then "panpsychism can be seen as a variation of panentheism."[23]

Ecotheology

As we've noted previously, ecospirituality, a postmodern refinement of panentheistic beliefs, suggests that (a) divinity inseparably suffuses or is synonymous with Earth in perceivable forms, (b) the divine Earth is the permanent home of individual humans while embodied and of the human species during its natural lifespan and is therefore sacred and holy, and (c) a special relationship with the divine through nature and with nature through divinity is possible and beneficial. This philosophical approach aims to synthesize the holistic findings of ecology and experiential discoveries of religion into a greater, more encompassing discipline with an underlying unity. As noted in the work of Thomas Berry, the project of admitting Earth (flesh) and Spirit (God) into the same dialogic requires the interweaving of two often estranged elements.[24] The expansion of each area into the other may require belief in and a search for unifying principles common to both and the explication of the syncretic and synergistic approach emerging from this alchemical process. Barry's suggested approach might constitute a worldview and resulting ethos designed for and conforming to the specific needs of the postmodern world that resembles NeoPaganism.

Ecospirituality's secondary mission is to heal the dichotomous abyss that has developed between Earth sciences (the study of our home planet) and the religious arts (the inquiries of metaphysics), and between objective observation and subjective experience. The expectation is that such a synthesis might result in a new epistemology – even a new form of spiritual connection

– emerging from deeper empathic responses believed to be hardwired into *homo sapiens* as products of divine creation through biological evolution.[25]

The term 'religion' often suggests concern with spiritual, metaphysical, or mystical areas of experience while leaving the physical world mainly to 'science.' CAW combines the two and as a religion includes geology in its theology: nature becomes the living voice of God/dess, an intimate and ubiquitous player in the divine drama, not only as Creation but also as a dynamic interface between humanity and the divine. If Earth is viewed by most members as a single intelligent being with a consciousness and soul of its own; theology and biology combine and the resulting religious symbol emerges as Gaea, partner and servant of God/dess. Although CAW does in some ways bicameralize the Goddess of soil, crops, and sea from the God of sky, heavens, and rain, it's the combination of the two in a complementary polarity that's the ultimate goal (internally) and reality (externally). Nature's balance relates to the health of Gaea, and humans are considered equal partners in nature's whole. However, just as an integral body part such as the heart or brain can become unhealthy, so is humankind, in the extremes of industrial civilization, viewed as unhealthy in the body of Gaea; therefore, humankind must be spiritually and physically healed. In my observations, most of what CAW professes and practices tends toward this greater therapeutic purpose.

Gender

CAW emerged from the feminist milieu of the 1960s and 1970s, and its imprint is stamped on Church tenets, whether as an emphasis on the Goddess or as an entrenched political stance on women's rights. However, I've noted that ultimately CAW's goal is the balance of what are considered 'masculine' and 'feminine' energies following generalized definitions common in many cultures: masculine (yang) is assertive, linear, and intellectual; feminine (yin) is receptive, cyclical, and emotive.[26] Of course gender polarities can degenerate into normative stereotypes, but as archetypes they influence CAW's system of complementary energetic polarities. The balance between these perceived polarities is believed to produce a healthy psyche at peace with itself.

In her 1992 book *She Who Is*, feminist theologian Elizabeth Johnson articulates the idea of gender balance by emphasizing the traditional role the feminine often plays and painting a grand historical picture of the female divine in the world:

> In a word, SHE WHO IS discloses in an elusive female metaphor the mystery of Sophia-God as sheer, exuberant, relational aliveness in the midst of the history of suffering, inexhaustible source of new being in situations of death and destruction, ground of hope for the whole created universe, to practical and critical effect.[27]

Undoubtedly, CAW developed in the zeitgeist of feminist liberation movements that questioned the patriarchal structure in society; however, the significance of gender harmony in the Church moves beyond women's rights into spiritual and metaphoric realms of meaning. Since Earth is considered a single sacred being, the goal of inner harmony between gender energies relates to external harmony among humans and between humanity and other species. Johnson sees in the female divine the mysterious wisdom deity whose energetic animation dwells within the world of suffering and transforms it with hope, and this is precisely how I've heard the Goddess described in many CAW rituals and services.

On the other hand, religious gender balance is more than Goddesses and High Priestesses – it also affects the socio-political realm of identity and liberation politics; that is, it translates into real-world equality between women and men as well as the abolition of forced gender roles. Women in CAW maintain what I'd describe as a fierce vigilance not only against domination by males but also against the oppression and violence many see as emerging from the extremes of patriarchy. In many areas – cultural equality of the sexes, sexualized energies, and divine bicameralism – gender harmony suffuses CAW's worldview and motivates much of its social activism in the name of gender rights, with the recent addition of transsexual and transgender rights.

Postmodernity

In the use of the designation *postmodern*, the condition of 'modernity' is historically bracketed and thus described as a whole phenomenon whose contours are known; however, considerable controversy exists within CAW over whether historical ages are in fact shifting and how much overlap continues between modern and postmodern. The former is generally associated with the Industrial Revolution and the notion of progress through rationality and organizational social structures while the latter seeks to move beyond the historical period containing such notions in response to contemporary issues apparently unsolvable by modern methods and assumptions.[28]

It's incumbent on those who suggest modernity has ended or is in the process of ending to define 'modern' in terms that illustrate the characteristics of a future without it. According to Dennis Carpenter, a NeoPagan scholar associated with Circle Sanctuary,[29] postmodern spirituality indicates a historical break from modernity. Carpenter describes the major spiritual contours of the contemporary Pagan worldview, particularly "spirituality within the postmodern context," and defines spirituality, quoting Charlene Spretnak, as "the focusing of human awareness on the subtle aspects of existence, a practice that reveals to us profound interconnectedness."[30] With this definition, Carpenter differentiates postmodernity from modernity through postmodernity's "creative synthesis of modern and premodern truths and values, including pre-modern notions of a divine reality, cosmic meaning, and an enchanted Nature."[31] Carpenter lists eight characteristics of postmodern spirituality from the work of author, retired professor, and Center for Process Studies director David Ray Griffin,[32] including:

- the reality of internal relations or interconnections
- nondualistic relation of humans to nature and divine reality to the world
- the eminence of both the past and the future in the present
- the universality and centrality of creativity
- postpatriarchy
- communitarianism
- the 'de-privatization' of religion, and
- the rejection of materialism[33]

Significant parallels exist between this list and CAW's basic philosophical structure; for example:

- the identity of the individual involves his or her familial, social, and environmental context and is capable of an organic sense of oneness with others and nature
- traditions of the past and future are of equal importance, and the world is determined by the co-creativity of divinity and humanity
- radical equality of the sexes results in health and harmony, and there exists a preeminence of family, local community, and bioregion
- reality should be re-connected to pluralistic religious values, and economics must be subordinate to values of sustainability and cooperation

Because of these parallels, it's appropriate to categorize CAW as a postmodern religion.

Human Nature

Although in my experience most NeoPagans emphasize application over theory, CAW contains theological ruminations covering a wide range of perennial questions – one of these concerns the nature of individual humans and the human species. Generally, Church members regard humanity with optimism as a species having considerable capacity for a positive future. They believe that hope overreaches reality even though most humans flounder in what is often thought of as primitive immaturity. The triumph of the peaceful will inevitably follow from the process of social development and bio-cultural evolution.[34]

One expression of this hopeful mythos is *Star Trek*, a television and film series beloved, or at least appreciated, by almost all CAW members. In the *Star Trek* universe, humanity has passed through a tumultuous period, including an almost catastrophic World War III with millions of casualties. From the ashes of near-extinction, humankind realizes in a collective shift of consciousness that it can survive only under a radically new global paradigm. The arrival of Vulcans, a race from a distant planet, catalyzes this shift as they mentor humans towards a unification of planetary awareness – humankind evolves into a single family within one generation. Just as racial segregation collapsed over a few decades, so the dream of peaceful diversity manifests because people become aware of their fragile existence and deep commonality. *Star Trek* begins after the 'United Federation of Planets' which is liberal pluralism expanded to a galactic scale and 'Star Fleet,' the quasi-military defenders of the Federation and explorers of a sometimes-hostile galaxy, are forming or have already formed. Although humans must sometimes defend themselves with force, their ultimate goal is to spread tolerance throughout the galaxy.

The 'nature of humankind' is best described using concepts from scientific theory, CAW mythos, and mystic spirituality: from a planetary organism perspective, the ultimate function of humans is as part of Earth's neural network and especially reproductive system. Oberon believes the former is better suited to the whales and that "if there were as many whales now as there were before we started slaughtering them, Gaea would have a fully functional cerebral cortex."[35] Oberon is familiar with Teilhard de Chardin's noosphere which has clearly influenced him to the point where he regards humankind as a contributor to Earth's "thinking envelope." Our comparatively large brains and self-awareness make us prime candidates for the secondary thought processors of the planet; however, whales have larger and more sophisticated brains so they serve as the primary Gaean mind.[36]

If whales exist to fulfill the majority of Gaea's cerebral functions, humans are the equivalent of celestial sperm: the planet's attempts over the last hundred million years to produce bipedal beings with opposable thumbs aren't random coincidence but intentional production of beings capable of building "seedpods that will spread the seeds of life to distant worlds."[37] In other words, Gaea, the generating force of life, has evolved humans with certain abilities, among them big brains, adept hands, and the desire to explore in order to propagate; thinking abilities and curiosity result in the construction of spacecraft enabling humanity to colonize other planets and thus spread Gaea's seeds of 'Terran'[38] life throughout the Milky Way galaxy, similar to *Star Trek* and its optimistic view of humanity's future as honorable and essentially non-aggressive space explorers.

Humans also act as spreaders of mythology, weavers of communicative energies around the artistic soul of oral creativity. Our language, images, archetypes, and intonations erect a vibratory web familiar from the womb and powerful on an unconscious level. CAW acknowledges and revitalizes the art of conscious myth-making: humans are storytellers, creating myths and legends by which the world is shaped, and fashioning "the continuity of culture that will carry humanity to the stars and throughout the universe."[39] Through storytelling, our experiences are explained and provided extra weight so that they expand beyond their original mundane reality and enter the noosphere as presences in the collective (un)consciousness. CAW works the storytelling realm, not as empirical fact, but as powerful consciousness-altering and community-unifying technique. As writers such as Brian Swimme[40] have emphasized, we live within a universe story that we have partly created to give form and meaning to our lives.

CAW myth places humans clearly within the complex matrix of Gaea, able to create intention based on the talent for perceiving and planning; in this view, consciousness serves as a reality filter interpreting, shifting, and shaping according to individual proclivities. Oberon sees this characteristic as providing the source of envisioning, mythologizing, and manifesting, and one of CAW's self-imposed tasks is to use the personal lifetime to further its future vision. Therefore, humankind is ordinary because it's simply one more aspect of Gaea and must fulfill its destiny; on the other hand, humankind is special because it has an irreplaceable task of actively participating in evolution within an optimistic psychological prerogative based on relational connection with the planet.

Some CAW members place the human species inferior to the Whole, and sacerdotal focus is on the greater amalgam of life from which humankind emerges and within which it exists. Like youths who believe the world revolves around them, humanity seems to believe the cosmos revolves around humanity – an understandable position since humans have radically disconnected from the Whole. If emergent developmental evolution continues, some members believe humankind will eventually acknowledge this fact and live an ethos reflecting the true nature of our kinships and destiny.

Cosmology

Religions typically seek to explain their theology and praxis by referring to larger mythic contexts such as stories about the beginning and nature of the world. Asking the question "How did the universe begin?" is both a spiritual and scientific inquiry because both approaches offer answers that are, from certain perspectives, incomplete alone. Science seeks to empirically explain the origins of the cosmos and offers a fascinating journey into the physical-material realm; religion takes a different approach based on spiritual reality and rich mythological stories that place humanity among the spirits and gods in the drama of Creation. CAW operates between the recent cosmological theories of astrophysics and the intuitive theories of the cosmos based on mystical experience. The human role within the vast reaches of space which stretches outward from the eyes of space telescopes can't fully replace the cosmogonies[41] of the ancestors, but in its way, a new cosmogony is forming, and the Church places itself firmly in both scientific *and* religious camps.[42] As in other areas, CAW seeks to discover the nature of the synthesis of the two and regards such hybrids as steps forward on the path of evolution.

The answer to the question "How did the universe get here?" involves the acceptance of *incompletion* since no complete answer is possible – Stephen Hawking[43] once said that asking what happened before the beginning of the cosmos is like asking what's north of the North Pole. There are different perspectives one can have about the nature of time, the two most obvious ones being the linear perspective (beginning, middle, end) or some version of the cyclical perspective (a circle or, if it includes movement, a dynamic spiral).[44]

CAW describes the origin of the cosmos using current

scientific theories such as the Big Bang, not the mystical stories offered in Genesis. Regarding models of time, CAW falls into the cyclical camp – not because of better empirical evidence but because the Circle is a theological metaphor in NeoPaganism at the core of CAW cosmology. Since cycles in nature are widespread if not universal, it's assumed spiritual realms are also cyclical, including the repetitive circle of birth, death, and rebirth. In addition, evolution indicates that time doesn't repeat but has directional momentum or trajectory towards the future. The most accurate description of CAW's cosmology would therefore be a spiral.

Morning Glory believed the short answer to the question of how the universe began is "it didn't; it's always been here."[45] Oberon believes time becomes circular as matter and energy pour into black holes and out again somewhere and "somewhen" else in an endless procession. With each cycle, the present becomes the past; the past gains volume and thus expands. Each galaxy creates a time loop in which the past continues expanding and pushing the future forward.[46] A great cosmic engine thus drives time in its unidirectional arrow towards the future where the universe grows progressively larger and more complex. In this way, the gap between science and religion is bridged and the two become inseparably intertwined to form a new cosmological structure – the consciousness of every being in the galaxy that has evolved over billions of years moves into infinity and eternity, essentially becoming divine.[47]

Progressively, the *omniverse*[48] gathers increasing amounts of spiritual energy just as it does matter and time, bringing with it an ever-increasing amount of cosmic consciousness which accounts for the continuing existence of spirit and divinity in the universe.[49] "Cosmic consciousness" describes a 'higher' and 'deeper' apprehension of reality than that ordinarily possessed by most people;[50] those who attain or are predisposed to such consciousness aggregately accrue, and often disseminate, vast quantities of accumulated and synthesized wisdom and awareness leading to a state of inner peace, personal balance, clear thought and emotion, and the ability to act as benevolent repositories for the human species' collective experiences and knowledge. Conversely, those who haven't attained such consciousness can't fully comprehend it. Oberon seems to view cosmic consciousness as material (in that it can increase in amount) and as free-floating energy manifest in individual persons. Apparently, he also views cosmic consciousness as the origin of "spirit and divinity," suggesting that the regenerative and progressive cosmic-galactic engine and its generation and renewal of cosmic consciousness are partly responsible for the presence of spirituality and the divine in the universe.

These speculations don't represent CAW dogma but rather are typical CAW ramblings about cosmological questions (e.g., divine evolution: the galactic core as god-maker) from the masters of 'theo-scientific rants.' Whether the content makes sense is beside the point; the interweaving of two disparate disciplines indicates the synergetic nature of CAW and challenges both disciplines of study to progress towards a transcendent and encompassing vocabulary. In CAW's universe, this process of integration has value because by reconciling apparent polar oppositions one attains spiritual wisdom and manifests the ecospiritual vision.

If a room full of CAW members heard Oberon's story, they would probably nod their heads in understanding, if not agreement; however, there would also be discussion, tangents, corollary ideas, and running commentary. According to CAW's activist beliefs, spirituality, the realm of religion, must take its progressive and emergent cues from science, technology, and evolutionary principles – as Oberon says: "So our theology must by nature be as radically (r)evolutionary as our science, as our discoveries, our perceptions."[51] CAW contends that spirituality must become a force in the progressive, emergent evolving of the universe, and religion must serve as guide to the project of synthesizing a new cosmic consciousness in the alchemical laboratories of ongoing and active relationships with Gaea and Divinity.

Life's Purpose

My observations of CAW reveals a complex matrix of interrelated ideologies, myths, practices, and visions, wrought from the adopted history of Paganism, the interwoven fabric of reconstituted Earth-spirit community, the imaginative worlds of science fiction, and the alchemical oven of modern industrial civilization. Beneath the frivolity and controlled decadence lies a serious theological system organically grown from the fertile soil of postmodern ecospirituality.

From this perspective and according to CAW doctrine, life's purpose is to:

- enjoy life and bring joy to others
- live out and encourage to fruition the CAW vision
- mature as a spiritual being

With this combination of altruism and self-actualization, the Church revels in what it considers the positive aspects of life and nests its theology within a starry-eyed worldview backed by an ethos of personal honor and celebration of diversity. It comes as no surprise, then, that Oberon's answer to the question "What is the purpose of a human's life?" is: "To become what we potentially are." Even more romantically, he continues: "It's the purpose of a seed: to produce a flower. And the purpose of the flower to produce the seed…so a seed might be a baby, but it might be an idea…" When I add that the "seed" could also be a vision, he agrees: "Absolutely. We're all Johnny Appleseeds. We're spreading our seeds, whatever we have, and our seeds are memes as well as genes."[52]

The "seeds" in the form of *genes* refer to biological

contributions, especially children. Raising the next generation of peace-and-planet-lovers means specifically respecting younger people in ways that allow them full personality and psychic formation and grant them a whole and open heart in response to the world. Many Pagan children are brought up within the Pagan faith, but most are exposed to other religions, other paths of living, and other ways of knowing. One of life's purposes, then, is to generate new humans to carry on the general CAW vision into the future through nurturing, but not indoctrinating, the next generation.

Another kind of "seed" comes in the form of *memes*, a unit of cultural information, cultural evolution, or diffusion propagating from one mind to another the way a gene propagates from one organism to another.[53] Examples of memes include music, axioms, beliefs and practices, fashion, architecture, and other transient popular styles. A meme one plants might be a work of art, a book or article, or a church, but in whatever format, the meme introduces an idea or object into the population that (if successful) spreads throughout that culture.

Oberon expresses his seed-planting in a very Pagan way, through the metaphor of the forest: he has watched his seeds "grow up to become great forests so they can spread their own seeds. Both literally and metaphorically, I've planted forests." Literally, Oberon's work has produced trees: a CAW subsidiary called Forever Forests plants seedlings and small trees, especially around Arbor Day, to replenish the Earth's supply of oxygen-exhaling flora. (Pagans in general have special feelings for trees and forests, perhaps due to genetically or mimetically transferred collective memories of the Old World's ancient forestlands.) Figuratively, Oberon has planted many meme-seeds through his work establishing and maintaining CAW, The Grey School of Wizardry,[54] and his other public and private efforts. Therefore, according to CAW doctrine, the purpose of life is also to:

- help, aid, and comfort other persons
- sustain the intertwined networks of mutual support, care, and positive energy within family, community, and world
- strengthen and deepen the relationship with the Divine from which Life itself flows

None of these can be accomplished under a cultural rubric of hyper-independence, social isolation, greed, or selfishness. Rather, a balance must be attained, internally and externally, allowing, as some members would say, *love* to course from the collective to the individual and from the individual outward to the collective.

Theodicy

The attempt to reconcile the reality of evil and suffering in the world with a compassionate and all-powerful God has fascinated many thinkers.

> The epistemic question posed by evil is whether the world contains undesirable states of affairs that provide the basis for an argument that makes it unreasonable for anyone to believe in the existence of God.[55]

The subject has elicited a range of responses, from German polymath Gottfried Leibniz' *Théodicée* [56] and philosopher Richard Swinburne's self-determined free-will,[57] to the mysticism of Advaita[58] and Dvaita.[59] The problem of evil has proven particularly thorny for most NeoPagans because no Satan, devil, or evil spiritual being exists to plague humankind. Certainly there are 'negative energies' but the tendency is to view horrors such as genocide as sickness rather than the work of demon possession or a malevolent fallen angel. CAW lacks a discrete personification of 'evil' partly because the marriage of religion and nature brings with it grudging acknowledgment of an amoral Earth where physicality is prone to disaster and death apparently uncorrelated to morality or ethical behavior – no matter how honorable some hillside town, it can be entombed in a sudden mudslide or volcanic eruption. Coming to terms with such events and incorporating their inevitability into one's theology challenges the black-and-white structure typical of good-evil dichotomies.

The concept of evil in CAW generates uncertainties common in NeoPagan traditions facing a world where cruelty and violence too often stain the hope of human potential. *Evil*, as a noun, tends to be subjective, but this doesn't suggest moral relativism: in CAW negativity or even 'evil' is defined as purposeful physical or psychological cruelty and/or violence. Evil becomes more than an "absence of good" but a reality on its own. For Oberon, "genuine evil" exists in the world on a personal level because he indirectly encountered the cold, callous reality of a murderer in his own life, exposing him to what he interpreted as substantive evil – the deliberate, calculated bearing of agony and misery to others as if embodying an amoral force of nature.[60] Evil becomes a separate entity (not merely the lack of good) and negativity assumes the form of an independent energy in the universe manifested not as a spiritually evil being but in individual humans carrying and inflicting malevolent energy. Although there's a sense of 'good' and 'evil' as discreet *energies*, they both fall under the aegis of divinity (Advaita) as symbolized in the incorporation of both light and dark within the Goddess and thus, panentheistically, the world.

What is the root cause of this kind of evil? Many CAW members consider the causes to be alienation from our physical home, separation from nature, the assumption that humans are superior to nature, and the subsequent belief that humans have the right to impose their will on other sentients.[61] Evil, in this form of thinking, originates from alienation, disconnection, and estrangement from mutual interdependence, connection, and kinship; pathology is created when the natural bond of empathic relationship severs. For many CAW members, evil resides in all persons as an indwelling negativity that must be acknowledged, controlled, and converted into productive anger, justified action, or compassionate determination. Hidden, it becomes a threatening shadow beneath the consciousness, potentially exploding into harmful rage. Everyone carries the seeds of separation and destruction within them; the difference is each person's response to their presence.

CAW's definition of evil is not exclusively anthropocentric, however, because it doesn't stop with human interactions; it extends beyond humankind to include negative human acts against nature. Someone who devastates a landscape, destroys an ecosystem, or consumes to the point of harming others or the environment may be considered malevolent. Evil, then, includes violence against Earth, wrought with the same motivations of greed, self-destruction, or malevolence that engender person-to-person violence. In this view, Gaea holds agency similar to that of people, a radical equality often debated in environmental ethics.[62] Breaking the primal vow of connection – that inter-relationship which contributes to forming the hardwired matrix of Life itself – cumulatively results in evil. Such extreme negativity emerges from an imbalance between creation and destruction. Life-enhancing creativity has imbedded within it altruistic tendencies – the willingness to share one's efforts and therefore connection, for example. Creativity benefits not only the individual through free expression of the self but also others through disseminating beauty and wisdom. The omniverse essentially contains goodness, so when creation and destruction find balance, good results from the equilibrium. Creativity becomes the antidote for evil as if the act of creating somehow mitigates, or at least positively balances, the negative energies everyone carries. The 'weight' of goodness exceeds that of evil, making it the more powerful force.

CAW posits a great deal of free choice with individuals for their behavior and suffered consequences. People choose to enter into pacts with or open themselves up to 'evil' as receptacles of negative energies, and so they endure most of the accountability. Certainly, nature and nurture influence the individual in combinations that can prove tragic, but the ultimate source of life's choices is in each person, a philosophically logical position for a religion that emphasizes individual autonomy. Evil represents violence and cruelty purposefully chosen and consciously wrought against other humans and against nature, the result of imbalance and disconnection from the *other* of humanity and Gaea. Adding individual psychological elements, a picture emerges of persons who become confused, angry, and ill in their hearts and minds to the point where the viciousness and cruelty of which humans at this stage of development are capable overwhelm the deep instinct of self-preservation and empathic interconnection.

Soteriology

Many religious traditions contain an element of personal salvation: from the saving grace of Jesus Christ in Christianity[63] or repentance and atonement in Islam[64] to the personal struggles of Hinduism[65] or *moksha* in Buddhism,[66] and through salvation religion offers transcendence of sin, imperfection, or physical constraints. In the West, the major factors motivating people to join religions (as opposed to adopting secular life-philosophies) seems to be the promise of salvation from (a) the weary world and (b) personal sin. The promise of a paradisiacal afterlife understandably draws many to the hope of release from the physical discomfort, imperfections, and sufferings of life – mitigated by grace and escaped after death in the experience of eternal bliss. The second factor concerns itself with control of personal 'demons,' positive modification of behaviors, and the easing of guilt. The conscience hardwired into most of us censures anti-social or wantonly destructive actions, and forgiveness (whether in a confessional, from others, or direct from deity) comforts the soul and relieves the burdens of culpability and remorse. Accomplished collectively, such pacification provides a powerful and widely sought experience.

Behind this confessional dynamic is a simple organizational procedure used by some religions: accentuate the negative aspects of life, elevate them to theological heights of consequence, and offer a simple, ego-managing solution within the embrace of religious dogma. The carrot-stick program of good-evil dichotomy acts, just as the ecospiritual dynamic, as the poles of a battery, one positive and one negative, driving the process from fallen to uplifted, supplying many churches with their motivational energy. However, most NeoPagan groups, including CAW, don't possess such a structure and don't appear to be maintained with a cosmic polarity of personal salvation. Oberon claims that salvation is not a factor in CAW, and that nothing in the Church's tenets or praxis indicates the need for salvation. The closest equivalent is probably that one will be happy if one lives the kind of moral, ethical, and honorable life the Church advocates but will be unhappy if one is violent, cruel, or dishonorable; in addition, there's a vague notion of karmic repercussion which adds an element of cautionary warning against bad behavior. It seems that one may be 'saved' from an unethical life by embracing CAW's beliefs and practices and find redemption through service to others, ecospiritual honoring of Gaea, and contributing to the evolutionary development of self and species.

In CAW, there doesn't appear to be a vengeful or wrathful God who punishes particular sins. God and Goddess either personify amoral nature, indifferent to human philosophical machinations, or represent the best of humanity, serving as exemplars for an ethical and joyful existence. NeoPagan deities seem just as likely to be jolly, wine-swilling hedonists as towering Apollonian figures of heavenly omnipotence. Therefore, the critical factors of soul-danger and immanent spiritual threat simply don't provide significant motivational energy, and with those factors gone, so are the main reasons for seeking salvation. There exists no discernable concept in CAW of either eternal bliss or damnation, and without the theological ideology of 'sin,' divine forgiveness is not imperative; the energy dynamic of the reward-punishment system doesn't power CAW's morality or ethics which are internal intuitive processes rather than externally influenced obligations. In fact, most members would regard such scare tactics as childish, fit for persons without internal behavioral compasses. Not that the Church doesn't admit the possibility of eternal bliss, including the concept of Heaven or Paradise specifically for those who sincerely believe in them, but eternal punishment is unequivocally denied as pathological.

One of the gravest criticisms Oberon has for other religions is their emphasis on personal salvation; he seems to view such interest as excessive self-indulgence, the opposite of concern with and service to others. The emphasis on personal salvation seems 'petty,' indicating a selfishness that excludes strangers, other life forms, and the planet as a whole.[67] In other words, CAW advocates an altruistic form of religion, one that seeks to serve the *other* rather than exclusively the self. Service becomes a central value and ethical prerogative over and above the personal which seems to contradict the devoted individualism in other areas of the Church but fits with its neo-tribal values.

Asceticism and Mysticism

Asceticism describes a life of abstinence from worldly pleasures, and implies belief in the separation of spirituality and physicality, presupposing that in order to grow closer to God, one must move away from attachments of material reality to the isolation of monastery or self-imposed austerity. The general assumption behind ascetic practices appears to be that Earth is low, dirty, and heavy but spirit is high, bright, and light, a sentiment exposing deep linguistic and psychological prejudices. In my experience, NeoPaganism combines hedonism and moderation in ways associated with tribal practices rather than modern religion. In CAW, spirit is embodied and nature is holy: the realms may be complementary polarities but they can't be separated in life. Mud and fungus partake in sacredness as much as the ascetic who devotes his or her life to solitary prayer; in other words, the tangible is as divine as the ineffable. For CAW, this doesn't trivialize divinity but lifts up the mundane miracles of matter to their proper status as blessed Creation.

The solitary natural life that some NeoPagans choose to lead doesn't usually develop into asceticism with its implied self-denial and world-renunciation, nor must they sequester themselves inside buildings to worship because – as with most Romantics – hill, dale, and woodland serve as cathedrals. In contrast to asceticism, most CAW members revel in their bodies, serve deity through ecstasy and joy, and honor the gods by manifesting pleasure and fulfilling desire within the world. Both body and soul serve God/dess and complete the circuit of life. The inclination to 'party for God' may appear contradictory, but once old assumptions about religion open to new possibilities, enjoying oneself becomes as worthy a path to the divine as sacrifice. Most CAW members seem to have little or no interest in the ascetic life, don't accept the assumptions behind it, and don't aspire to join with deity through paths of separation from the sacred experiences of a life robustly lived. If physicality is sacred then so is the body, and if the body is sacred so is sexuality – all logical conclusions with which the Church builds hedonistic spirituality into an organic institution.

Mysticism suggests the pursuit of communion or identity with divinity through direct experience and/or intuition and marks the departure from purely spirit-matter confluence to the exploration of profound truths underlying and unifying everything.[68] Through mystically experiencing ultimate sources of reality and existence, one may acquire gnosis, wisdom, and perceptions unavailable to the physical senses or empirical reasoning. In CAW, mystical understanding and journeying occupy a recognized position. Earth can be touched, smelled, and tasted, but to perceive it as a meta-being with which one may communicate requires cultivation and use of the mystic mind.

Oberon imagines the mystical as a mysterious land one may visit, but in which one can't permanently live; the realm of the "unknown, unknowable, intangible, and speculative – the places where the sidewalk ends" utterly fascinates many in CAW because such places are beyond human conceptualization.[69] Glamour surrounds the enigmatic universe and arcane levels of reality that lie over the hills and far away. In my experience studying CAW, mysticism takes on nuanced meaning not wholly within the classic definitions: the magickian's journey crosses under-explored boundaries and consciousness flows into the collective unconscious, into spiritual places where new information resides and becomes available. Such is the power of speculative possibility that a coherent ethical, theological, and futurist vision may be nurtured into an entire religious system.

Since CAW originally formed under the rubric of Heinlein's *Stranger in a Strange Land*, creative, imaginative, and innovative flights of fancy reside at the core of Church consciousness and motivate many of its beliefs. Science fiction is considered a mystical literature and the "contemporary equivalent to the mythic literature of all time, the mythology of the future";[70] in other words, science fiction provides a mythological glimpse into the (possible) future, both dystopian and utopian, which in turn supplies CAW with an endless store of images, techniques, methodologies, and consequences of the future toward which the Church collectively strives. While the past suggests mythic foundations for Christianity, Islam, and many other traditions, CAW's mythic/mystic structure derives from its visionary future and those theological beliefs and practices viewed as efficacious for its manifestation.

Ethics

Ethics, whether concerning right conduct or 'the good life,' can be divided into normative (moral theory), meta-ethics (analytic), and applied (contemporary application).[71] The last category applies ethical philosophies to specific issues and therefore allows moral philosophy to be related to the relationship of humanity and nature as *environmental ethics*,[72] which is "the discipline that studies the moral relationship of human beings to, and also the value and moral status of, the environment and its nonhuman contents."[73]

Environmental ethics pragmatically inquires into the duty of humans towards land and other species, especially as described through the 'land ethic' of Aldo Leopold,[74] religion and ecology studies of Mary Evelyn Tucker and John Grim,[75] sacred Earth advocacy of Roger Gottlieb,[76] and ecofeminism of Rosemary Radford Reuther.[77] Even as environmental ethics remains a fundamentally secular philosophical pursuit, the overlap with NeoPagan theology through deep ecology and Goddess mysticism serves as rich sources for the discussion of ecospirituality as it relates to CAW. A reading of the authors and works mentioned above reveals an academic response to the philosophies of Earth religion and many of the titles are included in CAW's official Bibliography.[78]

Applied ethics is frequently a topic of discussion in CAW in areas such as future vision, sexual and ritual etiquette, and general organizational deportment, including social relations, self-awareness, cultural tolerance, pluralism, accountability, conscientiousness, and authenticity. Above all, however, CAW embraces the (Wiccan) Rede[79] which restricts harming anyone and is usually interpreted as an ethical imperative prohibiting physical injury to another person without extreme justification or without his or her consent. Most CAW ethical standards reflect and support The Rede yet most ethics emerge not from external textual, prophetic, or historically based proscriptions but from internal and empathy-based intuition. Both the Golden Rule[80] and The Rede have ancient origins, and the adaptation of either indicates commitment to living an ethical life; however, a purely harmless existence is probably impossible, even if one were to become an orthodox Jain, so perfection is not the leading indicator of ethics. There exists a sense of tolerant practicality to the fact, for instance, that both dedicated vegans and ravenous meat-loving omnivores inhabit CAW's membership, and that they have to get along by respecting each other's choices (even while engaging in endless debates about the relative merits of each choice).

CAW's typical reaction to those outside the Church who violate The Rede indicates its ethical commitment: how one is treated can't always be controlled, but how one responds to negative treatment is controllable in that one can choose to act compassionately.[81] Dedication to compassionate response seems to abound in the Church, which is why almost everyone admired the actions of the Amish in Pennsylvania in 2006 after a deranged man murdered several children in an Amish schoolhouse – they brought food, forgiveness, and comfort to the killer's shocked and grieving parents. Such unequivocal forgiveness garners much praise and appreciation in CAW since almost all members strive to emulate it. Forgiveness and a uniquely Pagan form of 'turning the other cheek' may receive mixed response among NeoPagans in general but most CAW members find the 'law of return' – the NeoPagan belief that there are logical consequences to negative actions – to be an opportunity to practice a form of positive magick. Having had people treat him ill, Oberon has found the time, place, and opportunity to come back to them with a "bouquet of flowers," often with transformative results.[82] Oberon expresses the common NeoPagan belief that "what goes around, comes around," a law of return playing out on the moral stage of humanity – if one creates suffering in this life, one may well have to suffer the consequences in this life (perhaps in prison separated from society). If one escapes consequences in this life, another life awaits that may result in a rebalancing through experiences that teach lessons and provide karmic resolution.[83] Also like the Amish, the highest response to unkind treatment is to 'hit them on the head with a bouquet of flowers.' In my experience, confronting cruelty with mercy instructs others in ways that often lead to a transformation of consciousness, individually and collectively.

What most CAW members dislike above almost any other non-violent but 'negative' form of behavior is hypocrisy[84]which is seen as both a character failing and an element behind many other problems in religion especially as exemplified by certain conservative clergy.[85] One example is that of the pastor who rails against adultery and fornication yet is discovered engaging in these acts. The solution to hypocrisy is careful self-introspection to determine one's identity and corresponding beliefs which can then be manifest in behavior. One of the most powerful ethical standards in CAW contradicts hypocrisy and encourages honesty, openness, and authenticity as a sign of personal spiritual development and maturity.[86]

Rationality

Rationalists (as opposed to empiricists) claim that information can be gathered by means other than the senses and adopt three claims: the *intuition-deduction thesis* (some propositions can be known by intuition alone), *innate knowledge thesis* (we have knowledge of some truths as part of our rational nature), and the *innate concept thesis* (some of the concepts we employ in a subject area are part of our rational nature).[87] If intuition is a valid form of gaining knowledge, then the rationality of this description allows for innate knowledge and thus opens up the possibilities of subjective, experiential knowing as valid.

As befits a church influenced by both spiritual mysticism and Enlightenment scientism, CAW honors rationality defined as 'clear thinking' and 'logical behavior' but doesn't see logic as the only source of knowing. According to CAW philosophy, spiritual maturation results in rational decisions based on intelligence, knowledge, careful consideration, and informed reason – all characteristics of what CAW considers a highly spiritual being. Rationality requires a firm commitment to experience and knowledge of an issue or subject before making decisions about it. 'Rational' also assumes an opposite role to confused and potentially dangerous thinking or behavior; it's the "logical, left-brain approach to things, as opposed to complete chaos"[88] and the destructive force of hysteria. "Rationality" opposes "irrational" chaos and ultimately, as in so many other areas, CAW seeks to balance rational with non-rational, intellect with emotive response, and reason with whimsy. The imaginative, creative, and emotional integrate with the rational to harmonize in the individual and culture, hypothetically producing a state of health.

CAW as an organization identifies continuous and repetitious behaviors it considers irrational (e.g., warfare, murder, and other forms of senseless violence) as a form of insanity. According to this belief, 'religious madness' proves especially heartbreaking since spirituality is seen as maturing and progressive, moving humanity beyond violence and conflict. Religious extremism, wherever it exists, is anathema to the CAW vision, and extremists of any ilk can display irrationality emerging from the confusion of reality with imagination – one can believe any manner of internally produced story but that doesn't necessarily indicate that the story is verifiable by observation and objective analysis. Implicit is the ability to differentiate between imagination and rational intuition; when one accepts one's imaginative shadow as fact or confuses it with intuition and acts upon that darkness, irrational behavior may follow.

CAW's acceptance of rational science doesn't necessarily indicate a preference for a hard, mechanistic worldview over an organic worldview. Being ecospiritual indicates a commitment to life as unique phenomena separate from but integral to the individual or collective constructs of humans. Science fiction, for instance, serves to explore cultural issues emerging from modernity, including the delineation between human/mind/Earth and machine/program/technology. Oberon, referring to the hyper-rationality of industrial modernity, ponders this issue and lands firmly on the organic end of the spectrum: he regards machines as fundamentally different from and inferior to humans because machines don't possess souls.[89]

In CAW, the soul is an individualized phenomenon integrated with the body, but it also partakes in the spiritual realm, untouchable and unmoving, infinite and eternal. According to Oberon, humans can't imbue objects with life nor grace machines with a soul; that's the work of a force superior to humankind. Regardless of CAW's love affair with science fiction, the Church remains a religious group imbued primarily with spiritual vocabulary and imagery reliant on (super)natural theology[90] balanced with healthy rationality and a dedication to reason. In my experience, this balance tends to discourage the more extreme behaviors and devotions typically associated with cults.

Afterlife

Almost every culture speculates on death, especially in a way that postulates the survival of the soul, personality, or other essence.

> In most cultures, this concern has taken the form of belief in some sort of personal afterlife, in which the same individual that lived and died nevertheless persists and continues to have new experiences.[91]

In the case of CAW, surviving death can be considered within a dualistic metaphysics where the indestructible soul is radically different from, and continues after, the death of the body. In the tradition of US religious hybridizations, CAW has adopted this view and advocates certain beliefs modified from the Vedic Traditions with New Age elements added. For CAW, death is a passage from one incarnation to another and from one body to another physical or spiritual form while retaining individual consciousness. What occurs in nature, CAW proposes, probably has an equivalent in spirit: since nature has cycles, the afterlife must also have cycles, and because conscious choice exists in this life, it's likely to exist in the next. In other words, the Church applies natural phenomena to spiritual realms under the assumption that they share an underlying structure (i.e. the panentheistic omnipresence of the divine). Death and the afterlife constitute parts of a continuum in which this life and the next enfold each other within a larger common matrix. The drastic demarcation that death seems to present becomes one of the Mysteries in need of exploration and deeper understanding.

Free from the pressures of eschatological menace and finality, CAW appears more relaxed and open about death, seeing it in the context of natural life cycles and seasonal spirals rather than linear apocalyptic judgment or annihilation of consciousness. The organic nature of CAW's beliefs evidently discourages inflexible, unyielding, static philosophical and theological beliefs; it embraces instead a holistic worldview capable of encompassing complexities typical of diverse systems in nature, applying them to human experiences. CAW also generally accepts concepts held by other religions as legitimate for the members of those religions, but most members find a linear model difficult to appreciate and punishment scenarios implausible.

Since CAW regards individuality as sacred, most members believe that the unique character of each person influences the nature of their afterlife experience – the afterlife becomes as diverse a place as there are unique individuals and groups envisioning it. If Christians, for instance, accept heaven and hell as real, CAW members concede that such may be their postmortem experience – the same for the Buddhist Nirvana, Hindu reincarnation, Muslim Paradise, and Pagan Summerland.[92] For instance, most CAW members accept that Morning Glory's mother, who died a devout Christian, went to heaven and became an angel because that is what she deeply believed would happen to her. On the other hand, CAW accepts that one's afterlife experience will reflect what is "embedded in our mythological psyche" and that one "might expect to encounter the mythic archetypal."[93] Oberon and several other Church members expect a:

> cute little girl wearing an ankh or some great big, tall, black-hooded skeleton with a scythe to show up and say, "Walk this way" and take us to the boat.[94]

CAW doesn't advocate a 'one-size-fits-all' religion, but rather an individual-based spirituality partially determined by the parameters of each person's own will. It isn't that some "cosmic universal happens you when you die" but that "different things happen to different people according to what you believe in."[95] Perhaps guilt-ridden Christians can invite upon themselves temporary suffering in the afterlife because of some personal need, but eventually they will be finished with this experience and move on to another more positive and mature one.[96] In other words, CAW conceives of a semi-personal reincarnation where the individual has limited influence over the form and content of his or her next life. The afterlife is seen as *partially personalized*, a mixture of what the soul requires for maturation and what it desires to experience and know – part cosmic guidance and part private crucible.

In CAW, death is therefore regarded as a continuation of

the soul's mythic journey. Destiny is not rigidly pre-set but a distinctive and remarkable product of the universal conjoined with the particular, a belief that places some, but not all, responsibility on the individual and how he or she chooses to live. In this model, the human soul gets many chances to make and correct mistakes, many opportunities to grow, learn, and mature – life after life. Consciousness transmigrates, remembering more and more of previous incarnations as the soul (re)cycles through various forms and experiences in order to learn the necessary lessons. The general feeling about this journey is that it's similar to a hike though a grand landscape (one filled, in some cases, with figures of the Jungian unconscious); however, there's no specific sense, as in Hindu and Buddhist traditions, of an ultimate goal beyond which the cycle ends.

For the miraculous human consciousness to cease existing defies credibility: if energy is neither lost nor gained but only transformed, then the massive energetic locus of a person doesn't 'wink out' of reality but rather expands its original form. According to its needs and desires, our indestructible self-essence continues its voyage of growth, learning, and maturation which are the fundamental goals as CAW views it. For the Church, this answers the perennial question, "Why are we here?" Development and advancement along an evolutionary path of body, mind, and spirit toward vaguely outlined (but not necessarily ultimate) goals satisfies the need for purpose even as CAW attempts to develop spiritual technologies that they hope will bridge the gap between this life and the next.[97] In the end, however, the Church doesn't obsess over the topic of after-life, being more focused on life and leaving what comes after for the time when it arrives.

Texts

Although there are many important written and oral texts in CAW, none is accepted as divinely inspired or infallible as are the Bible or Koran; NeoPaganism bases its theology and practices on revitalized traditions of pre-Christian European folk religion and the internal voice of ethical intuition, not on external textual hermeneutics. The "text" of contemporary Pagans consists of historical association with the ancient and subtle intuitive communication with nature and the Earth; however, many books (and films, games, and music) are considered sacred in the sense that they reflect the NeoPagan vision of the divine or complement NeoPagan religious values and practices.

CAW considers many 'texts' sacred, including the cave paintings at Lascaux and Altamira which are revered as highly as the writings of Confucius.[98] The written word itself holds a singular fascination (regardless of its medium[99]) and serves as the archival repository for the *inside* of history – the thoughts, feelings, myths, stories, and accounts of people living in different times. (One example of wisdom writing is the works of Imhotep, the ancient Egyptian polymath, whom Oberon calls the "first recorded wizard.") Unlike buildings, cities, or pottery, an archeologist can't dig up this inner world and dust it off as an artifact; it must be understood through either oral heritage, which changes over time, or writing, which retains more of its original flavor.

CAW's penchant for archiving and storing its contributions to NeoPaganism and religion emerges, in part, from the love of and protective feelings for books – going so far as to declare that destroying books or libraries is "a crime against the future and the past."[100] Such sentiments toward libraries seem logical in light of the devotion to the printed word's wisdom-spreading capacity. Libraries are also viewed as important because knowledge can no longer be destroyed with the loss of one book or one library – information has been replicated and multiplied around the world. This spread of humankind's literary legacy inspires Oberon to pride and jubilation since there's more information available to humanity than has ever been possible before, and for a few dollars one can get one's own copy of almost anything.[101]

The logical result of global communication and data replication is the increasing intelligence and wisdom of Gaea. Oberon identifies the Internet as an intermediary stage between the written word and virtual reality[102] – a science fiction-inspired vision of virtual reality interfaces and holodecks – concluding with conviction that "the Internet may very well be the way that Gaea is truly growing a noosphere."[103] Nature is also declared a text, and while Oberon postulates that it's "the greatest book of all," he gives a scientific rather than mystical answer, admitting that one of his favorite 'texts' to read is the geologic record. Nature, as the geological documentation of Earth's history, serves as a holy book to read and understand, for in understanding the planet's history one can know more about human nature and even conjecture about the future. Science thus contributes to an increased knowledge about Gaea which leads to wisdom concerning the omniverse.

According to CAW, nature exists as the ultimate material reality beyond human constructed contexts[104] – science can tell us much, but observational methodologies limit its scope and depth, so that real understanding of nature comes through *relationship* with it. Nature is the reality for which other texts serve as analogs;[105] nature becomes a religious object in that it provides the ultimate and irreducibly grounded reality on which are founded all other human and nonhuman enterprises and existences and from which, in fact, they partly emerge. Nature is the other half of the hybrid, along with spirit, which creates the world and provides an intimate element in consciousness; thus, it serves as half of the sacred text to which CAW appeals for wisdom, and as the medium by which sacredness emanates into consciousness.

Goals and Means

CAW's goal seems to be to manifest a visionary future by acting as if that future already exists, at least within the limits of Church influence. Members act out their vision in the present as though they were vanguards of a coming (r)evolution bringing CAW's ethical and moral version of the future into the world. It's considered a magickal working to manifest into reality the central beliefs and practices of NeoPaganism; generally, the goal is not to replace diversity with a monolithic pan-Pagan worldview but to make intellectual room for that worldview in the belief that evolution (Gaea) will select the most sustainable and well-adapted behavior pattern.

Achieving these goals requires the restoration of what Oberon believes is the fundamental moral lesson of US democratic culture: the bad guys lose and the good guys win. For CAW's founders and for many youths during the 1960s, questions began to arise about whether authority figures and institutions were genuinely advancing the basic ethical litany drilled into their heads by Superman's "truth, justice, and the American way." The original goal of CAW, therefore, was to restore what Oberon and his friends saw as fundamental US values, especially as reflected in television shows and pop culture icons; the "assignment" was to create a religion that actually manifested those values and within which they could be lived and strengthened. The institutional matrix chosen to create this haven of traditional US standards was religion, a discipline whose job description includes morality and ethics. The adaptation of NeoPagan religion supposedly served as the means to attain these goals – an odd choice, certainly, to actuate the era's popular Americana. Evidently, Oberon's memories get filtered through childhood, softened by a fondness for specific visions and beliefs shared by many of his generation, socio-economic class, and educational propensities. He did not grow up black, poor, in an urban ghetto, or as a woman so he did not experience the difficulties faced by these groups – his is a middle-class entitlement vision wrought through the dreams of science fiction writers and the overwhelming assumptions of technological progress and better living through chemistry.

CAW eventually adopted the progressive worldview wherein time acts as an agent to introduce innovations along a specific line of advancement, leading, in this case, to greater freedom and justice. Inspired by examples such as the civil rights and other social justice movements, several CAW members see their task as preparing the way and being the next step in human development[106] – the mechanism for progressive actualization turns out to be human evolution. Science again provides the means by which the progressive agenda might be explained and justified as being an inevitable process of nature. Hitching one's belief system to the forces of Earth lends a certain power to human philosophies; suggesting a divine connection to one's beliefs lends even more weight to the Church's ideations. Add a substantial dose of altruism based on modern utopian visions of the triumph of reason and one arrives at a religion reflecting the common goal of creating a better world through evolutionarily transcending this one.[107]

Through living out an ecospiritual life now, CAW hopes to create the means for human transformation in an effort to overcome global tribulations and to progress into a new age. Mutual support in the task of envisioning and living the vision of a better future through the machinations of natural evolution explains the origins of CAW and describes one impetus for its continuation. This is a unique combination, to be sure, but one that many members believe may prove integral in a shift to Earth-based spirituality stimulated by an actual or perceived environmental crisis.

Tolerance

CAW practices a form of tolerance that borders on xenophilia – whatever is new, original, and innovative appears to excite most members. Since their future vision differs significantly from present reality, radical ideas and controversial practices are sought out and developed. CAW not only tolerates differences and diversity, but tends to celebrate them as superior to conformity and similarity. Under the rubric of "unity in diversity," uniqueness and individuality become elevated to the sacred. From the very beginning, the unusual found a home – according to Oberon, misfits were always welcome, and in one early meeting of Atl at Westminster College, attendees included a seven-foot-tall albino, a thalidomide victim with flippers instead of limbs, and a tattooed Maasai warrior exchange student who had killed a lion for his initiation.

Embracing diversity – even strangeness – as an ethical imperative always seemed to be part of the CAW character, partly acquired through the medium of science fiction, especially *Stranger in a Strange Land*. How much of a rebellious and shock-value element was contained in this ethic remains uncertain but it's likely there was a tendency to accentuate the freakish side in order to break from the stifling conformity of middle-class American life at the time. When CAW was founded, NeoPaganism probably fit these tendencies, for what would be more disturbing than a tradition so closely linked in the popular imagination to the occult?

CAW's inclusiveness extends to religious affiliation: a member can retain loyalty to any chosen religion and still participate in the Church. One can be Christian, Buddhist, Jewish, or atheist – it's not about what one believes, but about "who you are and what you do, the way you show up and participate," a sentiment connected to the positive concept of tribal religion.[108] CAW bases itself on the belief that variety equals richness and that accumulation of knowledge and experience are valuable and spiritually enhancing. Like a vibrant city where people from all over the world open restaurants and serve their unique food, life is seen as a banquet to be sampled and enjoyed with zest and gusto – the model is one of an open-hearted embrace of what exists, within ethical limits, not what *ought* to exist according to an inherited tradition.

From CAW's perspective, some religions see themselves in a contest to win adherents and in competition against other traditions; exclusive religions, the ones who claim universal or select righteousness, fall under the "win-lose" structure. This mindset erects valuated hierarchies with one religion at the top, a system that has caused considerable violence and suffering throughout history. Most CAW members admit confusion over the motivation for such behavior, especially in religion, and a common response is the question, "Who cares what other people do?" Evidently, such incredulity stems from a lack of the emotive responses and historical experiences held by members of more evangelical groups; not being experienced directly by its members, CAW tends to dismiss them as invalid and destructive. Accordingly, some members blame the religions themselves for the actions of a greedy and power-obsessed few so that history mythically emerges as a bloodbath of violent oppression against Pagans. Such an interpretation seems skewed in the direction of a victim mentality useful to contemporary Paganism and appears to cause CAW to sometimes engage in boundary-less and indiscriminate inclusivity.

Chapter 5

CAW's Practices

Based on its beliefs and worldview, CAW's practices reflect and embody its values, commitments, and ethos. Sacred actions support and encourage mindsets and behavior patterns commensurate with CAW's stated mission, literature, and clergy. Practices also aid in (inter)connecting members with the movements of planets and stars, the cycles of Earth, and the highest and deepest elements of the self. Each heading in this section begins with a quote from *The Church of All Worlds Tradition*, a pamphlet written by Liza Zell[1] with the approval of Oberon and Morning Glory and distributed among the membership in response to institutional dissolution in the early 2000s. These practices seek to embody CAW's beliefs, philosophies, and worldview while providing common ground to an otherwise diverse group.

The Wheel of the Year

> Like almost all NeoPagan traditions, the Church of All Worlds Tradition celebrates the cycles of the seasons, especially the traditional quarters and cross quarters: Yule, Imbolc, Ostara, Beltane, Litha, Lughnasad, Mabon, and Samhain.[2]

As part of CAW's Earth-as-divine-being theology, the eight traditional Sabbat celebrations and ritual structure are generally observed.[3] Marking the seasonal equinoxes, solstices, and cross-quarters, Sabbats continually reconnect members to planetary cycles and rhythms, each weighed with its own symbolism and significance.[4] By linking personal lifespan with seasonal changes and larger cycles of planetary history, such celebrations serve to imbue daily existence with greater meaning and consequence as part of an ongoing meta-story of the human species, the grand heritage of a roughly 4.5 billion-year-old planet, and the grandeur of the cosmos. In addition, the Sabbats provide a reason for community gatherings, which afford a measure of social cohesion in an otherwise diverse and scattered religious community. The Church also takes the opportunity Sabbats afford to congregate and express its hedonistic style of worship – Sabbat Circles grant space-time partitions from mundane existence to (re)create sacred energy, worship embodied divinity, and concretize concepts of embodied devotion.[5]

For CAW, the Wheel of the Year represents the cyclical movement of Earth as well as changes in the psyche and the physical and psychological development of the typical lifespan. Although many Wiccans recognize Samhain as marking the start of the New Year, some CAW members choose to begin at Yule, the longest night, when the daylight begins its ascent to primacy again; others prefer Beltane, when Spring has, for the most part, completed its thaw and warmer days begin in earnest.

The names of the Sabbats come from different Pagan sources: "Ostara," for instance, comes from the Germanic Goddess of dawn, Eostre; "Lughnasad" from the Irish mythic deity-hero Lugh; and "Samhain" from the Celtic term for 'summer's end.' When Christianity first spread across Europe, the old Pagan holy days were kept in order to pacify the rural folk and encourage conversion, but renamed as Christian holidays; so, for example, Yule became Christmas, Ostara became Easter, Lughnasad become Lammas, and Samhain morphed into All Hallows Eve. CAW celebrates the original holy days not only as an acknowledgment of Earth's seasonal cycles but also to emphasize corresponding attributes.

The illustration below is an artistically rendered example of a representative Wheel of the Year, indicating Sabbat names, approximate dates of occurrence, and significant energetic and lifecycle correspondences. Pre-modern myths, contemporary collective stories, and post-modern sensibilities meet in the celebratory cycles represented in the Wheel of the Year. For instance, the upper half of the year, from Ostara to Mabon, is often identified as the 'lighter' side while the lower half is designated the 'darker' half, generalizing the level of energy, activity, and mood or 'vibration.'

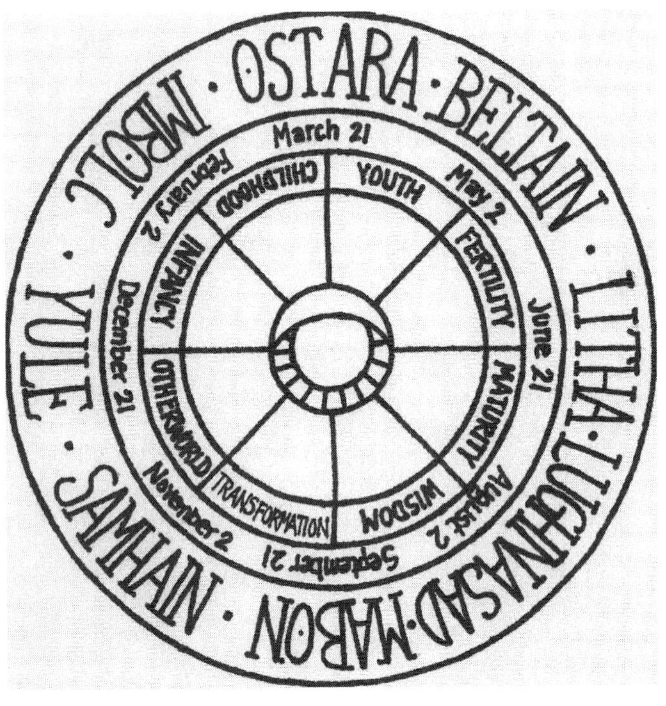

In addition to seasonal changes, each Sabbat celebrates developmental markers in the lifecycle; for example, Yule is birth, and the time from Yule to Imbolc acknowledges infancy with all that level of maturity suggests: basic survival, dependence, innocence, and newness. Imbolc, on the other hand, is marked by first speech, the end of infancy, and the start of childhood which holds until Ostara, the rite of First Moonblood or Seed (the onset of puberty), ending childhood and initiating youthhood. Beltane

(May Day and mid-Spring) represents the end of youth and the beginning of adulthood, with analogous attributes of sexuality, fertility, and beginning one's own family. In CAW, this Sabbat often translates into orgiastic festivities, the honoring of new adults or families, May Games, or all-night vigils centered around traveling to the faerie land. While these associations are fluid and unique to each Nest, and while they aren't universally adopted or recognized, they do point out symbols connecting CAW practitioners with the natural cycles of Earth and body.

The Rede

> Most Church of All Worlds practitioners support the Wiccan Rede as a foundation: *If It Harm None, Do As You Will.* However, in the Church of All Worlds Tradition, it's understood that *all magick, whether it serves personal ends or not, is intended to move towards the best outcome for all.* The Church of All Worlds Tradition looks beyond the perennial spiritual value of non-harming and actively contributes to the evolution of the whole. What form this takes varies widely.[6]

The (Wiccan) Rede[7] is a polarity-dynamic axiom acknowledging freedom while delimiting excess and is the central ethical statement of NeoPaganism and CAW. Conceptually, The Rede stands as a bargain between humankind and the cosmos, rewarding active acceptance of moral responsibility with otherwise uninhibited freedom of self-expression. It's believed that either of these polarities alone creates rifts in the balanced harmony of dualisms (including intellectual-emotional, physical-spiritual, and body-metaphysical, among others), resulting in either oppression of individual liberty or overindulgence in selfishness. The most basic interpretation of The Rede is if a person refrains from causing involuntary physical or significant material harm, hurt, or injury to another person, then he or she has the right to express fully his or her individual will. The rights of others logically bound such rights, and though it's admitted that arbitration will often be needed to articulate and maintain those boundaries, The Rede unifies most NeoPagans under a common ethical commitment and sets clear areas of activity to be avoided.

Beyond the usual moral and ethical patterning of behavior, however, The Rede additionally prohibits *magickal* harm. Since CAW is a magickal tradition that accepts the efficacy and potency of magickal work, The Rede covers subtle and mystical realms of action – all magick must be intended and manifested "towards the best outcome for all." Although vague, this proscription conforms to the general consensus that magick serves the best interest of everyone involved in the working, even when desires appear to be at odds. The guiding philosophy seems to be that since deity possesses superior knowledge and understanding of the circumstances around motivations and needs, it alone can successfully create solutions that maximize positive results. For this reason, "for the good of all" is a frequent disclaimer to otherwise self-centered magickal efforts. Not all NeoPagan groups abide by this ethical injunction, especially the "left-hand" paths[8] that may have no compunction about attempting to force their will on others if they feel justified; in CAW, however, there's little question that such behavior is inappropriate.

Casting a Circle

Practitioners of the Church of All Worlds Tradition frequently cast a circle by ritually drawing it with a blade, wand, or other power object. The circle then serves as a place of protection, holiness, and power in which religious and magickal acts are accomplished. The ideal of every action and relationship inside the circle is *perfect love and perfect trust*.[9]

The basic physical and metaphorical structure of the NeoPagan religious service is the Circle; as both a noun describing the service and a verb describing the action, circles and circling mimic the major progressions of life such as seasons, life spans, planetary evolution, and cosmic time. As pointed out by Mercia Eliade,[10] sacred space/time events like Circles attempt to create a temporary boundary between the extraordinary and the mundane worlds in order to access the incomparable properties of the manifested sacred he calls "hierophanies." These events evidence the religious psyche as set apart from the mundane or profane world of ordinary consciousness.

> For religious man, space is not homogeneous; he experiences interruptions, breaks in it; some parts of space are qualitatively different from others...It's not a matter of theoretical speculation, but of a primary religious experience that precedes all reflection on the world.[11]

There's a purposeful delineation set aside for religious, spiritual, and magickal worship and work that is identifiably different from profane space/time – ordinarily, a Circle is cast by ritually separating it off from mundane space/time. Many CAW members believe casting actually forms an ethereal barrier that insulates and centers magickal energy; it seems to change the consciousness of the participants in ways facilitating ceremonial and magickal efficacy. The resulting psychological 'bubble' acts as an alchemical oven, holding in the generated heat of energy work and focusing perceptual and intuitive concentration as mediated attentiveness and directed willpower. Most CAW practitioners maintain that magickal work of this kind has repeatedly proven effective, giving further credence to those who believe collective or hive mindsets empirically alter group psychology and may even effect objective changes as a result of pliable morphic fields[12] or other para-scientific phenomena.

The image of *radiant circles* comes from the tradition of gathering in circles as practiced by many cultures and from the ubiquity of the *circle* as a spiritual and socio-cultural symbol, the prime metaphor of what we're studying. The radiant circles of personal and planetary transformation through ecospirituality and devotion to the divine offers hope for the present and a vision of the future firmly grounded in material immanence and ecstatically focused on the transcendent.

Circles are all around us: humans collectively form them to communicate as equals,[13] roundness permeates forms in nature, and circles symbolize infinity and eternity because they have no beginning or end. A circle can also indicate a fellowship or community, such as a circle of friends or the circle of life.

When a circle moves, it's a *cycle*. Of course, nature has constant cycles: days and nights, moon phases, seasons, and years. The Moon revolves around Earth, Earth rotates on its axis and moves about the sun, and the sun makes its way through the zodiac. Even our galaxy spins slowly through space every 240 million years. Cultures and societies cycle through emergence, dominance, and decline, and civilizations rise and fall. Humans have biorhythms, menses, and moods that shift during a day or month. It seems that almost everything is in constant motion.

When a cycle moves, it becomes a *spiral*. The spiral of time, for instance, cycles around but doesn't remain in the same groove: it pushes in one direction towards the future. You can't really go home again or step into the same river twice – unidirectional change seems to be an inevitable characteristic of the universe. Spiral designs appear throughout nature, from nautiluses to galaxies. People have walked labyrinths (stylized spirals) and danced in undulating circles for centuries. Spirals are three-dimensional, bringing dynamic depth to the cosmos.

According to CAW's *Membership Handbook* (1995), the Church's liturgical structure follows a distinct pattern:

- Banishing/Cleansing
- Grounding
- Casting the Circle
- Calling the Quarters
- Invoking Deities and Spirits
- (Magickal) Working (Power Raising/Releasing)
- Communion
- Thanks and Dismissal of Elements and Spirits
- Opening the Circle

Casting the Circle itself contains several parts: walking the circumference with a tool (i.e. blade, wand, or crystal) or with the hand, and/or everyone dancing the circumference with chanting, singing, and visualization, enclosing sacred space.[14] One example of the spoken portion of Circle casting was provided by CAW member Mike Fix:

We cast the circle of ancient lore
Waves upon a timeless shore
With no beginning, nor an end
Always knowing foe from friend
Ouroboros, of legends old
Rings of power, forged in gold
Wheel of the year, circle of stones
Cycle of life, from birth to bones
A ring around the silv'ry Moon
We cast you now, o ancient rune![15]

As this example demonstrates, readings or recitations are highly eclectic assemblages from disparate sources – in this case old English lore, traditional Witchcraft, Tolkien, Alchemy, and Nordic mythology. Such historical and cultural eclecticism typifies CAW's open attitude of pluralistic multiculturalism shamelessly plundering the world's cultural coffers in the pursuit of a global wisdom. Members of CAW unabashedly research and utilize elements from all planetary cultures, mixing them in an alchemical cauldron to create a blended style (that occasionally descends into a messy swill of conflicting ingredients). In fact, such merging is one of the hallmarks of CAW in its continuing attempt to create a synthesis of the world's religions and spiritual traditions, a postmodern conglomeration resulting in what is hoped to be an evolutionary leap to a new level of conscious actualization and spiritual development.

Within the Circle, the call for "perfect love and perfect trust" seems to involve an attempt to create an atmosphere conducive to magickal working, commonweal, and protection. Since Medieval Europe and Colonial America were often hostile environments for tribal, polytheistic nature traditions – trust between Pagans was required, serving as protection against discovery and the resulting social harassment or legal persecution. Circling in unqualified love and trust emerged from the needs of an illegal minority religion but has since expanded in meaning to include the basic human desire for closeness, comfort, security, and empathic relationship with co-Circlers and spiritual peers.

The Five Elements

> Practitioners of the Church of All Worlds Tradition often use the traditional elements, Air, Fire, Water, Earth, and Spirit and the corresponding directions East, South, West, North, and Center as important parts of religious practice.[16]

Wherever CAW places the center of its Circle, the compass directions are constant, and a conscious or unconscious attempt is made to connect to the planetary grid or geomantic "ley-lines"[17] popularized in New Age lore. The five Elements simultaneously represent the historically recognized elements of Earth, the Elementals (magic[k]al beings), and aspects of the human condition of being. For instance, Air indicates the breathable atmosphere, breezes, wind, and other empirical phenomena, but it also includes the Elementals of air such as Zephyrs and sprites, and finally symbolizes the aspects of intellect, thought, reason, rationality, intelligence, and mind.

A typical CAW Circle begins in the East with the element of Air, celebrating the aspects noted above. It then moves clockwise to the South, element of Fire (celebrating passion, zeal, will, power, creativity, and innovation); West, element of Water (dreams, daydreaming, intuition, inner gnosis, contemplation, and meditation); North, element of Earth (physicality, embodiment, grounding, stability, and manifestation); and finally The Center (above and below), element of Spirit (divinity, deity, the soul, mystical realities, and the unknown, ethereal, and transcendent). Together, these ideas, conceptualizations, metaphors, natural elements, environmental signifiers, and religious associations produce a Circle.

Evoking the God and Goddess

> Practitioners of the Church of All Worlds Tradition often choose individuals in their circles to serve as focal points and expressions of the Divine Male and Female. Divinity is also invited into the ritual circle on its own without being invited into a particular individual.[18]

Being polytheistic, CAW regards divinity as pluralistic rather than monistic, and being a highly educated and typically curious group, members tend to research and explore various subtle forms and manifestations of divinity. One historical activity has been the allowing of spiritual beings' entrance to the body in oracular or ecstatic fashion.[19] The title of Adler's *Drawing Down the Moon* is an example of one such ritual that seeks to attract the energy and divinity of the Moon down to the Earthly realm and into a specific person prepared for hosting such energy. Based on a depiction on an ancient Greek urn, the ritual specifically requests a goddess or the Goddess to descend into the body and psyche of the High Priest or Priestess and to speak through him or her. Such communication is considered highly significant much like Spiritualism or New Age channeling.[20] As parental surrogates, bountiful lovers, and erotic co-creators of the omniverse, deities form a central part of CAW. To invite such a deity into oneself is usually considered a privilege and an adventure, and the recipient of such an honor requires proper personality traits and training to accomplish the task well. Since the gods who enter a Circle are considered benevolent, little thought is given to negative forms of possession and their potentially unfortunate consequences – as long as the energy and intent of the Circle remains positive, conventional wisdom suggests the results will be equally positive.

Bardship

> The Church of All Worlds Tradition is a rich source of song, chant, ritual, art, lore, scholarship, vision and so on. The practitioners of the Church of All Worlds Tradition who have made major contributions to the creative life of the NeoPagan movement and the broader culture are too numerous to name. Innovation and creativity are valued and nourished.[21]

Bard enters English through the medieval Scottish-English word *bardos*, referring to professional poets, musicians, singer-songwriters, satirists, chroniclers, and keepers of local or regional stories, legends, and family lineages. Bards typically travelled from court to court, town to town, or, if fortunate, secured a sponsor, providing entertainment and social commentary.

CAW's collective celebrations, punctuated by a compendium of songs, chants, dances, and stories, evoke its neo-tribal side –

at any given Pagan gathering, one is likely to find a Bardic Circle where anyone from the assembled may sing, play an instrument, tell a story, or engage in other crowd-pleasing performances. Usually encircling a fire, Bardics seek to recapitulate ancient tribal and medieval traditions and re-stimulate their memories in the audience; this bardic activity seems to create an aura of communal unity through re-membering the act of sharing creative talent and performance drawn from members of the community. CAW is not unique in recording and archiving its creative endeavors, but it does have one of the largest collections, including works by Church member Gwydion Pendderwen, who was, according to the admittedly biased official CAW website,[22] a "gifted songwriter and performer."

> This music has continued to be very influential in the resurgence of Pagan culture in the US and beyond. Beyond that, these songs stand the test of time for their artistry and listenability. Now may they continue to inspire future generations of bards and poets.[23]

Pendderwen is an example of the compendium the Church has developed and continues to nurture; CAW even has a 'Bardic Guild' made up of performing artists within the Church to exchange samples, comment on each other's work, and generally develop their craft. Members have published songbooks, ritual poetry, and fiction recognized within the NeoPagan community.

Influences from Other Traditions

> The Church of All Worlds Tradition enjoys and embraces influences from all the world's religions and traditions in ways that complement its basic principles and practices.[24]

Exclusivity stands as normative in many religious traditions in that there's one right way to the exclusion of all others; in most of NeoPaganism, however, there exists a sense that not everyone will or should be attracted to Pagan values and practices, and if one is Pagan, one can also be an active member of any number of other religions as well. What might be called an *ethic of inclusivity* or *interfaith covenant*[25] based on the perception that diversity serves to enrich the whole, pervades contemporary Paganism and reigns supreme in CAW. This inclusivity produces not only the acceptance of other traditions (even those in apparent opposition to CAW) but also an active integration of other traditions into the Church's core tenets and practices. I've frequently noted that when faced with the passion and power of non-Pagan religions – with the exception of violent extremist fundamentalism – CAW members usually react with either courteous neutrality or engaged interest.

Most members seem to desire knowledge about the world, and though they may have their own personal opinions, they generally seek to expand their knowledge and understanding of others, either through accepting other religious paths (as best for their adherents) or in practicing certain elements of that tradition as part of their participation in the Church. CAW incorporates other religious and spiritual traditions into itself, especially those that complement its basic principles and practices.[26] While such adoption is meant as complementary, it does occasionally tend toward questionable co-optation, especially in regard to Native North American traditions – often the adoption process alters the original inspiration in ways that aren't always appreciated by members of the original group. Again, CAW, being of "all worlds," sees the entire world's spiritual catalog as fair game for adaptation and incorporation.

Reverence for the Earth

Practitioners of the Church of All Worlds Tradition revere, honor, and protect the Earth. Most believe that our planet is

> a conscious living being. Most revere Her as a manifestation of the Great Mother Goddess worshipped by human beings from the dawn of time.[27]

As previously noted, one of the primary spiritual foci of CAW is the immanent and panentheistic planetary meta-being Gaea, whose embodied form is the Earth and whose embodiment *is* Earth. Several books on Gaia as a potentially conscious entity have been published,[28] but CAW's view of the Earth as "a manifestation of the Great Mother Goddess" is central to understanding the inner dynamic of the Church and represents an inventive synthesis of Gaia theory and Pagan spirituality. NeoPaganism is itself a Goddess spirituality tradition, responding to the traditional 'mother nature' model of a feminized Earth and to what NeoPagans perceived as dominance-heavy patriarchal excess and the resulting extremes of industrial civilization; CAW seems to advocate this sacred feminism with intense devotion to feminine energy and feminist ideology. The 'Earth as Mother' motif expresses this orientation in its nurturing form while the Earth as Great Goddess expresses it in its more power-full[29] form.

To "revere" is to feel respectful awe, as in the veneration of statues, icons, and images surrounded by fresh flowers, candles, and offerings. In CAW, reverence for Earth indicates the same sense of sacredness applied to an anthropomorphized planet from two sources: Earth as a deity or divine being worthy of worship and Earth as Elder deserving honor and respect. Because an Elder has lived long and learned much of life through longevity, he or she is recognized as a valued source of wisdom and authority. In a similar fashion, Earth as Gaea is considered a biological and spiritual authority figure, often envisioned as mother, senior partner, or dominant lover, by virtue of the millions of years of evolutionary development and acquired planetary wisdom 'She' has accumulated.

Reverence and honor for Gaea implies religious and spiritual reverence toward the Earth, but *protection* suggests an active and often activist environmentalism with religious and spiritual motivations. Through various subsidiaries such as Forever Forests and Peaceful Order of the Earth Mother (POEM), CAW works to protect nature, especially forests, and in general to spread the message of sustainable cohabitation with the natural world in which humans are embedded. For this reason, some Church members are also eco-activists – through public groups such as Greenpeace or Earth First! or privately through personal lifestyle modification, or both.

Thou Art God/dess

> Practitioners of the Church of All Worlds Tradition honor the God and/or Goddess as immanent in every human being, voiced in the common greeting, "Thou Art God" or "Thou Art Goddess." The deepest experience of the Divinity in other people and things comes through the process of *grokking*. Literally, *grokking* means "drinking." In practice it means expanding one's identity to include the whole being of another person or thing.[30]

When the statement "thou art God" is found in the Bible, it's addressed to the God of Israel and is traditionally interpreted to mean that He is the universal transcendent Creator and only true God – an assertion of monotheism or at least of superiority among deities.[31] One example of these Biblical statements is the passage from 1 Kings 18: the Prophet Elijah's denial at Carmel that the Pagan god Baal has any reality, divinity belonging to Yahweh alone. The statement may also refer to the religious philosophy that all beings contain within themselves some essence of the Godhead, such as the Hindu saying *Tat Tvam Asi*, "Thou Art That," which stresses the divine nature of the human soul and emphasizes the creative and spiritual power within each individual.

"Thou Art God" is also a statement of divine immanence integral to CAW's theology, taken directly from *Stranger in a Strange Land*. Within the context of the book, "thou art God" stems from the novel's premise that beings can become integrated with each other on a fundamental level that includes shared knowledge, senses, neural processing, and capabilities. In order to know and appreciate something fully, the main characters in the book become part of that thing – in *grokking*[32] God, therefore, those characters necessarily *become* (a limited human version of) God insofar as they totally integrate with the divine. The belief that intimate empathic (inter)connection is possible inhabits the heart of CAW where interactions of human, nature, and divinity involve the ongoing effort to grok in such a way that their interdependence becomes explicit; thus, the vision of a peaceful unified world is not considered utopian but rather a practical matter of developing those inherent empathic abilities that allow "eco-psychic" unification based on mutual recognition of the deep familiarity and sacredness of all.[33]

Another aspect of being God is a panentheistic view of life, wherein God stands separate from the world, yet simultaneously and radically whole with and within it – theologically, divinity is simultaneously transcendent and immanent, more than the world but irreducibly present *as* the world. Therefore, the CAW greeting "Thou art God" acts as a reminder that God/dess dwells within each person, and, because divinity exists, in part, as physical reality, *is* each person. The belief that all persons actually *are* God is not meant arrogantly but in acknowledgement of the intimate immersion and immanence of divinity in all existence; while not the totality of God, each person embodies the divine, which mystically inhabits all life concurrently.

Sharing Water

In harmony with the process of *grokking*, the water that is

> essential to all life is the primary Sacrament of the Church of All Worlds Tradition. Water is Blessed and passed in a chalice, or otherwise shared. Often the last drops are offered to the Divine. Usually when a chalice is passed, the person passing blesses the person receiving the chalice by saying, "Never Thirst," "Thou Art God," "Drink Deep," "Don't spit in the cup," or other appropriate words. This ritual, more than any other, is the common practice of the Church of All Worlds Tradition.[34]

Because water is essential for all life on Earth, the ceremony of sharing a cup or glass of water, representing various possible levels of relationship, is integral to CAW observances; this value is partly derived from *Stranger in a Strange Land* in which the fictional Martians who raise Valentine Michael Smith to adulthood treasure water greatly because Mars is a very dry planet. As a CAW sacrament, water represents the blood of the Mother, the main ingredient in our bodies, and the major element of the biosphere – water exists as an underlying substance, one of the inescapable foundations of civilization. In this sacrament, the unity and inter-relationship of human and Earth receive repeated recognition.

Various phrases usually accompany water sharing, including "Thou art God" or "Thou art Goddess" (depending on the gender energy claimed or dominant) and other humorous comments such as "Be ever hydrated" – sharing water is rarely solemn unless the ritual context encourages it. Oberon often signs his correspondences with "NT" for "Never Thirst," a phrase again drawn from *Stranger in a Strange Land*. As an aside, it may also be noted that in sharing a cup of liquid, DNA in saliva is passed among the participants, another subtle but symbolically pertinent exchange.

A loose parallel might be drawn between sharing water that is ceremonially consumed and baptism in water that is ceremonially sprinkled or used to immerse. Both are symbolic acts of blessing through contact with a natural element, and for CAW, the emphasis is on the life-giving and sustaining aspects. As previously noted, because it's ubiquitous, water symbolizes the unity and coherence between life forms and beneath life itself.[35] More readily utilized and handled than other substances such as air or sunlight, water (along with its Piscean and Aquarian implications[36]) remains central to the Church's search for the underlying ecospiritual harmony among its members, in nature, and throughout the cosmos.

Water Kinship

The intention of the Water Sharing ritual is to affirm bonds of kinship. Depending on the intimacy of the circle, four levels of this bond are common:

- Affirming our connection to each other and to all life
- Affirming belonging to a tribe or tradition
- Affirming friendship
- A lifelong Commitment of deep communion, friendship, love, and compassion, which may or may not have an erotic element[37]

Involvement in CAW tends towards familial bonds rather than congregational or community models – acquaintances tend to be encouraged to develop into friendships then nurtured into kinships that imply a deeper sense of responsibility and attachment, with all the benefits and challenges thereof. Unfortunately, this model, which is part *SISL* idealism and part hippy communalism, wreaks havoc with Church cohesion because families tend to argue and fight in ways other models of community usually don't. My experience is that the various trials and 'breakups' in CAW's history emerge partly from the emotional intimacy engendered by the Church's organizational proclivities. Affirming a sociologically 'neotribal' connection involves self-identification with and ongoing commitment to the members and ideologies of the group; water sharing (re) establishes those bonds in CAW and reaffirms the kinship of belief and practice. Tribal bonds are more familial than other types, involving worshipping and even communally working together, and at deeper levels, water-sharing can indicate significant voluntary commitment.

As discussed above, affirming the connection all humans have with each other as a common species and with the Earth lies at the core of CAW's worldview and vision of the sacred. In advocating close, mutually sustaining bonds between members and then anthropomorphizing and sacralizing the planet at the highest level of human honor, Church members hold as ideal the application of loving bonds to the Earth and to each other. Affirming the bond of deep communion represents the most intimate water kinship in CAW – while not a marriage contract, it represents a freely chosen and occasionally life-long merger. Although this state can be (and often is) temporary as relationships ebb and flow, there are many stories confirming its depth; for example, in 2006 when Morning Glory was diagnosed with cancer, former lovers and beloveds, some of them her friends from the 1960s, traveled thousands of miles to gather at her bedside with healing energy and love. Such efforts affirm that what was originally forged existed and was maintained at a significantly deep level. At its most erotic and binding, deep communion can be polyamorous, the closest non-marriage kinship in the Church.

Nests

Nests are the basic grouping of the Church of All Worlds Tradition and are usually composed of at least three people who have a consistent commitment to the Tradition. At

> least one member, the Nest Coordinator, should have at least one year experience and the blessing of other long-term practitioners of the Tradition. A Nest may begin with no experience and work towards the ideals of Nesthood. Some Nests are families. Others are social networks, or ritual working groups. They are usually small and intimate. Sometimes several Nests may form a Branch.[38]

The idea of 'Nests' also comes from *Stranger in a Strange Land* wherein Valentine Michael Smith establishes groups to gather and study 'Martian'; in CAW, Nests are analogous to branches, congregations, or parishes in other traditions. Nests register with the main Church in California but remain highly independent entities, establishing their own methodologies, tenets, and practices so long as they exhibit minimal connection to the CAW Tradition and don't aggressively violate basic rules of ethical behavior. Anyone may assemble two other like-minded people and start a Nest,[39] and typically when a Nest grows larger than thirteen, it will hive off and form two smaller groups. The Nest format encourages both involvement with CAW and independence within a small group dynamic that is decentralized and intimate.

I founded and facilitated the Holy Oak Nest from 1991 to 1999; at its height, Holy Oak had about twenty members, monthly meetings, outings, Sabbat celebrations, and a newsletter. The Nest dissolved shortly after I left to study for my Master's degree. One of the most challenging tasks was to juggle the various energies and talents in the group while maintaining the energy level needed to keep it engaging and beneficial – it was important to balance the needs and abilities of everyone into a synergistic whole that became more than the sum of its parts. Currently, the Solantis Nest has taken up where Holy Oak left off.

Fun

> Humor, enjoyment, play, fantasy, and all forms of pleasure are central to the ways that practitioners of the Church of All Worlds Tradition come together.[40]

In my experience, religion is often treated as serious business encompassing deep spiritual seeking, monumental historical events, awesome miracles, consequential moral proscriptions, and/or eternal judgment. Many religions do contain and even encourage fun, especially as joy, contentment, and non-physical (or proscribed physical) pleasure, but in CAW, fun stands as a central religious precept that is as important as all other tenets. In addition to being intimately crucial to Church praxis, the definition of fun expands greatly to include fantasy, play, imaginative games, and "all forms of pleasure," including the sensual and erotic.[41] In contrast, Catholic priests and nuns are charged with celibacy and the pleasures of the flesh open to ministers, pastors, most Indian and Oriental monks, and clergy around the world remain variously circumscribed, at least in the ideal. Clergy in CAW usually lead lusty, sensual, sexually robust, and erotically charged spiritual lives; the joining of the light-hearted erotic pleasures of the physical within the realm of the religiously sacred makes CAW unique.[42]

Because the Church doesn't contain eschatological judgments or moral condemnation (at least not for activities conforming to The Rede), there exists a lightness of being, a sense of comfortable co-existence with embodiment and its pleasures or challenges. Members seem to play and seek fun constantly, not as harried obsession but simply because they see the world and life as sources of amusement and adventure made meaningful by zestfully embracing life – even most NeoPagan deities know how to have fun and are joyous beings of spontaneity and mischief. Tragedies and sorrows aren't fun, of course, but they are powerful sources of growth, learning, and wisdom to be experienced and then moved beyond into the normal state of happiness which, according to CAW, is our human birthright.

A Tradition Looking Equally to Future and Past

> Four of the five practices above derive directly from *Stranger in a Strange Land*...Some members of the Church of All Worlds Tradition glow with pride over this fact, while others are embarrassed and don't wish to be identified with the book. There's no question that many aspects of the book are increasingly outdated. What will never be outdated, however, is the Church of All Worlds Tradition's embrace of the mythology of the future and of science and technology as sources of wisdom as valid as the sacred traditions of old. The Church of All Worlds Tradition honors the ancient past and looks, with equal reverence, to the future.[43]

Most religions, including CAW, emerge from and rely on some past experience, avatar, or ritualized praxis to draw the past forward into the present. For instance, the Eucharist reenacts the declaration of Jesus to remember Him through transfigured bread and wine; it recalls and celebrates the existence of the Savior Christ as a historical figure, spiritual intercessor, and holy guide. As Margot Adler notes, CAW is a "religion from the future";[44] although as a NeoPagan organization the Church looks to the past for vital mythological heritage, in my experience its emphasis remains on nurturing the future, mainly influenced by *SISL* and the tendency of science fiction to explore speculative and imaginative realms of possibility. As the 'literature of tomorrow', many science fiction authors have tried to establish themselves as modern futurist prophets and harbingers of (possible) things to come, at least within the parameters and zeitgeist of modernity. A religion influenced by such an artistic tradition will likely expand the usual borders of spiritual praxis to include a long-term view of the future and a worldview formed to bring those visions, rather than only an established past, into the present – CAW's emphasis, therefore, inverts the usual pattern of remembering a sacred past in lieu of manifesting a sacred future.

Robert Heinlein, aspiring futurist prophet though he may have been, suffered from temporal limitations in his writing; being a novel of its historical time and geographic place, *SISL* expresses personal quirks such as certain patriarchal and racial attitudes no longer acceptable to most visionaries.[45] Since CAW membership is decidedly liberal, Green, and/or radical, these aspects of the book cause consternation; nevertheless the basic vision remains central to CAW's self-mythos: multiple open intimacies and close, complex familial relationships within one household expanded to form networks of intentional community based on love. These are the qualities envisioned as elements of a paradisiacal future, one in which all religious and secular visions are welcome within the limiting and proactive mandate of The Rede.

Freedom of Expression in Intimacy and Family

The Church of All Worlds Tradition is associated with open attitudes towards intimacy and sexuality. How this is practiced differs widely from person to person and Nest to Nest. Practitioners of the Church of All Worlds Tradition affirm and support the broadest diversity of intimate and familial expression consistent with a sustainable and ethical life. For example, Church of All Worlds practitioners support same-sex bonding through marriage, handfasting or other means. While quite a number of practitioners of the Church of All Worlds Tradition are monogamous, all support the full range of choice in relationship, including intimate relationships and familial bonds that contain more than two adults; in other words, polyamory.[46]

In no area is CAW more unconventional than in its institutionalized attitudes towards sacred sexuality.[47] Because the Church adopts what it considers a pre-modern and neo-tribal stance in combining religiosity and eroticism, it stands well outside the normative parameters set by Abrahamic (and many Eastern) traditions that share a subtle or obvious emphasis on the transcendent or non-physical quality of spirit and the religious life. Some non-Pagans mandate a secondary role for the material realm, or even discredit it as illusory, corrupt, or evil – physical pleasure often is considered a distraction from the real work of inner spiritual development, and erotic pleasure is sometimes regarded as counterproductive to spiritual efforts.

NeoPagans, however, seek to recombine and reconcile the physical and spiritual realms which they mainly view as having deteriorated into an unhealthy schism. Regarded even within the NeoPagan community as radical, CAW consciously strives to break down normative – and what the Church see as oppressive – models of intimacy and family. To do so, CAW reaches into the past and outside 'civilization' for non-modern sexual and familial forms and envisions a future in which the scope of acceptable behavior is widely inclusive. As such, CAW is firmly embedded in the modern democratic and pluralistic milieu, emerging from and dependent on the post-Enlightenment emphasis on freedom and individual rights against collective standardization.

Within CAW there's almost unlimited latitude afforded to and expressed by members; within the accepted ethical confines of The Rede, free expression of physical pleasure and eroticism is common. Some members regard marriage between one male and one female as emerging from normative dualisms of gender inequality, patriarchal control issues, and paternity rights which have been institutionalized to such an extent that laws prohibiting polygamy, 'fornication,' or 'adultery' exclude other relationship or familial models. Although the majority of CAW members appear to have monogamous relationships, they almost universally accept and support polyamory and collective sexuality for those who chose it. Most members suggest that the ultimate truth of poly choices is not mere hedonism or selfish gratification but the striving for love, companionship, and stability.

Polyamory

> Among the more intriguing aspects of CAW is its espousal and practice of *polyamory*. The term is typically defined as the practice or lifestyle of being open to having more than one loving, intimate relationship at a time, with the full knowledge and consent of all partners involved. Persons who consider themselves emotionally suited to such relationships may define themselves as polyamorous, often abbreviated as *poly*.[48]

Although the practice is recognizable as far back as the 1920s, the word *polyamory* was coined by Morning Glory in her 1990 article "A Bouquet of Lovers." Morning Glory wrote therein, "The goal of a responsible Open Relationship is to cultivate ongoing, long-term, complex relationships which are rooted in deep mutual friendships."[49] Therefore, poly people are those who consciously choose to enter into a relatively stable collective relationship with more than one intimate partner, all of whom also choose such a relationship and approvingly know about each other.

Polyamory's origins are inseparably intertwined with the origins of CAW in the mid-1960s. The original impetus towards polyamory was Robert Heinlein's science fiction classic *Stranger in a Strange Land*, in which sexual love is joyfully practiced among members of family "Nests." The novel concerns a human boy who is stranded on Mars after the death of his parents and their entire Martian expedition, and who is subsequently raised by Martians to young adulthood, acquiring special abilities and radically different morals. His name is Valentine Michael Smith, and one of those special abilities is "grokking," which is defined as "the perfect understanding, the mutually merging rapport…that should exist between waterbrothers."[50] A special and deeply empathic relationship is created between voluntary "waterbrothers"[51] both in the novel and in the real-life CAW. To "grok" is to understand something (ideas or people) so profoundly as to in essence become that thing. This relationship relies on the use of the brain, in its most complex emotive context, to establish an interconnected and roughly telepathic consciousness between persons, which forms the basis of polyamorous groupings in the fictional version of CAW.

Groups in the novel practice polyamory (though it isn't called that) as extended family units somewhat akin to hippy communal structures, but with an important difference. To grok means that people are able to understand each other so well that if misunderstandings, anger, jealousy, or other destructive emotions emerge, they do not have a chance to fester. Conflicts are minimized as each member comprehends and accepts the foibles of the others. Of course, this means that everyone in the group must have considerable communication skills, which is why CAW's real-life version of polyamory also requires these skills. It might even be argued that the Church's function is to teach the language of deep empathic grokking, which in the novel is metaphorically called "Martian."

Smith takes polyamorous love for granted as a virtue and, in an exchange with his friend Jillian, the absence of jealously does not indicate indifference. Speaking sexually, the dialogue introduces a kind of innocence relating to sex:

"Jill, you would not want Duke?" She heard an echo of "water

> brother" in his mind.
> "Hmm...I've never thought about it. I guess I've been 'being faithful' to you. But I grok you speak rightly; I wouldn't turn Duke down – and I would *enjoy* it, too! What do you think of *that*, darling?
> "I grok a goodness," Mike said seriously.[52]

This isn't merely a middle-aged SF writer in the early 1960s rebelling against monogamous morality; it's an attempt at revealing another mode of joyful, mutually sustaining relationship. In Smith's CAW, people live together in comfortable surroundings, usually naked and sexually uninhibited, bound together by Smith's charisma and the desire to live what's perceived as a healthier and more evolved lifestyle. Next to the door of the Nest is a sign that says, "Did you remember to dress?" The exact same sign was displayed next to the front door of the early CAW meetinghouse in St. Louis, Missouri.

In a way, water brotherhood and Heinleinian polyamory are like marriage: a substantive commitment, but between more than two people. Describing it, one character says to another:

> You *are* married. After tonight there will never be any doubt in your mind." Duke looked happily pensive. "Ben, I was married before...and at first it was nice and then it was steady hell. This time I like it, all the time. Shucks, I *love* it! I don't mean just that it's fun to shack up with a bunch of bouncy babes. I *love* them – all my brothers, of both sexes.[53]

Forgiving Heinlein's early 60s patriarchal attitude, love is an irreplaceable element in the equation of his SF universe and has become an undeniable part of CAW mythology. Heinlein describes love as "that condition in which the happiness of another person is essential to your own"[54] – a sentiment which requires a steady altruism, challenging even for many CAWers.

The supreme benevolence of love, practiced deeply and authentically, allows the complex interchange of energies and personalities in a poly relationship.

In *SISL*, polyamory is described by Jubal Hershaw, the major character after Michael and the one closest in spirit to Heinlein himself, as "plural marriage – a group theogamy, to be technical."[55] "Theogamy" – marriage between gods – is something of an inside concept, without any attempt at blasphemy, implying the immanent divinity of all persons. To survive a polyamorous relationship, one almost has to accept such personal divinity, not only as theology, but in order to claim one's individual right to follow an inner voice rather than external social pressures.

Jubal also discusses the morality of polyamorous arrangements:

> Yes, I think what those people – the entire Nest, not just our kids – are doing is moral. I haven't examined details, but – *yes*, all of it. Bacchanalia, unashamed swapping, communal living and anarchistic code, everything.[56]

Jubal's description is a rather dusty but accurate picture of polyamory. The elements included begin with "Bacchanalia," by which is implied hedonistic, even orgiastic pleasure within the group. Indeed, this is still a part of CAW today. Pleasure, fun, and enjoyment, both intellectual ("sacred bullshit sessions") and sensually embodied ("growing closer") are integral parts of CAW worship and continue to function as two sides of an integrated coin: both spiritual and physical ecstasy are considered equally valid forms of worship. Pleasuring another person is considered roughly equivalent to pleasuring the gods because the physical body and its erotic capacities are of divine origin and therefore sacred, and the gods literally dwell within each person.

The second element is "unashamed swapping" which implies sharing sexual partners. This is a firmly accepted practice, and its recognition as virtuous is requisite to learning the lessons of deep empathic connection, free of the poison of guilt, shame, or jealousy. No person is owned or possessed by another, and the real-time acknowledgment of this fact enhances the ability to share one's body, and by extension love, with others. Sharing ecstasy closely relates to sharing water since humans are made of water – a circular recognition of the unity of spirit, matter, and the immanent divinity of humankind.

Next, we have "communal living," which suggests intentional, cooperative, and extended family or community. Cooperation indicates common effort beneficial not only to the self but the whole as well. Acting to assist others, with no immediate or direct reward (except warm feelings of inclusion and altruism) calls for a sense that benefiting the whole is beneficial to the self, which means that the individual voluntarily identifies with the collective and senses himself or herself to be a functioning, valuable, and honored part of that collective. Communal living requires the capability of extending the self and its capacity to love outward towards others.

Finally, we have the "anarchistic code": socio-political philosophies wherein hierarchical authority is rejected in favor of free-flowing consensual structures, radical equality, and total freedom. In this case, anarchy isn't violent chaos; it suggests the absence of need for power-over authority figures and oppressive political systems and is the most spiritually advanced social structure because it functions only when practiced by emotionally, psychologically, and spiritually advanced people. The assumption is that when one reaches a certain level of maturation, one becomes a self-regulating entity no longer requiring external control. Polyamory tends to attract people who are already predisposed to open relationships or communal living, and who are, at least in theory, more sophisticated along a personal evolutionary path that allows for alternative styles of loving. Not that everyone ought to "evolve" into a poly relationship – many people will never be interested in it – but some will, and society as a whole will mature when it accepts these alternative lifestyles.

Jubal continues with a pointed critique of the hegemonic structuring of relationships. He, and thus CAW, sees the polyamorous communal "Nest" structure as arising from a different but coequal morality extant in religious history.

> Ben, this pattern has been offered to a naughty world many times – and the world has always crushed it. The Oneida Colony was much like Mike's Nest – it lasted a while but out in the country, not many neighbors. Or take the early Christians – anarchy, communism, group marriage, even that kiss of brotherhood – Mike has borrowed a lot from them.[57]

From these sentiments, Jubal criticizes mainstream sexual morality, finding in it a source of needless suffering, a critique as pertinent now as in 1961:

> The ethics of sex is a thorny problem. Each of us is forced to grope for a solution he can live with – in the face of a preposterous, unworkable, and *evil* code of so-called 'Morals.' Most of us know the code is wrong, almost everybody breaks it. But we pay Danegeld by feeling guilty and giving lip service. Willy-nilly, the code rides us, dead and stinking, an albatross around the neck.[58]

As the Man from Mars – a true stranger in a strange land – Michael is the radically alternative 'other,' an outsider who views Western morality from a unique perspective and rejects it because it is anachronistic and immoral. Thus, he serves as symbolic representative of real-life CAW members who are made to feel like the 'other,' as if they had been born elsewhere and immigrated, or been assigned to dwell amidst the dominant culture, living in uncomfortable co-existence or outright conflict with its mores and rules. The goal of many CAWers is personal and social transformation, in part through liberating the libido. Jubal observes:

> I see the beauty of Mike's attempt to devise an ideal ethic and applaud his recognition that such must start by junking the present sexual code …monogamy, family pattern, continence, body taboos, conventional restrictions on intercourse, and so forth…[59]

Most CAW members see beauty in the ideal ethic laid out in *SISL* and resonate with it through grokking its goodness. Polyamory is an integral part of CAW as a spiritual organization and social movement, part of the grand quest for sexual liberation and freedom. Jubal declares: "Now comes Mike and says: 'There is no need to covet my wife…*love* her! There's no limit to her love, we have everything to gain – and nothing to lose but fear and guilt and hatred and jealousy.' The proposition is incredible."[60]

It would be a mistake to believe that all CAWers practice polyamory, but it would be safe to say all accept those who choose it. Nor are most CAWers so naive as to think that everyone should embrace polyamory; clearly, it isn't for everyone. However, they do defend their right to practice it without harassment or interference, and evidently practice it with considerable joy and some success, despite its indisputable unconventionality. Only deep desires could stimulate such devotion; as one *SISL* character says: "It looks as if the whole family will be home."[61] Home and family are clearly two of the primordial human needs sought and often fulfilled in polyamorous relationships. To understand this dynamic is to begin to grok polyamory.

A Bouquet of Lovers

Although a group originating in the late 1950s called Feraferia was probably the first to advocate polyamory, it was Morning Glory and CAW that popularized the practice and developed its parameters through practical experience. The ethics of "pan-erotic freedom"[62] were described, and the basic outlines of polyamorous relationships delineated, in the 1990 Green Egg essay "A Bouquet of Lovers," which contains a wealth of information and opinion still relevant to the practice today. Beginning with a quote from the Crosby, Stills & Nash song "Triad," Morning Glory lays the foundation for success with two "Rules of the Road": "Honesty and Openness about the polyamorous lifestyle" and "All partners involved in the Multiple Relations must fully and willingly embrace the basic commitment to a polyamorous lifestyle."[63] Although many may find them difficult to authentically embrace, these rules appear to be unequivocally prerequisite: "Honesty and willing Polyamorous Commitment are the basic building blocks all partners must use to build a lasting Open Relationship."[64]

The first rule concerns the capacity for courageous authenticity and the ability to remain emotionally open to others even under stressful circumstances. This implies willingness to form, and rudimentary skills at maintaining, relationships not based on possession, jealousy, or codependency, and thus requiring people who are at a certain stage of consciousness and maturation in these matters. Without such attributes, one can't maintain the inner balance that results in outer harmony, and negative responses will emerge from the unconscious to subtly or overtly sabotage the relationship. The second rule concerns the necessary awareness of everyone involved about what they and others are doing. All partners must be fully conscious of the poly lifestyle and be committed to it. Even if they do not specifically use the term "polyamorous," they must still possess delineated ideas about the extended open relationship model and a few of the basic tools needed to make it work.

Another of Morning Glory's rules is "Never put energy into

any Secondary relationships when there is an active conflict within the Primary. This has to be bedrock or the Primary will eventually fold."[65] The basic structure is this: two poly people who love each other form the "primary" relationship, to which other "secondary" relationships can be added within agreed guidelines to create a threesome, foursome, or larger extended affiliation, which is then considered a single unit. CAW even has a non-legal ceremony appropriate to multiple unions called *handfasting,* generally recognized as a binding religious ceremony within the NeoPagan community. Morning Glory addresses the common struggle with jealousy stimulated by poly-loving through emphasizing focus on the primary relationship:

> Territorial jealousy has no place in a polyamorous agreement. However situational jealousy can arise over issues in the relationship when one or more of the partners is feeling neglected. Obviously the best cure for neglect is to focus attention on what has been neglected; the relationship will prosper when all partners are feeling strong and positive about each other. From that strong and healthy center it becomes possible to extend the love to others.[66]

For many people, it might seem challenging enough balancing the needs of one other person, never mind two or more, and it does require mature people dedicated to the poly arrangement. Nevertheless, clearly the author not only considers such arrangements desirable but also confirms its viability through personal experience. For instance, there is this bit of procedural advice:

> If a Secondary becomes destructive to the Primary partnership, one of the Primary partners can ask the other to terminate the threatening Secondary relationship. It is wise to limit this veto to the initial phase of Secondary relationship formation. After

> a Secondary relationship has existed over a year and a day, any difficulties with the partner's Secondary must be worked out with everyone's cooperation. If you are not all friends by that time, then you are not conducting your relationships in a very cooperative and loving manner. When all is said and done, what we are creating is extended families based on the simple fact that lovers will come through for you more than friends will.[67]

The basic elements are comprised of honesty about one's own feelings, commitments, and personal boundaries (which requires a certain level of introspection), openness to new sexual arrangements, communication skills, and the ability to love another, not as possession, but as independent and autonomous *other*. A high level of intelligence, integrity, and maturity nurture this particular "bouquet." In Morning Glory's description, there is even an element of ritual in patiently waiting a year and a day before confirming the solidity of a new flower in the arrangement. The ultimate goal, however, isn't merely an intellectual exercise in collective relationship, as if it were some objective, scientific experiment; the whole systems is founded on emotive response, as ancient as our species, and the need for acceptance and joy. Friendship, cooperation, and love, in this order, constitute the journey that must be taken by anyone hoping to have *any* deep, lasting, and mutually satisfying relationship.

Finally, Morning Glory includes a section on "Staying Healthy," which was, and still is, of prime concern when the "thorn" of VD is joined by the "poison" of HIV. As the author puts it, poly lifestyle requires developing "an impeccable honesty that will brook no hiding behind false modesty or squeamishness." Safety demands full disclosure within a "Condom Commitment" wherein all members of the group agree to wear a condom with anyone not already in the group and/or tested HIV negative. If all this sounds a bit preconceived and passionless, it actually becomes second nature, taking a back seat, so to speak, to the traditional elements of genuine love, pleasure, and fun. The extra time, thought, and energy suggested by "Bouquet" recedes into the background but remains an integral part of surviving the emotional turbulence and physical concerns multiple partners can create. As Morning Glory states:

> Adherence to the Condom Commitment and to the other Rules of the Road may seem harsh and somewhat artificial at first, but they have evolved by way of floods of tears and many broken hearts. Alternative relationships can be filled with playful excitement, but it isn't a game and people are not toys. The only way the system works is if everyone gets what they need. The rewards are so rich and wonderful that I personally can't imagine living any other way.[68]

The religious aspects of polyamory relate to CAW's commitment to self-actualization[69] as a spiritual enterprise and to the cultivation of love in corporeal form. Love for others as erotic embodiment of divine nature isn't unique to NeoPaganism or CAW, but its form as a new religious movement has brought it into the twenty-first century in a way that challenges many long-held moral beliefs and their resulting legal proscriptions. Therefore, polyamory is integral to the CAW vision; Morning Glory concludes:

> I feel that this whole polyamorous lifestyle is the *avante garde* of the twenty-first Century. Expanded families will become a pattern with wider acceptance as the monogamous nuclear family system breaks apart under the impact of serial divorces. In many ways, polyamorous extended relationships mimic the old multi-generational families before the Industrial Revolution, but they are better because the ties are voluntary and are, by necessity, rooted in honesty, fairness, friendship

> and mutual interests. Eros is, after all, the primary force that binds the universe together; so we must be creative in the ways we use that force to evolve new and appropriate ways to solve our problems and to make each other and ourselves happy.[70]

Polyamory serves several functions within the Church. First, it conforms to the futurist orientation of CAW's founding principles, including its original inspiration in *SISL*. The Church seeks to make religion and spirituality relevant to postmodern sensibilities and thus renew its power into the future as a moral and ethical force in society. Second, it provides an alternative familial and relational context within which to reestablish collective security, stability, and primacy of caring love in the face of the decline of the modern nuclear family. Third, it promotes the "primary force" of the universe, *eros* – love's erotic energy – that creates and sustains all life. This isn't a philosophical position but a simple fact: we all come from the act of mating (even test-tube babies are born of the energetic synthesis of sperm and ovum), and until humans create living beings out of molecules, life will be the creative combination of entropy-defying primal forces. Finally, at the heart of polyamory lies happiness, for those who desire or need more than one person to love and for society in its journey towards acceptance of the *other*. Most of us desire happiness, yet live in a world of minefields constraining and threatening our happiness, including those whose ideal family is a postmodern version of the pre-industrial extended biological family.

Clearly, polyamory serves sociological as well as religious functions in CAW. On the one hand, bonding ceremonies and bonded states help create the close-knit neo-tribal confluence of energies and personalities that constitute the "Nest" with a familial element that places members in a stronger obligatory relationship than the common congregational model. Also, possessing an alternative relationship ethic not only sets CAW apart from other NeoPagan groups, it also places the Church in a unique position within the greater culture as vanguard of evolutionary growth towards acceptance, which is one of CAW's missions.

CAW Precepts

The morals and ethics of CAW emerge from two sources: the general morals held by NeoPagan traditions (especially exemplified by The Rede) and the humanist ethics of modernity (exemplified by the United Nations Declaration of Human Rights). These Precepts, as published in the CAW *Membership Handbook*, seem whimsical in presentation but, as I've observed, actually stand as rather firm guidelines for member behavior – not as externally coerced by Church leadership but rather as descriptions of typical Church members. The type of person attracted to CAW evidently already conforms to most, if not all, of these principles and agrees with Oberon's introduction which refers to integrity of our actions and strength of character that inspires others to grow and transform the world.

Be Excellent to Each Other!

> Thou art God/dess. To truly honor the Divinity within each other is to treat each other with respect, kindness, courtesy, and conscious consideration. This involves honest and responsible communication, including the avoidance of gossip and rumor-mongering, and the willingness to reach for understanding rather than judgment. Learn how to communicate in a positive, life-affirming way. We prefer to avoid us/them and either/or thinking, and to instead take an inclusive systems approach that sees the Divinity in all living things. To this end we also deplore coercive behavior that doesn't respect the free will of others. We prefer to lead,

> not by guilt or coercion, but by inspiration and example; not only to be excellent to each other, but to strive for excellence in all our endeavors, no matter how seemingly insignificant. Tribal values we hold include Loyalty, Generosity, Fairness, and Hospitality.[71]

Most of this Precept is recognizable from other religious traditions, and some of it derives from Christianity (the cultural milieu in which CAW grew up and exists). The statements seem rather old-fashioned, but I suggest they are perennial and exist as part of an unceasing flow of ethical advocacy stretching back to long before the tablets were delivered at Mt. Sinai.

The first statement that "Thou art God/dess" connects CAW's ethics to the fact that members see themselves as divine beings by virtue of the panentheistic ubiquity of Deity and the capacity to grok, compelling them to act in ways representative of, and responsive to, divine morality. To "truly honor the Divinity within each other" indicates that the God/dess, as perceived in CAW, desires people to "treat each other with respect, kindness, courtesy, and conscious consideration." "Respect" and "kindness" become qualities of the Divine, and like most religions, CAW views the divine as a reflection of itself.

CAW members attempt to communicate with each other in ways that maintain a level of conscious respect due all divine carriers of being. That is, words matter: in magickal work, words contain power, changing consciousness and therefore altering subjective reality. "Honest and responsible communication" is more than politeness or courtesy; it serves to continence magickal influence and focus power in positive directions, namely "life-affirming" paths in line with the Church's ethical vision and away from destructive and life-negating paths – be they personal, ecological, or spiritual. Most CAW members accept that positive communication encourages positive energy, so kindness and deference engender more of the same in a cascading effect.

Another interesting feature of this Precept is the support of panentheism through *systems theory,* which suggests that physical phenomena can be seen as a web of interconnected relationships and that all such systems share behaviors, patterns, and properties that give them a fundamental underlying unity.[72] The theory expands in CAW to describe the theological position of panentheistic divinity and thus highlights the Church's efforts to combine ecology with theology through reference to an underlying, overarching, and ultimately unifying reality.

Neo-tribal values are defined as "Loyalty, Generosity, Fairness, Hospitality," standards so revered they are capitalized as proper nouns. As previously noted, Pagans have historically been loyal to one another out of necessity and can be fiercely protective of their small faith community; CAW takes generosity and hospitality further with the promise members make to each other that none will ever go without food, shelter, or love. A sense of fairness also emerges from *SISL* in that several members of Valentine Michael Smith's fictional CAW are "Fair Witnesses," officially certified and legally recognized observers, somewhat like turbocharged Notary Publics who can attest to the truth of a situation through training in stringently objective and dispassionate scrutinizing and reporting techniques. Again, these values materialize from a familial or semi-familial grounding wherein the good of the whole is everyone's personal responsibility.

Be Excellent to Yourself!

> Again, Thou Art God/dess. Divinity resides within as well as without, so how you treat yourself is how you treat that Divinity. Self-abuse, whether through irresponsible use of substances, overwork, self-denial, self-deception, or simply running those tapes that undermine self-esteem, are all insults to the Divinity within. Treat yourself kindly, with compassion

> rather than judgment and it will be easier to treat others that way. Take care of your body, home, and possessions, as a piece of Gaia that has been entrusted to you. Be a conscious guardian to the Temple and the God/dess within.[73]

Beyond the sometimes-narcissistic indulgences of the New Age movement lies a balance between service to the *other* and care for the *self* – while some religions emphasize just one of these two, CAW members claim to work toward a harmonious equilibrium empowering both. Returning to the theme of immanent and indwelling divinity, care for the body, mind, and spirit becomes a religious obligation honoring the interior deity. The 'God within' is seen as deserving no less than the 'God without,' so attentiveness to personal needs and desires constitutes a holy act.

Viewing the self as an incarnation of God forms the basis for self-preserving avoidance of self-destructive conduct – since divinity dwells in all persons, Church members accept a special responsibility to note harmful self-indulgence or dangerous behavior patterns developing in them. Gentle self-criticism notwithstanding, the point is to respect and nurture the self as divine being and to love oneself as prerequisite to loving others. This introspection is not meant to encourage selfishness or egotism but rather the acceptance of one's own divinity and reverence of the authentic self – the body is not just a temple, it's a palace, and the soul is not merely a carrier of the divine spark, it's a portion of God wrapped in flesh.

Less clear is the issue of material possessions and acquisition and how this intersects with being excellent with the self. Few Pagans are ascetics, but voluntary simplicity has found favor with a few CAW members for whom the adage "live simply so that others may simply live" is meaningful; on the other hand, more than a few members revel in material prosperity, viewing it as blessing.[74] With increasing social and global awareness of environmental issues, more self-reflective consideration is being given to lifestyle choices and their impact on the Earth. For CAW, being excellent to the self doesn't require gluttony, self-absorption, or egocentrism; it requires love.

Honor Diversity!

> In Nature a diverse ecosystem has more stability. There are many styles of living and ways of living, each of which has something to offer to the overall puzzle of life. Be open-minded and receptive to new ideas because this usually manifests in growth of the spirit and the mind. Learn about differences rather than judge them. Be willing to explore others' creative abilities to manifest a sense of well-being and confidence in their own Divinity. Sexism, racism, or rude remarks directed towards other's sexual preferences, body type or personal habits (insofar as they don't harm others) have no place in this community. All life is sacred.[75]

NeoPagans seem constantly to observe and consult with natural systems for hints on how to live: metaphorically and literally, Earth is considered a carrier of wisdom in its processes and biological forms available for humans to mimic.[76] The idea is that Earth is a superior being compared to humanity – an enveloping whole within which the physical aspect of humanity dwells and with which spiritual communion is possible, desirable, and perhaps inevitable. Diversity is one aspect of Earth wisdom that, according to CAW, humans must emulate for the health of the species. Since multiple crops often prove more viable than mono-cropping, human variety – and the social acceptance of that variety – might prove equally important. CAW possesses a 'nature is Mother' (i.e. older, wiser, smarter) motif; therefore, humans (i.e. younger, less skilled or less intelligent) should mimic Her ways to produce a healthy society and sustainable biosphere.

In human and nonhuman realms, diversity provides the ingredients for stability so that human diversity is seen as necessary for our species to survive and flourish. From the inclusion of humankind in the multileveled, ecological sophistication of nature emerges an ethic of co-existence, and from the model of the Earth and its diversified meta-systems comes the moral prerogative to honor and even celebrate differences in people. CAW members exhibit an easy-going openness and curiosity, resulting in an acceptance of other worldviews and behaviors as perfectly valid *for their adherents*. Difference is not usually perceived as threatening or offensive but completely natural.

Along with appreciating human and nonhuman diversity, CAW members see themselves as learning, growing beings open to an omniverse of possibilities and willing to enter speculative, imaginative, and creative territory in anticipation of discovery and enrichment. Beyond self-enrichment, however, lies the further ethical imperative to help others in reaching their potential. 'CAWers' see themselves as not only learners but also teachers, offering the Church's worldview, beliefs, and morals to anyone interested. As a 'religion from the future,' some members consider themselves missionaries or explorers from the future with gifts of wisdom, knowledge, and visionary stories from an optimistically rendered Earth of tomorrow. Remember that in the Star Trek universe, two hundred years from now, the bridge of the Enterprise[77] contains every race, gender, and ethnicity (even nonhuman aliens) working together without thought to their differences, and CAW generally finds any behavior inconsistent with that state of affairs distasteful.

Objections raised in CAW against capital punishment, abortion, warfare, and other forms of violence can be partly traced to the belief that "all life is sacred": in an animistic sense, God/dess inhabits, and in fact *is*, all living entities and even all "inanimate" objects are alive and/or inhabited by spirit, so all living things, including all humans, must be granted the honor of individual selfhood. To do less is to dishonor divinity itself and to engage in reductionism wherein the *other* becomes abridged in value in order to facilitate power-obsession, emotional corruption, and oppressive dominance behaviors,[78] the source of which is often declared at best immature and at worst psychotic. Bigots, racists, and chauvinists inhabit an inferior place in CAW's universe as either substandard throwbacks or unenlightened souls lost in a miasma of ignorance.

Take Personal Responsibility!

> The necessary counterpart to individual freedom is the willingness to be personally responsible for all of our actions, and for our effects upon the planet. Only through the practice of personal responsibility can we become responsible collectively and live a life of freedom and maturity. We aren't a religion of gurus, Mommies or Daddies who can tell you what to do. As a religion that respects equality, we must take equal responsibility for making things happen, preventing harm, or cleaning up mistakes. To this end we also advocate one of the principles taught in kindergarten: Clean up your mess![79]

In CAW, there seems to be an ongoing attempt to balance The Rede in daily life and within the Church with an emphasis on individual responsibility. The Rede strongly suggests that in life one ought to balance the pleasure of doing what one wills with the responsibility of harming none, but even further, it implies a wider context for the harmonious equality of positives and negatives, including giving and taking. Obviously, many in CAW consider a good deal of life to be under individual control (or at least influence); while this doesn't ideally involve power over others, it focuses Will in the free choice of actions and the willingness to own up to the results. In other words, consciously choosing positive behavior and facing the outcome forms the basis for "taking personal responsibility." Most Church members indicate that failing to do so reveals a person who blames others for his or her circumstances, complains about a situation (but doesn't correct it), and/or inaccurately claims helplessness or powerlessness in the presence of an undesired reality. CAW lays a substantial burden for "fate" on the individual's shoulders, confirms that unwanted events in life can usually be modified, places accountability on choices made, and seeks to empower the Church's membership through magickal systems of consciousness-shifting, energy manipulation, and divine invocation.

In my interaction with CAW members, those unable to accept such personal responsibility are considered childish and immature; an adult has, by definition, the capacity to move purposefully through the world and the ability to admit and rectify errors. According to the Church, adults don't live in a fantasy world of disconnection from actions and their consequences. Maturity is the acquisition of experiences and knowledge resulting in wisdom, forthrightness, and positive choices. Through personal responsibility, the adult becomes free and no longer abuses his or her freedom; freedom becomes the logical reward for assuming personal responsibility. If one creates a mess, one's task is to make sure it's cleaned up, and the same principle is valid for the collective, so if most members of society contribute to making a mess, everyone is responsible for cleaning it up – the relationship of this principle to current environmental and social justice issues is obvious.

Walk Your Talk!

Talk is cheap. It's fine and well to proclaim to be a feminist or environmentalist, to preach heady Pagan gospel, or to play holier than thou. It's only in practice that words become Truth, and change becomes manifest. But don't be afraid to fail, for in order to grow, our reach must exceed our grasp, and it's through failing that we learn.[80]

Many religious traditions advocate honesty and authenticity while condemning hypocrisy and deceit; this CAW Precept evokes both authenticity and action. According to some CAW members, the nature of spiritual growth and maturation is that as a person develops, he or she becomes less needful of alter egos, alternate personas, or false pretenses, and therefore becomes more real, openhearted, and genuine. The old adage "talk is cheap" implies a comparison to action – activism is highly honored in CAW, which prides itself on doing over believing, ritual over belief, and problem-solving over endless deliberation.

I've observed that in CAW, *truth* refers not to an exclusive Truth held solely by the Church but to anyone's truth, be they Amish or Zoroastrian, deeply religious or adamantly secular. Truth confirms itself through experience, intuition, and critical analysis, a triad reflecting the balance between emotion and intellect that most members seek; elements of consciousness in harmonious synchronicity are seen as complementary to each other and holistically complete.

The changes sought in CAW's future mythology must be manifested (literally "given a hand") by activists publicly declaring and resolutely working to bring such changes to reality, both within the self and outwardly in the culture. For these and other reasons, a minority of members meditate regularly while most can be found developing rituals, writing books, running poly groups, or parading in demonstrations.

Success doesn't necessarily follow every attempt, of course – being at the radical end of NeoPaganism and vulnerable to infighting, CAW frequently fails to achieve its goals when faced with the larger social audience. This failure is generally accepted by members because, they believe, society is simply "not ready" to hear and incorporate Church ideas; in time, it's thought, most people will evolve into a deeper understanding of the world, themselves, and others, leading to positions closer to CAW's mythos and ethos.

In addition to these CAW Precepts, the *Membership Handbook* also contains a section concerning "Sexual Etiquette" that follows the general Precepts; since many members practice sacred sex, this section appears to be a response to the sensitive nature of sexuality for many in and outside of NeoPaganism.

> Sexuality and the Sacred Freedom thereof is one of our prime values, so respect it. Sexual activities that are engaged in by informed and mutually-consenting adults are *no one else's business*, and aren't to be condemned or censured.[81]

The discussion in the *Handbook* includes "Sexuality and the Sacred Freedom," reaffirming that mutually-desired and consented sex is positive; "Minor Issues" discouraging adult-child sexuality; "Be sure you interpret signals correctly," urging clear and plain-spoken communication of desires; and "Practice safe sex!" involving a condom compact with strangers.

My experience with the CAW Precepts has been that most members strive to live an ethical life in emulation of mythic exemplars, such as the compassionate Goddess, and out of a general sense of what constitutes positive energy, right action, and the good life as exemplified in modern humanistic, pluralistic, and progressive ethics.

Initiation

CAW resembles an academic degree program almost as much as a church: its initiatory requirements for progression include rigorous reading, personal growth, and ecospiritual activism. RINGS – an acronym for "Requirements Invoking Network Growth System" – is arranged as three Rings of three Circles each, totaling nine steps, one for each of the nine planets.[82] It's possible for a member to remain at a basic level of participation indefinitely according to his or her desires and capacities, but the opportunity exists to advance along a series of steps whose ultimate fruition is clergy ordination. Each step increases in complexity, adding more demands and intensifying personal involvement. However, this doesn't suggest cult indoctrination; in my experience, the process more closely resembles a series of college courses in an unconventional religion department logically building on prerequisites and deepening the student's knowledge.[83] Those who are sympathetic with CAW and maintain a minimum connection to its beliefs and practices can choose to join and take advantage of RINGS at their own pace. As stated in the *Membership Handbook*:

> Many members are perfectly content to remain in 2nd Circle indefinitely, and only a very few feel called to become Priestesses or Priests. But if you should wish to become more involved in the workings of CAW, and to help evolve a network of Pagans interested in changing themselves and the world around them, here's how…[84]

The RINGS system begins with simple assignments allowing members to test the Church's waters. The First Ring – Seekers – contains the Circles "Contact," "Getting to Know Us," and "Growing." "Contact" occurs when anyone makes connection with a CAW member or attends a meeting; in this way, just talking to a CAW member puts one into Circle One. "Getting to Know Us" takes place after six months at Circle One and after *Stranger in a Strange Land*, *Drawing Down the Moon*, and *The Spiral Dance* have been read – three substantial texts required just to get to Circle Two. Circle Three, "Growing," involves:

- Engaging in some form of magickal training
- Establishing a *regular* spiritual practice

- Developing social skills and relationships
- Spending time in "intimate contact with Mother Nature"
- Initiating an exploration of the Church's Bibliography
- Subscribing to another Pagan journal besides the online Green Egg
- Training in "Communication skills and group dynamics"
- Exploring your own issues from childhood
- Becoming a water-sibling with at least one other CAW waterkin[85]

RINGS requirements consist of magickal knowledge, interpersonal skills, hands-on experience in nature, psychoanalysis, and connection with CAW through relations with another member – a somewhat involved list that hypothetically prepares one for the next Ring: Scion.

The Second Ring term *scion* means a cutting from the branch of a plant that can grow another whole plant, an apt botanical comparison for the middle three steps which theoretically lead members into a state wherein the whole of CAW holographically rests in the individual. A Scion is more advanced than a Seeker but is not yet Clergy, and the purpose of the level is "Service," indicating a more active role in the Church and in one's own transformation, as well as the task of serving others. After a membership of at least six months, one must find a "scion advisor" and then write an essay demonstrating an "ability to think critically and express yourself knowledgably about Comparative Religion"; the academic structure continues with further Scion requirements down one of four "Tracks," namely Support Services, Earth Stewardship, Magickal Guilds, or Ministers.

Circle Four – "Serving" – asks members to accept such tasks as assisting in local Nest rituals, teaching community classes, and developing in the areas of counseling, drama and liturgy, and religious studies as well as becoming "familiar with the

History of the Craft, the development of the Goddess religion, its downfall and resurgence."[86]

Circle Five – "Creating" – requires:

- Creating and leading Nest rituals and Sabbat festivals
- Starting one's own Nest or Circle, if possible
- Teaching CAW classes
- Facilitating meetings, offering meditation or conflict resolutions
- Serving on a CAW governing board
- Creating new events in one's community
- Becoming water-siblings with yet another, more advanced, kin[87]

At this point, the member stands well within CAW structure, familiar with its ways and means and with several other members in some sort of Nest or group context. Circle Six – "Ministers and Postulants" – is reserved for those planning to become ordained ministers or those wishing to pursue the Priesthood. (For instance, I completed Circle Six, was granted ministerial credentials, and have continued with postulancy to become a Priest.)

The third and final Ring – Priesthood – has as its purpose "leadership in Her Majesty's Sacred Service,"[88] and follows the most demanding course in the CAW. If one declares postulancy at Circle Six and fulfills the stringent requirements, then one may enter Circle Seven – "Leading" – which is the regular offering of ritual in the larger NeoPagan community, then Circle Eight – "Fostering" – involving official interface with the non-Pagan community, and finally Circle Nine – "Grokking" – which no one (not even Oberon) has yet attained. All postulants must display and submit the requirements to sitting clergy and each level is awarded through consensus agreement of the clergy.

Expectations and qualifications for the Priest-(ess)hood include the following:

- Establish a link between God(s) and community, and help people make that link themselves
- Administer sacraments
- Accurately communicate the body of lore or doctrine of the Church
- Have a sense of presence that is inspiring to others
- Have personal credibility through lack of hypocrisy
- Effectively lead others without using "power over"
- Evoke a sense of affection and respect
- Maintain clarity of vision for the community
- Be able to deal with administrative issues effectively, appropriately, and timely
- Be able to raise power magickally
- Lead regular services
- Be water-siblings with several other Priests and Priestesses[89]

One interesting yet unattained requirement of the Ninth Circle is to be able to speak to animals; everyone awaits the first communicator at this lofty level of grokking.

RINGS constitutes a mutually-nurturing cycle wherein members work on the Church's behalf and help sustain its prosperity but also are supported by the Church and are guided (and self-guided) toward personal growth and transformation. The *Membership Handbook* offers a more in-depth explanation:

> The concept of life as an interconnected living web is the basis for our internal structure within the Church. The RING web is an interconnected egalitarian support network, utilizing our strengths and addressing our weaknesses. It's a system of nine concentric interconnected Circles, ever leading toward the consciousness of the Goddess/God within.[90]

The term "interconnected" is used several times in this quote, suggesting that the secondary purposes of RINGS include (a) connecting members to the Church, other members, and the dynamic elements within the self; and (b) promoting interconnectivity between members and both the nonhuman world and the Earth meta-consciousness. Since the planet is regarded as a conscious being, connection with its myriad manifestations as well as its collective super-human consciousness hypothetically provide members with empathic awareness and sensitivity, glimpses into the wider and deeper perspective of the Whole, and an energetic faith in primordial processes and presences older and greater than humanity. Although people remain ultimately responsible for environmental protection and social justice, neither our species nor our physical states are final or superior; there exists much more in the perceivable and imperceptible 'omniverse' than we know. Acknowledgement of this fact seems to encourage humility and determination in many CAW members.

Criticism of CAW

Much criticism of CAW comes from outside the tradition, occasionally reflecting ignorance of the Church's internal workings and motivations. In general, critiques may be summarized in three accusations: the Church is either:

- a cult
- a superstitious anachronism
- a transient fad

Occasionally CAW is erroneously included in anti-cult activities;[91] often associating Paganism with Satanism,[92] some cult-watchers inaccurately assume CAW condones violence or practices 'black magick' when actually these behaviors are no more NeoPagan than Christian. Most Church members with whom I've spoken regard Satanism as the reverse side of Christianity, dependent on Christian theology for its own structure. In 1979, NeoPagan author, Druid, and friend of CAW, Isaac Bonewits, wrote and disseminated the *Cult Danger Evaluation Frame* which can be used to appraise the risk for psychological or physical manipulation of any group. Using this chart, which admittedly was designed by a NeoPagan but has been deemed useful for objective evaluation, CAW ranks as a non-cult.[93]

On the other hand, some rationalists dismiss CAW, most NeoPagans, and even religion in general, as regressive mystical superstition, and modern pundits accuse CAW of being composed of bored suburbanites practicing pop witchcraft.[94] For some modern secular humanists, civilization progresses in a trajectory of advancement over time, each era replacing previous forms with more advanced ones. The past is generally seen as inferior and attempts to return to it are regarded as reversion to more primitive states.[95] According to this thinking, if society has moved away from old Pagan beliefs and practices, it's for a good reason, and Paganism should be abandoned to history. Pagans thus become anachronistic and obsolete throw-backs, retreating to a former level of progression – to pre-civilizational tribe-ways. In my understanding, this modern worldview sees humanity as progressed inevitably past such credulous practices to a new day of rational thought and reasoned behavior. Among Christian apologists, secular humanists, and atheists with whom I've spoken, much chagrin accompanies calls for the reinstatement of certain ancient practices.

The third common criticism is that CAW is a pop-culture fashion, an excuse for members to feel cool and hip while granting themselves a certain illusion of control and power.[96] Magick, especially, is seen as the result of the hopelessness and isolation of modern people as they attempt to regain a sense of empowerment through the opiate of a special occult relationship with divine and (super)natural forces. CAW emerged from the hippy milieu of the 1960s, and because hippies are sometimes considered passé, organizations based on their values and principles are also ephemeral – CAW is seen as outdated, utopian, and idealistic, sadly disconnected from the real world and stubbornly sanguine. This judgment gives CAW a fleeting lifespan whose relevancy has already passed.[97]

Another criticism emerges because CAW's founding was inspired by a science fiction novel – such unorthodox origins are bound to elicit doubt in many whose model of religion evokes avatars, saviors, ancient texts, and time-honored traditions. I should point out that many religions began as unconventional breaks with their cultural norms (Jesus, Buddha, Mohammed) and that being inspired by speculative fiction might well be in this pattern, prescient to the norms and needs of the twenty-first century. Nevertheless, origins in a fringe literature logically make for a fringe religion whose legitimacy and longevity has yet to be tested by history.

My personal criticism of CAW centers on the fact that for all its lofty ideals and futurist vision, the Church has so far lacked the power to inspire dedicated members who are able to work together for common goals. Despite the claimed ideology of tribalism and community, CAW is spread hopelessly thin around North America and Australia without strong central leadership or even inspiration. Members appear too consumed by their own lives and egos to cooperate and coordinate within a collective. The dissolution of the Church in 2004 and subsequent decline in membership exposes what appears to be a serious flaw in CAW's structure: an inherent conflict between the desire for a do-it-yourself religion with large amounts of freedom to express one's individuality and the desire to form a church around which passionate enthusiasm and spiritual growth may communally manifest. In some cases, individual egos dominate and cause unnecessary and ultimately destructive quarrels, ensuring that CAW will be caught in cyclical booms and busts, at least until the implementation of a systemic organizational structure and strong leadership that attracts more altruistic members.

Conclusion

The Church of All Worlds views itself as a postmodern NeoPagan religious organization emerging from 1960s experimentalism and influenced by speculative fiction. It consists of a hybridization and synthesis of several historical, socio-cultural, and philosophical influences, including Romantics, Spiritualists, Teilhardians, hippies, New Agers, cultural creatives, pre-Christian reconstructionists, postmodern liberal humanists, contemporary Witchcraft revivalists, and science fiction visionaries. CAW stands solidly within the NeoPagan religious milieu with its emphasis on sacred naturalism, seasonal holy days, Gaea worship, ecospirituality, and commitment to environmental activism; therefore, it's a Western religious tradition that's followed a different historical track with a radically dissimilar perspective from what might be called the mainstream majority culture.[1] CAW represents the congruence of youthful yearnings, liberal values, New Age syncretism, cultural innovation, progressive optimism, and the ascendancy of integral Earth spirituality. Its traditions reflect an emergence of ecological awareness, its beliefs have reclaimed elements of magick, panentheism, and polytheism, and its practices resound with pre-modern culture, postmodern identity politics, and Bohemian unconventionality. From the mythic past emerge the theological nuances of kinship and interconnection with people, nature, and the divine, while the *other* is enveloped in a relationship inspired by liberalism, futurism, and resistance to personal alienation.

As a religion, CAW reveres unknown realities beyond empirical science, yet it embraces the authentic explorations of science and the development of biomimetic[2] technology. Its theology is experientially confirmed rather than belief-based, its mysticism grounded in the sacredness of soil, oak, ocean, and sky. CAW attempts to balance into harmony energetic and gender polarities, endeavoring to reconcile dualities and integrate apparent opposites. It absorbs the influence of Enlightenment democracy in its commitment to plurality, diversity, and equality but also accepts the inheritance of shamans, wise folk, and mythology from around the world. CAW's covenant may be different from the Great Religions, but it nonetheless includes established ethical boundaries to accompany its dedication to hedonism.

Although CAW draws inspiration from the past, it emphasizes envisioning the future in ways markedly influenced by speculative literature, the worldview of emergent evolution,[3] and the utopian paradisiacal yearnings of Western religion.[4] Like Christianity, Judaism, and Islam, CAW sees the future in terms of its own deepest hopes and reflections, so to call the Church "postmodern" is to recognize that its vision constitutes a reaction to the social and ecological issues of modernity's 'shadow.' Not all of these values and visions are authentically lived by all members – error and ego occasionally thwart the Church's best intentions, and tension between CAW's ideals and the imperfections of those drawn to it make for periodic eruptions of internal chaos. Whether CAW's well-meaning utopian organizational model is viable at all remains uncertain.

CAW's place in wider mainstream society can be described as (a) supporting the liberal Western tradition in the United States, and (b) synthesizing religion and ecology into a single ontological worldview. CAW offers a unique opportunity for worship, influencing Western cultures in directions needed to survive what has been called the modern crisis.[5] CAW is quintessentially global and energetically supports those values and freedoms on which the developed 'West' was founded – the liberal tradition of which I speak can be encapsulated in the US Constitution and the right to "life, liberty, and the pursuit of happiness." Rather than being nationalistic, the Church seeks to maintain those values and behaviors it sees as perennial, the ones it believes are hardwired into humanity – from avoiding physical suffering in others and the self to insisting on high ethical standards.

Life, liberty, and happiness are claimed as inalienable rights, but in CAW these rights are expanded beyond their common definitions to reflect the Church's values and beliefs. For example, theoretically, all citizens have the right to *life* under the Constitution of the United States,[6] but the Church develops the meaning of 'life' to embrace all living beings, from phytoplankton and earthworms to timber wolves and the Amazon rainforest. Life-forms other than Homo sapiens have the right to survive, based not only on ethical ideals of compassion and tolerance but also on a pragmatic understanding of the ecological interconnection of all living entities.[7]

Liberty means freedom from oppression and freedom to live an individually satisfying life; one must have autonomy to choose in order to manifest one's ordained life-path, but CAW widens this right to include socially unconventional non-violent behaviors – if one religion is free to worship in formalwear with an alcoholic sacrament then NeoPagans are equally free to worship naked with cannabis. CAW represents a challenge to genuine plurality and acceptance as codified in the Bill of Rights. It's always possible that CAW will play a political role in the expansion of these rights – it supports the full diversity found across the United States, draws from ancient forms of culture currently out of (modern) social fashion, and envisions a future based on the logical extension of peaceful liberal progressivism.

The pursuit of happiness is meant to allow people to fulfill their dreams, usually focused on vocational success or material prosperity; happiness is acknowledged as a legitimate pursuit and worthwhile state for cultivation, but CAW broadens the definition to encompass many new paths to happiness, limited only by proscriptions against physical violence. CAW's versions of joy, contentment, excitement, and adventure span such a swath of reality they could not possibly fit into the constraining category of 'religion' as currently defined in popular consciousness – the term will have to be restructured and enlarged to accommodate the varieties of happiness that freedom allows to develop.

In 1776, only white, land-owning adult males could vote – that the United States has not remained at such a limited level of emancipation indicates that the liberal project (the widening of inclusion in agency and liberty) has so far been successful. CAW pushes the boundaries further and envisions great expansions of liberty and sustainability as difficult for some to imagine at present as the Civil Rights Act would have been to most eighteenth century slave-owners. While some fear and despise these changes, I can barely contain my fervor for them – the time may arrive when the Constitution will be tested and the dichotomy between regional and religious intolerance – with its narrow interpretation of life, liberty, and happiness – will confront the expansive ethic of CAW.

In addition to supporting liberal progress, CAW is part of the larger project to reunite religion and ecology, in this case within an established religious tradition. I submit that Heaven and Earth have been estranged in the minds and hearts of many Westerners and the sacredness of nature fundamentally dismissed as primitive. I'd further argue that Earth divinity has not been part of the modern worldview and that even most contemporary religions have assigned the divine a mostly transcendent existence: God is more or less removed to other ephemeral realms or restricted to a direct line to the special human soul, leaving only scattered indigenous and aboriginal peoples to continue the 'unified tradition' wherein Earth remains the dwelling place of deities and spirits. CAW stands in contrast to many of the world's great religions in locating the divine on a sacred Earth and refocusing transcendent divinity away from embattled ideologies and towards physical realities that all humanity shares during life.

The synthesis of immanent and transcendent divinity – rejoining spirit with universe, body with soul, and God/dess with nature – is, I submit, a vital work for the future. Once considered radical, the ecospiritual synthesis is gradually becoming more accepted as humanity's environmental impact increases. However, some of the practices associated with this reunification can still be uncomfortable: in CAW, nudity (whether casual or ritual) is considered a tenet, yet it remains illegal in many places; using marijuana or hallucinogenic mushrooms as sacraments is forbidden on pain of imprisonment under 'drug' charges; and the worship of nature as the embodiment of the divine leads to accusations of tree hugging and nature worship as though these activities were at least unsavory and possibly dangerous. Since the Church is a religious organization advocating these unconventional beliefs and activities, even at its diminutive size, its impact may prove substantial.

Being unconventional and somewhat ungrounded in history (aside from a mostly self-created mythic past) allows for some mobility in addressing current issues through cultivating theological innovation, challenging cultural assumptions, and offering timely solutions. The reunification of thought, intellect, and dreams with the reality of soil, oceans, atmosphere, and ecological interactions emerges from the (spiritual) crisis of modernity where assumptions such as infinite population growth, ever-expanding industrialism, abandonment of tradition, and the primacy of material accumulation are being questioned and challenged.[8] CAW addresses these issues in ways that link theory to application by yoking ecological knowledge with religious passion. I believe that in the history of the United States there has not been so large a movement directed toward restoring the balance between the natural world which supports life and the spiritual yearnings of the incorporeal spirit. This movement is made possible in part, I believe, because CAW is not significantly bound by historical convention and sees itself as outside modern assumptions.

CAW sees itself as having a specific place in the future of planet Earth: with early twenty-first century issues like global economics, the spread of democracy, regional unifications,[9] and environmental issues, NeoPagans appear to hold beliefs, practices, and rituals that answer some of the questions of the millennia. While Christianity served as the Western religion of the Middle Ages and Renaissance, NeoPaganism may well serve as the Western religion for the coming Anthropocene. As humanity comes to terms with its place in the physical world and life on the planet, our bodies, emotions, and semi-conscious wounds cry out for healing, and the meek may well inherit the Earth and usher in a period of peace and love. These sentiments might seem romantically idealistic, but they are at the inspired core of many religions and overtly command allegiance in CAW.

CAW tends to deal with the future in optimistic terms, reveling in affirmative possibilities and carrying forward what it sees as a continuous sub-cultural perspective. This view promotes peace, advocates loving relationships, opens itself to growth and maturation, and celebrates radical freedom, utter joy, ecstatic adventure, and individual rights and responsibilities within an ethic of co-existence – a worldview emerging from the developmental progression of planetary consciousness hardwired into life and spirit. Such teleological imperatives can be deeply grounding, weighing the human species towards Earth, centering it in physical being, and focusing on ethical imperatives even while they open up the heavens so that we may explore our spirits and cultivate our psyches to their unknown potentials. As one line of the CAW membership pledge reads, "Like an ancient tree, I would have my roots deep in the Earth and my branches reaching for the stars."[10]

I think this optimism requires a particular type of faith: one must have confidence that Earth possesses an inherent wisdom in its complex matrix, that divinity cares *for* and *about* life, and/or that there's a plan and logic in the universe beyond human understanding. In other words, the future may well require a spiritual awakening as profound as any awakening in history in order to shift consciousness away from obsessions with death, destruction, conflict, and fear toward being, creativity, peace, and courageous love. If one trusts in divine evolutionary progress based on its billion-year history, then time and the very fabric of the cosmos is on the side of life. Since the divine is equal to, but also more than, the cosmos, God/dess itself cheerleads for the prosperity of each soul and all Creation – with such support, optimism is justified.

In this section, I endeavored to show the common parameters and historical continuity of CAW and to suggest that its vision is tailor-made for the particular needs and issues of this era: optimi, organics, ecology, and ecumenicism – all buoyed by the rich spiritual heritage of humanity. From cave paintings to cyberpagans, this inquiry moves through time, following a thread of consciousness culminating in CAW's establishment with its re-intuited concept of Gaea as a function of emergent evolutionary progress set in the deep logic of material reality. As the cultural historian William Irwin Thompson writes:

> The furthest development of industrial technology and its extension into space brings about a classic enantiodromia as technology triggers a mystical change in consciousness in which an *object* becomes a *presence*. But it also brings about a cultural condition in which the spiritual unconscious, or Gaia, is precipitated into consciousness.[11]

The "spiritual unconscious" dwells at the fringe of culture in artistic, mythological, and religious visions, emerging into consciousness with the re-cognition of Earth as an in-dwelling but ultimately transcendent entity within which we exist as *holons*.[12]

The world-changing and human-transforming power of this shift becomes perceptible to the consciousness when a critical mass of information and need coalesce into sacred revelation. Referring to British anthropologist and cyberneticist Gregory Bateson,[13] Thompson continues:

> Bateson's analysis of the ecology of Mind is the transition from the uncovering of the intellectual unconscious to the precipitation of the spiritual unconscious. This revelation takes two forms: first, the unconscious becomes experienced as the body not identified with and hitherto seen as 'the other,' namely, the environment; and second, the environmentally compressed social consciousness integrates under the threat of crisis to precipitate, not a literate civilization, but a collective consciousness.[14]

Movements such as NeoPaganism exemplify the transition from intellectual civilization to "collective consciousness" by revealing the unconscious assumptions about the environment as displaced "other" and by defining prosperity as the task of re-establishing the lost relationship of humanity to nature through an empathic planetary awareness. The (perceived or actual) ecological crisis acts as stimulant to hasten this reawakening just in time to serve as cyclical apocalypse in the continuing drama of the Gaean experiment in awareness and transcendent being. CAW stands at the threshold of a possible groundswell of transformative energy revealed as both a continuation of the original process of human evolution and a fresh ontological perspective needed by an overpopulated and over-industrialized planet.

One fundamental question is: if Earth is a conscious being,

do humans have the capacity to empathically (inter)connect and communicate with Her? If so, an unprecedented new source of knowledge and understanding becomes available to the human species, and many of our current problems may fade into obscurity. The only way to discover the answer is through intellectual and psychic research.[15] The project for deep global empathy holds the promise for global peace and profound (planetary) wisdom, and it can be accomplished in several ways.[16] One, the mystical mind – that part of us able to converse with the divine – should be pursued with the same dogged commitment as the study of stem cells and pulsars. Initiated by humanity's earliest recorded mystics and refined in the Middle Ages by 'researchers' such as Julian of Norwich, the human capacity for mystical experience remains an under-investigated phenomenon.[17] Perhaps corollary to the mystic mind are the explorations, initiated in the 1950s and 1960s, of mind and consciousness-altering substances such as LSD and various mushrooms and cacti.[18] Can these chemicals unlock a gateway to otherwise inert observational abilities?

Experiences with psychoactive substances may be creative fantasies of the mind or they may open Huxley's doors of perception[19] to other realms of reality unavailable to the ordinary mind – shamans have claimed the efficacy of trance journeying for centuries, but the investigation of these claims has been thwarted by legal obstacles and social stigma. Other related areas of investigation include Extra Sensory Perception, psychic ability, and paranormal phenomena – all, I submit, at the fringes of legitimacy and therefore poorly or sloppily researched. One difficulty in the attempt to understand the role of the 'religious experience' recorded in the history of the human species[20] is that the scientific method is not always an appropriate tool for exploring esoteric truths; innovative ways of charting these territories must be investigated and new structures devised to comprehend an expansive definition of 'reality.'

A twenty-first century meta-narrative, which may be necessary to address all the issues discussed, would be based not on ideology but on the embodied perception of a physical presence in an interactive, sacred, and precious world – recognizing Earth (and *de facto* all its inhabitants) means acknowledging deep empathic (inter)connection with all life, not as an ideal but as emotionally confirmed reality. Our commonality rests in the physicality shared across political, regional, and cultural boundaries, and in our capacity for suffering and healing. Such experiences may be profoundly shared if the CAW belief in the subtle, integral, and spiritual relationship of humanity and omniverse proves correct. The Church's postmodern project involves stimulating, developing, and utilizing what it considers the evolutionarily-inevitable integral consciousness present in the written and oral compendium of so many wisdom traditions. According to CAW, this planetary ontology wherein physical reality and spiritual truth merge into a synthesis that eventually fades into the background noise of human consciousness, marks one step in the (r)ev-olutionary progress of our species. Because certain aspects of modernity have proven unbalanced and destructive, many modern assumptions and practices may no longer be tenable; spirituality offers the transformative and transfiguring energy needed to move into a new era. Furthermore, since religious reality mainly results from the interface between spirit and matter – prayer emotes from lips, worship from a centered mind, joy from the heart – CAW represents a seminal synthesis. Earth and all its wonders finds us among it, welcomes us as family, and delights in our progression, and in turn charges us with responsibilities to nurture Ecotopia,[21] invest it with affection, and infuse it with joy.

As noted, Margot Adler's 1989 tome *Drawing Down the Moon* provided the nascent NeoPagan community with its seminal handbook, describing Witches, Wiccans, and other Earthen folk. CAW's chapter in the book reminds us that the Church's mission is in part to invoke the future into the present and live as if inhabiting the 24th century of *Star Trek*. Many members see themselves as belonging to that time-period, acting as missionaries from that tomorrow, holding controversial worldviews because a couple of centuries from now, no one will care about what people fight over today. Apparently, this is the way of evolution: like awkward old yearbook photos, it mocks what we regard as all-important, laughs at our fashions, ridicules our obsessions. Time relegates the present to the museum of history, where it belongs.

In addition, we can't go backwards into the arms of nature to find our solutions; that path offers only deception & suffering. Let's not deceive ourselves: living in the natural world is dangerous business. Mother Nature tries to kill us with unceasing vigor and enormous creativity – we can be injured by accidents, attacked by animals, harmed by weather, or infected by microbes and diseases, so it's no wonder we've struggled to distance ourselves from nature's elements through urban cityscapes, medicine and surgery, industrial processes, climate-controlled buildings, and sturdy clothing. These innovations emerge from instinctual self-preservation and the simple desire to live as long and comfortably as possible – and this is precisely what civilization offers: a modicum of security and the chance to thrive. In fact, we may be entering a post-biological Anthropocene, and it may prove a profound relief and liberation.

In 2009, Earth's population crossed an unprecedented threshold: for the first time in recorded history, more humans live in cities than outside of them, which may suggest that evolution pushes towards urbanism as the natural structure of human habitation, with attendant 'urbane' behaviors. The circumstances making such a hyper-urban future possible include deep empathy – co-feeling and co-thinking with each other – which permits humankind to gather into denser and denser habitats while gradually abandoning horizontal urban sprawl because of its unsustainability and allowing Earth's 'rewilding.' In other words, non-human nature will continue in one direction, while humanity moves into large human-made habitats. The future bends in a surprising direction: not back-to-nature but to relative human isolation in super-dense vertical structures called *arcologies*, leaving the natural world relatively free of human intervention and destruction to follow its own evolutionary trajectory.

From Naturalism to Arcology

As the 21st century progresses, and if the stark reality of climate change becomes evident, crisis solutions such as lifestyle shifts, de-industrialization, post-capitalism, and calls for re-harmonizing humans and nature proliferate and clamor for attention. If climate changes are as significant as currently predicted, human civilization may need to adjust itself to the new reality in radically innovative ways or face decline. This adjustment process provides yet another opportunity for humankind to display its versatility, cooperation, determination, and innovative spirit. The planet forces us to rise up, move beyond our old ways, and become better versions of ourselves.

Presently, human progress and the integrity of nature can appear to be oppositional forces. Won't the spread of civilization require increased consumption of resources? Doesn't the inevitable growth of cities mean converting more wild lands to domestication? Won't industrialization mean continuous pollution dumped into the planetary commons? If we attempt to envision the future based on current practices, the outlook appears grim, but if we speculate about human advancement – not just scientific and technological, but also sociological and psychological – the vision becomes more optimistic because, as noted, emotional, mental, and social development tends towards greater complexity and adaptability that produces new Homo sapiens better adjusted to environmental changes.

This was always my complaint about *Star Trek*: it wowed with technological wizardry, but cast the people with 20th century hang-ups and morays. Even so, scripts occasionally expressed explicit progress of the human psyche, manifest as compassion, integrity, maturity, and intelligence. For instance, in *The Next Generation* episode "The Neutral Zone," a 20th century man revived after being in suspended animation for hundreds of years desperately asks Captain Picard what he is to do now that he finds himself in such a radically changed future:

> "Then what will happen to us? There's no trace of my money. My office is gone. What will I do? How will I live?
> Picard replies, "This is the twenty-fourth century. Material needs no longer exist."
> The man remains skeptical, "Then what's the challenge?"
> "The challenge, Mr. Oppenheimer, is to improve yourself, to enrich yourself. Enjoy it."

On *Star Trek's* Earth, money, warfare, and inequality don't exist, an optimistic ideal emerging partly from a belief that humanity progresses over time in a uni-directional manner towards greater mental acuity, emotional maturity, and sociological complexity. The notion that evolution has a positive trajectory, deeply held by visionary writers such as Pierre Teilhard de Chardin, seems especially pertinent concerning global climate disruptions.

Stimulated by this potential crisis, environmental movements have evolved, bringing attention and possible solutions to a multifaceted set of ecological variables. Regrettably, some of these movements have proven relatively ineffective, falling well short of influencing real change on the necessary scale. As noted earlier, one major problem is that some of them are simply exercises in nostalgia, proposing solutions that oppose and retract from many positive aspects of modern civilization. Regressive nature-lovers and organizations such as Earth First! typically express such sentiments, and although some of their ideas are not entirely without merit (they can stimulate behavioral changes in some activists), the basic premise – that modernity has ruined nature and we have to get ourselves back to the garden – is faulty because it assumes humans can and will, without trauma or suffering, return to earlier stages of evolutionary development, that people can and will voluntarily regress to some fanciful past when we lived harmoniously with the land – conveniently ignoring the sorrows and discomforts of life before modern conveniences, medicine, and social stability.

It should also be pointed out that these well-meaning calls for human re-naturalization usually come from thoroughly civilized and modernized persons, often writing from comfortable climate-controlled and electrified homes on networked computers by authors who have sufficient food, fresh water, and safety to contemplate the fate of the natural world from a place of wellbeing and security, reminding us that some environmentalists expediently disregard the movement's glaring ironies, such as driving internal-combustion cars everywhere or flying to climate change seminars. People in the past weren't any better about resources than we are. In fact, one could argue they were worse. Bottom line: popular environmentalism comes nowhere near its stated goals and is both ineffective and occasionally hypocritical about itself and its back-to-the-land, love Mother Earth ethic.

Take a house, for instance. As the comedian George Carlin once said: houses are for storing your stuff while you're out getting more stuff. He was an American, of course, and perhaps nobody can acquire as much stuff as Yanks can. As of this writing, I live in a four-bedroom two-bath in a small tree-canopied suburban neighborhood at the edge of town. It's like living in a forest with a drive going through it circling a pond, and in Spring, the birdsong is riotous, joined by a cacophony of frogs in Summer. I like the house, ordinary as it is, and occasionally I will spend all day in it, going out only for the mail, working in my room, then kitchen for a meal or smoothie, and family room for a movie. It is its own tiny world, and through the windows I see the cold of winter, but I'm warm and snug, or heavy thunderstorms, and I'm dry and content. It is a life that would have struck my ancestors dead with envy and awe, and yet so many of us take it for granted, as though such a level of comfort and security was always our birthright, and would always be the norm. A house or apartment – wherever home may be – is a microcosm of civilization and its benefits.

Because of human social and psychological evolution, and the world's increasing urbanization, and because we may need to abandon nature to its primordial devices, one solution may be insulated mega-structures called *arcologies*. An arcology is a self-contained, hermetically sealed vertical city, popularized by visionary architect Paolo Soleri, who envisioned collective living in the flush of 1960s idealism by building Arcosanti, a community of like-minded visionaries and structures in the Arizona desert, a project that continues today. The arcology stands as a complete community, with hydroponic farms, 3-D print/manufacturing, commercial shops (if mercantilism endures), parks and recreation areas (free of most natural dangers), hospitals (advanced healing centers), educational centers (in conjunction with democratized and dispersed learning), and residences (mostly single person). With the ability to house hundreds of thousands of people, arcologies are reasonable alternatives to horizontal cities in that they have relatively small physical and carbon footprints, can be maximally energy efficient, and as insulated habitats, can weather climate changes. Dense living environments are possible because of psychosocial evolution, and technology will make interior lives richer, healthier, and longer. Nature would return to wilderness as Dark Greens envision, making arcologies win-win propositions.

Vertical cities are not socially engineered utopias; they will not solve the world's problems, nor be the end of history.

As Soleri writes, "Every stage in the evolutionary process contains within itself the preceding stage." He suggests that human activity naturally results in density: "The ecological reorganization of nature caused by the intrusion of large social aggregates will produce the bio-technic city." Arcologies are logical extrapolations of current evolutionary trends, which may or may not continue (thus are the pitfalls of futurism). They point out the general drift of humanity, and offer a solution to the growth of human populations set against the need for functioning ecosystems, which are at present too complex for humans to fully replicate. They satisfy the urbanites and their cosmopolitan aspirations towards a more peaceful world, and they satisfy the naturalists with their back-to-the-past idealism and ecological regression.

Part of Soleri's undergirding philosophy included the inevitable evolution of ethics.

> The sharper knife, to produce a more 'controlled' statuette is the symbol of the technological world, and its justification. It just happens that a healthier individual, physically, psychologically, ethically sane, will make a better, more complete use of the knife. Thus, science, technology, ethics, providing better shelter, better diets, better communication, better understanding so that the hand guiding and powering the knife will be better willed, more powerful, more reflective, reverent, super-rational...[22]

Which brings us back to CAW: we noted that it draws its ethics and vision from an idealized, but possible, future where humanity has evolved beyond the need for violence, and has advanced in the areas of healing, interconnectivity, and world-centric morality to extraordinary degrees, attempting, by its beliefs and behaviors, to draw that future into the present, but the way they suggest humanity might arrive at this happy juncture is by evolving as we have been for millennia: *away* from nature.

I don't mean to suggest that this path forward will be without problems and setbacks, nor without a grieving process. Just as the excitement of leaving home for the first-time mixes with anxiety and the grief of abandoning familiar surroundings and support systems, leaving nature – striking out, as it were, on our own – produces similar effects. Why shouldn't we glance back with some nostalgia (and even homesickness) on the innocent circumstances of our youth? Yet we know we cannot live in our crib forever, dependent on parents for our sustenance; we must individuate, and that means separating to some extent from childhood. In the same way, humankind cannot remain in the embrace of, or direct dependence on, Mother Nature. Even though we may require Her basic elements indefinitely, the relationship has to change, and we become less child and more peer. Neither regressive immaturity nor matricide will do; we must forge a new equality with our planet.

So the arcology stands as a complete community, graced by empathy and empowered by technology, with hydroponic farms, manufacturing, commercial shops (if mercantilism endures), parks and recreation areas (free of most natural dangers), hospitals (advanced healing centers), educational centers (in conjunction with democratized and dispersed learning), and residences (mostly single person). With the ability to house hundreds of thousands of people, arcologies are reasonable alternatives to horizontal cities in that they have relatively small physical and carbon footprints, can be maximally energy efficient, and as insulated habitats, can weather climate changes. Again, dense living environments will be made possible by psychosocial evolution, and technological innovations will make interior lives richer, healthier, and longer. Nature would return to wilderness as dark greens and many NeoPagans envision, making arcologies potentially win-win propositions.

According to Jeff Stein in a 2012 TED Talk, arcologies answer the question "How shall we live?" and offer radical new answers combing architecture and ecology as "two parts of a single whole system to which we as humans belong." The problem, according to Stein, is not population but patterns of inefficient horizontal urban sprawl, an incoherent, destructive, anachronistic, and unsustainable design. He notes that 'life favors two conditions above all: miniaturization and complexity;' using the brain as analogy, he advocates dense, interconnected living, working, and playing arrangements that maximize energy, communication, and transportation efficiency, networked like neurons, not a thin and isolating veneer spread across a surface. "Crowding," he says, "is the maker of life."[23]

If we allow ourselves to speculate about the form of a typical arcology, we might begin with a mega-structure of potentially hundreds of levels.

The bottom several levels contain hydroponic farms, efficiently growing fruits, vegetables, nuts, berries, and grains which could be eaten separately or in liquid nourishment, cared for by those interested in, knowledgeable about, and possibly communicative with, plants. Meat is absent or artificially cultivated because growing and eating animals remains prohibitively inefficient and, if the empathic circles embrace non-humans, morally repugnant. In fact, there may be few if any animals in the arcology; in the effort to rid humankind of parasites and diseases, non-engineered animals would be a liability.

- The next levels up might include recycling systems, where all solids and fluids are treated as needed and returned to use; then workshops, where mechanical parts, supplies, goods, and electronics are created or upgraded using future versions of 3D printers and recycled materials.
- Above this, 'shops' distributing items by category

and attended by experts in each field, with additional artesian and handicraft space for innovative research and development (although I doubt the 'shops' will utilize retail capitalism as it currently operates).

- Other levels have labs and additional research and development facilities innovating in such areas as health, transportation, communication, and energy, filled with people engaged in this work.
- Another level is occupied by centrally located but minimal administrative offices for processing and archiving personal 'legal' interactions or resolving disputes (although negative behaviors are quickly perceived and have auto-pre-set consequences) and above this healthcare facilities using light therapy and other non-invasive techniques to solve issues not already genetically screened out before birth.
- Above this, parks, meadows, forests, botanical gardens, and recreational facilities, with grass, trees, pools, playing fields, and edible plants carefully maintained to be safe and enjoyable escapes into cultivated nature, lit naturally by windows and a distributive reflection system, and by full-spectrum sun lamps.
- Upper levels house residences, mostly single individuals (because we've developed encompassing interior lives), of similar size and design, with glass-enclosed balconies, interactive walls, and ubiquitous connection to decentralized AI interface more like a 'meta-consciousness' (perhaps also involving voluntarily connected human participants), holographic entertainment, food dispensers, and almost everything else needed, as already explored in *Star Trek.*

The arcology's structure itself is in some sense alive, perhaps even conscious in a bio-mimetic fashion. The 'building' produces all energy requirements, capable of communicating with people, archiving knowledge, adjusting technologies, and generally being self-sufficient and self-maintaining (with assistance from human specialists, as needed). In other words, the structure itself is a member of the arcological community. Returning to *Star Trek,* the exploration of conscious artificial intelligence produced an android member of the crew named Data, whose desire to be more human threads through the series.

Concluding Thoughts

Eco indicates a commitment to the preservation of the planet's life-giving bio-systems, including humanity. Evolution engenders compassion and empathy needed to live peacefully with other humans and all life. Yet, it will no doubt be challenging for humankind to quit the field of direct interaction with nature. Long have we been forged in the crucible of its survival conflicts and natural disasters, and like an apple tree that is stressed to produce the sweetest fruit, our past struggles mark our present bodies and minds. But time may come when we must leave the nest, strike out on our own, and engage in a more mature relationship of mutual respect with our biological (nature) and spiritual (religion) parents, and grow into the species toward which our physical and spiritual evolution seems to have guided us. As we move away from virtual slavery to our biology and add an "entirely novel structure of consciousness" which differentiates "the noosphere and the biosphere,"[24] we may find ourselves liberated from nature, free to explore fully our unique humanity within our own distinctive environment. This new life of the mind pulls us farther away from our bodies, just as it pushes us away from nature. "That is, the noosphere is just emerging, the mind is just emerging, and as such it's still relatively undifferentiated from the biosphere, from the body and sensorimotor intelligence."[25]

> ...thus the cure is not to reactivate the tribal form of ecological ignorance (take away our means [of eco-destruction]), nor to continue the modern form of that ignorance (the free market will save us), but rather to evolve and develop into an integrative mode of awareness that will – also for the first time in history – integrate the biosphere and noosphere in a higher and deeper union.[26]

My sense is that the new integration will involve nature in one realm and the human mind in another, the latter at last able to know (bio-gnosis) the physical universe as we could never know it as hunter-gatherers, or even in the twenty-first century, when we still till the soil (albeit with machines), eat and eliminate food, breathe air, communicate by sophisticated grunting noises, and are generally at the mercy of natural functions and environmental life-support systems.

The notion that we might, in fact, isolate ourselves from nature's embrace and eventually disengage from the natural world altogether seems counterintuitive. Yet, if current trends continue, isolation may become a prerequisite to survival, and super-dense mega-structures for everyone the norm. When I look out of the window of my house, I know I'm protected from the elements, both cold and heat, and from the local wildlife, whether coyote or mosquito, and that I do not enter nature without proper precautions, nor would I wish to live in the trees of my back garden. So it is that humans have gained some separation from the environment which we have fought hard to attain and which we ought not to carelessly surrender.

In conclusion: certain people serve as visionaries, pointing to the future and the requirements to get there; human bio-cultural evolution naturally increases empathy over time in ever widening circles of inclusion and compassion; empathy allows for increased habitat density because we can get along peacefully; density superheats civilization; civilization increases evolution. The Church of All Worlds stands as an example of these socio-cultural dynamics. The circle feeds on itself in a continuous spiral moving away from nature toward human meta-habitats, arcologies. Ecospirituality will allow non-human nature to prosper and follow its own evolutionary path, and allow humankind, by virtue of our evolved sense of compassion and wholeness, to live together with increased individual freedom and greater interconnection. We can leave the natural world alone, while living in a world of our own creation, and so peacefully co-exist – the ultimate goal of ecospirituality and those who envision it.

So we end where we began, in a forest where the Moon dances with the ground, and the skyclad children of the Goddess swirl around the circle filled with warmth and joy, suffusing land and heavens with radiant energy and love. The trees form a council of elders, the cool breeze brings messages from celestial realms beyond our kin, the fire blazes at the center, and water courses through everything, carrying the mysteries of consciousness. Together light and dark spiral from microbe to galaxy, and from dreams to infinite distances, wrapped in time, passages of voice, and the enfoldment of Gaea, Mother of all worlds.

Endnotes

Chapter 1 Introduction

1. Harris 2014: 6-7
2. Harris 2014: 78
3. Based on Genesis 1:28.
4. See "An Evangelical Declaration on the Care of Creation" at www.creationcare.org/resources/declaration.php
5. See Folz' *Worldviews, Religion, and Environment.*
6. J. Baird Caldicott (2002), in an encyclopedia published in 2004, as quoted in Bron Taylor's "A Green Future for Religion?" in *Future Journal,* available online at http://www.clas.ufl.edu/users/bron/bron/Taylor--GreenFuture4Rel.pdf.
7. Taylor 2010 ix
8. Taylor x
9. Ibid 4
10. Ibid 4
11. Taylor 15
12. Taylor 29. Quoted from Goodall's *Reason for Hope.*
13. Ibid 47
14. One EF! slogan, for instance, is "Back to the Pleistocene!"
15. Taylor 6
16. This "reality" could be a personified Earth deity, or a modified monotheistic God, or any number of diverse forms.
17. Taylor 2010: 188-99
18. Taylor 2010: 197
19. Taylor 2010: 197
20. G'Zell 1971
21. Starhawk 1989
22. G'Zell 1971
23. Wilber 1995
24. Taylor 2010: 7

25. MoonOak 2010
26. Vaidyanathan, Gayathri, "Can Humans and Nature Coexist?" Scientific American, Nov 10, 2014.
27. Callenbach, Ernest. *Ecotopia*. Bantam Books, 1975.
28. https://www.cpcc.edu/programs/sustainability-technologies
29. 2011
30. Elias in Pinker 2011
31. Pinker 32
32. Pinker 611
33. Pinker 583
34. Pinker 694
35. Singer 1981, 2011
36. Pinker 691
37. Pinker 691
38. Pinker 689
39. Beck; Cowen 2005
40. Wilber 2007: 7
41. Teilhard de Chardin 1959.
42. Rifkin 430
43. Rifkin 171
44. Rifkin 461
45. About 65 million years ago.
46. Teilhard de Chardin, *Phenomenon of Man* and *Hymn of the Universe*.
47. The theory that life has a tendency to move along a uni-directional path due to an internal or external driving force.
48. Describes the maximum possible level of complexity and consciousness towards which the cosmos is evolving.

Chapter 2 Ecospiritual Visionaries

1. John Stewart, "Evolution Toward Global Cooperation," *Kosmos*, 7(2): 56-58, Spring/Summer 2008.
2. Stewart 2008

3. Among them da Vinci, William Blake, Jules Verne, Bucky Fuller, Arthur C. Clark, Jacque Fresco, and many others.
4. http://www.earthcharterinaction.org/content/
5. "Eutopian" meaning 'good place' rather than "utopian" meaning 'no place'
6. Charles Reich, *The Greening of America* (1970), 4-8.
7. Reich, *Greening*, 24.
8. See William Whyte's *The Organization Man* (1956, 2002).
9. Reich, *Greening*, 66.
10. Ibid 241
11. Ibid 242
12. Ibid 323
13. Ibid 327-328
14. Ibid 382
15. Ibid 418
16. Ibid 419
17. Ibid 419-420
18. See Heelas, *New Age Movement*.
19. Ferguson, *Conspiracy*, 29.
20. Ibid 23
21. Ibid 23
22. Ibid 26
23. Ibid 57
24. Ibid 61-62
25. Ibid 362
26. Ibid 363
27. Ibid 405
28. Ibid 407
29. Ibid 409
30. Ibid 417
31. Thompson, *Pacific Shift*, 7.
32. An inner guide or helpful attendant spirit.
33. Thompson, *Shift*, 37.
34. Ibid 37-39

35. In which oppositions are seen as complementary polarities rather than competitive dichotomies.
36. Thompson, *Shift*, 35-62. Also graphically presented in the Appendix.
37. Ibid 62
38. Ibid, 159
39. Ibid 154
40. Ibid 181
41. Ibid 182
42. Ibid 123
43. Citing Catholicism's inherent patriarchy, resistance to female leadership, clerical celibacy, and even feminized raiment, the author wonders why pedophilia has not been even more rampant.
44. Thompson xv
45. ---, xvi
46. At least most of us do. Age clearly doesn't guarantee maturity.
47. Cummings 1
48. Ibid 37
49. Ibid 25
50. Ibid 79
51. Devall and Sessions 66
52. Berry 131
53. Berry, Swimme
54. See Berman's *Reenchantment of the World.*
55. Berry 136
56. See Dowd's *Thank God for Evolution.*
57. Ray and Anderson, *Cultural Creatives*, 4.
58. Ibid 4
59. Ibid 4
60. Ibid 8-16
61. Ibid 27
62. Ibid 31-32

63. Ibid 39
64. Ibid 140
65. Ibid 141
66. Ibid 194
67. Ibid 244
68. Ibid 263
69. In Hinduism, the enlightened being chooses to return from the bliss of Nirvana and teach others.
70. Ray and Anderson, *Creatives*, 341.
71. Hawken, *Blessed Unrest*, back page blurb.
72. Ibid 4
73. Ibid 12
74. Ibid 18
75. Although Hawken argues that the movement is actually a majority of the world population.
76. Hawken, *Unrest*, 25.
77. See Swimme and Berry's *The Universe Story: From the Primordial Flaring Forth to the Ecozoic Era* (1992, 1994).
78. Hawken, *Unrest*, 141.
79. Ibid 142
80. Ibid
81. Ibid 142-158
82. Ibid 163-164
83. Ibid 164-165
84. Ibid 182
85. Ibid 184
86. A term coined by German philosopher Karl Jaspers to describe the period from 800 to 200 BCE in which similar spiritual ideas and figures simultaneously emerged in China, India, and the West.
87. Hawken, *Unrest*, 188.
88. Ibid 188
89. Ibid 188
90. Ibid 189

91. Rifkin, *The Empathic Civilization.*
92. Hubbard 2
93. Such a journey brings to mind the Buddhist path from being victim of one's thoughts and emotions to achieving some measure of governance over them.
94. Hubbard 8
95. Singer, Peter. *The Expanding Circle: Ethics, Evolution, and Moral Progress* (Princeton University Press, 1981).
96. Hubbard 9
97. Ibid 18
98. Ibid 19
99. Ibid 29
100. Ibid 41
101. Ibid 46
102. Ibid 46
103. Ibid 47-49
104. Ibid 49
105. Hubbard 54
106. Ibid 57
107. Ibid 60
108. Ibid 63
109. Ibid 69-76
110. Beck, Wilber
111. Hubbard 97
112. Ibid 114
113. Abraham Maslow
114. Hubbard 126
115. Ibid 128-129
116. Ibid 131
117. Ibid 135
118. Ibid 153-158
119. Ibid 172-184
120. Ibid 206
121. Ibid 209

122. Ibid 209
123. Ibid 121
124. Dowd 9
125. Dowd 42
126. Dowd 16
127. Ibid 24
128. TED talk
129. Ibid 52
130. Dowd 56
131. Dowd 75
132. Dowd 300-302
133. Dowd 307-310
134. Dowd 307-310

Chapter 3 The Church Of All Worlds

1. Ray and Anderson 2000
2. Wilber 1995
3. Intimate relationship of more than two people.
4. According to most estimates, the largest five religions in terms of adherents are: Christianity, Islam, Hinduism, Chinese Traditional Religions, and Buddhism. It's interesting to note that "Secular/Non-religious/Agnostic/Atheist," while not a religion, ranks number three on this list, between Islam and Hinduism.
5. Gerald Gardner was a British civil servant who visited what he believed was a surviving coven of Witches in New Forest, England. He then hybridized that tradition with some of his own proclivities (such as ritual nudity) into the first NeoPagan sect.
6. In 1401, the first act in English Act of Parliament declared sorcery or divination a heresy punishable by execution. In 1735, George III replaced the ecclesiastical belief in witchcraft with new laws against con artists claiming to be witches, along with lesser penalties. Apparently, 1944 was

the last time anyone was punished under anti-witchcraft acts. Current consensus suggests that Gardner's work was precipitated by the repeal of all such laws in 1951, and it's likely that many who deemed themselves Witches or psychics felt some liberation to speak and write more freely.

7. Defined in his 1971 article "Theagenesis: the Rebirth of the Goddess." First published in *Green Egg: the Journal of the Church of All Worlds*, July 1971.
8. First formulated in the late 1960s by James Lovelock and Lynn Margulis, co-authors of "Atmospheric Homeostasis By and For the Biosphere: The Gaia Hypothesis," and further elucidated by Lovelock in *Gaia: A new Look at Life on Earth*.
9. Magick – differentiated from stage 'magic' – is variously defined as the ability to alter consciousness, and/or the external environment, at will. To alter one's consciousness affects external perceptions, leading to a desired change in circumstances. There is also a sense that forces in nature and divine realms can be called upon to aid in magickal endeavors.
10. The 'mytho-poetic' perspective relies on images and symbols, the language of poetry, affecting the soul or 'heart' rather than intellect.
11. The story many NeoPagans view as their mythic history includes primal age shamans who, by lost arts of spiritual communication and activity, healed, called game animals, and communed with the realm of spirits and ancestors in ways and by means no longer generally cultivated in modern times. A good examination of this mythic cycle can be found in Hutton's *Triumph of the Moon*.
12. *Goddess and Gods of Old Europe*, *Language of the Goddess*, and *Civilization of the Goddess*.
13. See Harvey's *Animism* and, for a more secular treatment concerning the presence of 'mind' in nature, see Skrbina's *Pansychism in the West*.

14. For instance, in Black Elk's writings. There can be considerable overlap between Native people and NeoPagans in a given region. Being (neo)tribal traditions, mutual gatherings occur; for example, at the Phoenix Phyre gatherings in Florida, Don Waterhawk, a Tsalagi (Cherokee) elder, performed my son's manhood ceremony.
15. See Harrison's *Elements of Pantheism.*
16. History records many instances of Christian discrimination and outright violence against Pagans, especially after Constantine's Edict of Milan in 323. When Gratian became Emperor in 375, Ambrose, Bishop of Milan, encouraged him to more forcefully suppress Pagans, their temples, and their practices. This was the common practice throughout the Middle Ages.
17. See Ong's *Orality and Literacy.*
18. The manifestations of this "Fear" and its tragic effects on small towns and rural villages of the agricultural peasantry were profound. See Gibbons' *Study of the Great European Witch Hunt,* Levack's *Witch-hunt in Early Modern Europe,* Barstow's *New History of the European Witch Hunts,* and Hutton's *Triumph of the Moon.*
19. See Hutton's *Triumph of the Moon.*
20. See Chryssides' *Exploring New Religions,* 332-341.
21. Charles Godfrey Leland was an American humorist, folklorist, and journalist.
22. Leland, *Aradia.*
23. Ibid i
24. Ibid ii
25. A contemporary version is available at http://www.reclaiming.org/about/witchfaq/charge.html.
26. Weston, *From Ritual to Romance.*
27. Murray, *Witch-Cult in Western Europe.*
28. Records of witch persecutions of the Benandanti exposed a wide variety of practices that Ginzberg describes as

evidence of a substrate of shamanic cults in Europe.

29. In England, passed in 1401, 1541, and 1563, making witchcraft a heresy, then a felony, punishable by death. It was replaced in 1951 with the Fraudulent Mediums Act, which was itself repealed in 2008.
30. Gardner. *Witchcraft Today*.
31. Gardner. *Meaning of Witchcraft*.
32. Founded in the early twentieth century and associated with Freemasonry, whose most noted leader was Aleister Crowley, the Ordo Templi Orientis has about 3,000 members, half in the United States.
33. Earth, Air, Fire, Water, and Spirit.
34. See the works of Bron Taylor, e.g., *Encyclopedia of Nature and Religion*.
35. See Miller's *Hippies and American Values*.
36. Ibid
37. See Jacob's *New Pioneers: Back to the Land*
38. Harvey 1
39. Ibid 15
40. Ibid 38
41. Ibid 88
42. Ibid 182
43. The esteemed psychologist Alfred Adler, founder of Individual Psychology and personality theory (including coining the term "inferiority complex," colleague of Sigmund Freud, and an influence over several other schools of psychoanalysis.
44. Adler 3
45. Ibid 4
46. Ibid 300-1
47. Ibid 301
48. Ibid 307
49. *Spiral Dance*, *Webs of Power*, and *The Fifth Sacred Thing*, and founder of Reclaiming, a national Pagan collective.

50. Starhawk 16
51. Reclaiming is a San Francisco-based Witch collective, described on their website as: a community of women and men working to unify spirit and politics. Our vision is rooted in the religion and magic of the Goddess, the Immanent Life Force. We see our work as teaching and making magic; the art of empowering ourselves and each other. In our classes, workshops, and public rituals, we train our voices, bodies, energy, intuition, and minds. We use the skills we learn to deepen our strength, both as individuals and as community, to voice our concerns about the world in which we live, and bring to birth a vision of a new culture.
52. *Green Egg* (*GE*), the official journal and 'flagship publication' of CAW, was published in hard copy from its inception as a one-page ditto sheet in 1968 to its cessation in print form in 2001. According to J. Gordon Melton's 1979 *Encyclopedia of American Religions*, it grew it grew over 80 issues into a 60-page journal, becoming the most significant periodical in the Pagan movement during the 1970s and made Tim Zell, its editor, a major force in NeoPaganism (a term which Zell coined). It was also the major instrument of the Church's expansion. *GE* continues in the present as an online magazine, available at www.greeneggzine.com
53. See Barker, *Of Gods and Men* and *New Religious Movements*.
54. For instance, its unconventional combination of science and religion, commitment to contemporary polyamory, and ecospirituality – all new phenomena in their CAW form.
55. Author of *The Encyclopedia of American Religions*, Melton is currently on the Board of Editorial Consultants and frequent contributor to *Nova Religio: The Journal of Alternative and Emergent Religions*.
56. Melton, *Encyclopedia*, 909.
57. Ibid 910
58. Ibid

59. Melton, "New Religions" 107.
60. Hutton 351-52
61. Ibid 352
62. See Kaldera's *Pagan Polyamory*.
63. According to Maslow's *Motivation and Personality*, self-actualizing people: (1) embrace the facts and realities of the world (including themselves) rather than denying or avoiding them; (2) are spontaneous in their ideas and actions; (3) are creative; (4) are interested in solving problems; (5) feel a closeness to other people, and generally appreciate life; (6) have a system of morality that is fully internalized and independent of external authority; and (7) have discernment and are able to view all things in an objective manner.
64. Atl, the Aztec word for 'water' and 'home of our ancestors,' is a group dedicated to raising human consciousness and thus precipitating social change. It continues to exist under the leadership of Lance Christie and, as I experienced it, represents a secular path that leads in a similar direction as its sister organization, CAW.
65. They used a technique wherein the horn bud of a young goat, which is initially unattached to the skin, is moved to the middle of the forehead and allowed to develop normally. Oberon and Morning Glory traveled for years with the Ringling Bros. circus showing their 'unicorns.'
66. Oberon and Morning Glory Zell, interview by author, February 26, 2006, Cotati, CA.
67. Oberon Zell, Church of All Worlds *Membership Handbook* 2nd ed., with the Church of All Worlds Clergy Council (Ukiah, CA: Church of All Worlds, 1995), 30.
68. Ibid 4
69. For instance, in Boas' *Mind of Primitive Man* and several letters to colleagues and newspapers suggesting a humanistic cultural relativism.

70. Teilhard de Chardin, *Phenomenon of Man*, 180-84. Teilhard sees human biological evolution as linked to planetary transformation through the development of the noosphere, writing, The biological change of state terminating in the awakening of thought doesn't merely represent a critical point that the individual or even the species must pass through. Vaster than that, it affects life itself in an organic totality, and consequently it marks a transformation affecting the state of the entire planet. (181)
71. See Benyus' *Biomimicry*.
72. Oberon, and CAW in general, continue to be influenced by Teilhard de Chardin's work, but envision a different hierarchy. The God/dess (a hybrid concept emphasizing the feminine aspect) is seen as infinite and eternal, partially beyond the scope of human imagination or contemplation. Gaea is one aspect of God/dess, an example of embodied divinity, and the most important example for humanity. Not everyone I know in the Church embraces this system, or even views it as critical, but it's a theology which favors all life as sacred and humankind as arbiters of progressive spiritual evolution among the servants of the divine, from amoebas to galaxies and beyond. To coin a descriptive term, I would call most CAW members *panentheistic mystics* or *mystical panentheists*.
73. As exemplified by Berry and Swimme's *Universe Story*.
74. See Driver's *Liberating Rites*.
75. See the works of anarchist and primitivist philosopher John Zerzan, including *Future Primitive and Other Essays* (1994), and *Against Civilization: Readings and Reflections* (2005). Also see Daniel Quinn's 'new tribalist' novel *Ishmael* (1992) and *Beyond Civilization* (2000).
76. Jean-Jacque Rousseau lamented the thwarting of the tribal self by modern society; neo-tribal organizational principles include voluntarily living and working among familiar

and/or familial persons and establishing geographically contiguous communities and cooperatives of such persons towards common social goals.

77. See various popular books, including James Nash's *Loving Nature: Ecological Integrity and Christian Responsibility* (1991), Ian Brodley's *God is Green: Ecology for Christians* (1992), Steven Bouma-Prediger's *For the Beauty of the Earth: A Christian Vision for Creation Care* (2001), and Calvin Dewitt's *Earth-Wise: A Biblical Response to Environmental Issues* (2007).
78. A term for 'death' used by the character Valentine Michael Smith and his followers in Heinlein's *Stranger in a Strange Land*.
79. Interesting but controversial work has been done on organizing fields of consciousness and "morphic resonance" by Rupert Sheldrake. Often accused by orthodox scientists of attempting to infuse magic into his work (a definite heresy), Sheldrake takes seriously telepathy and a "probability photograph" composite theory of evolution. See *New Science of Life*, *Presence of the Past*, and *Rebirth of Nature*.
80. Zell interview, February 26.
81. Often attempts at collective and cooperative living arrangements in CAW have centered on polyamory, with extended families, mutual business ventures, and common land. However, the inexperience of participants, external social indifference (or hostility), complex emotional pitfalls, and financial disputes have usually prevented the Church from manifesting this neo-tribal vision with any breadth or duration.
82. Zell, interview, February 26.
83. Ibid
84. Ibid
85. Maslow's process of reaching 'self-actualization' begins with satisfying his 'hierarchy of needs' (Physiological,

Safety, Love/Belonging, Esteem, Self-Actualization). This satisfaction leads to the full expression of an individual's potential, defined as the desire to become more than what one is – in other words, the capacity to grow and improve. See Maslow's *Motivation and Personality*.

86. Zell, interview, February 26.
87. Ibid
88. Japanese animation
89. Japanese comics, drawn in the distinctive anime style.
90. See Blackmore's *Meme Machine*.
91. Arweck, *Researching New Religious Movements*, 59.
92. Zell, *CAW Membership Handbook*, 33
93. Ibid 33-34

Chapter 4 CAW's Beliefs

1. *Politics of Women's Spirituality* and *States of Grace*.
2. Spretnak, *Grace*, 136.
3. *Chalice and Blade*.
4. *Gaia and God*.
5. *Rebirth of the Goddess* and *Re-Imagining the Divine in the World*.
6. *She Is Everywhere!*
7. Starhawk 91
8. First published in *Green Egg*, July 1971.
9. Developed in the 1970s by James Lovelock and Lynn Margulis, and popularized in Lovelock's 2000 book *Gaia: A New Look at Life on Earth*.
10. Zell, "Theagenesis," 1.
11. Ibid
12. Devall and Sessions, *Deep Ecology*
13. Ibid
14. Ibid 2
15. Ibid
16. Originally indicating community or commonwealth, the

current meaning suggests common welfare or public good; its usage in the book implies the common good of the whole Earth community.

17. *Church of All Worlds Tradition*, a pamphlet published in 2005, endorsed by Oberon and Morning Glory Zell. Pamphlet pages not numbered.
18. See Greer's *World Full of Gods,* Paper's *Deities Are Many*, or Miller's *New Polytheism*.
19. Adler, *Drawing Down the Moon*, 4.
20. One of the 'philosophers of identity' (i.e. Schelling and Spinoza), Krause (1731-1832) sought to reconcile monotheism and pantheism, that is, the God of faith and conscience with the sensory world. For Krause, God was not a limited being but an essence (*Wesen*) containing the universe within itself. He called his attempt to reconcile theism and pantheism *panentheism*; in this view, the world constitutes an organism, and therefore the universe – which is contained by God – is a divine organism. Ultimately, Krause saw evolutionary development as leading to identification of the world with God by means of the 'Perfect Law' of absolute freedom and liberty – until humanity finally merges with God. This theory in turn influenced, along with Kant's idealism and the Vedic traditions, the American Transcendentalists such as Ralph Waldo Emerson, especially in his *Nature* (1836) which can be seen as panentheistic. I submit that in some future paper a lineage might be drawn from Krause to Lovelock, Matthew Fox, and the Gaea theories of CAW. Krause's principle works include *Entwurf des Systems der Philosophie* (1804); *System der Sittenlehre* (1810); *Das Urbild der Menschheit* (1811); and *Vorlesungen über das System der Philosophie* (1828).
21. Fox, *Coming of Cosmic Christ*, 57.
22. Skrbina, *Panpsychism*, 21.
23. Ibid

24. One of my favorite expressions of Berry's ecospirituality (possibly because of its brevity) is an interview by Betty Didcoct in the journal *In Context: A Quarterly of Humane Sustainable Culture* (Winter 1984) available online at www.context.org/ICLIB/IC08/Berry.htm. A list of ecospiritual books includes Berry's *Dream of the Earth,* Berry and Swimme's *Universe Story,* Swimme's *Hidden Heart of the Cosmos,* and Capra and Steindl-Rast's *Belonging to the Universe.*
25. Some scientists and theologians insist the two disciplines are, and should remain, separate; others advocate integration, particularly Teilhard de Chardin (Omega Point) and Ian Barbour (process philosophy and theology).
26. As reflected in such popular books as John Grey's *Men Are From Mars, Women Are From Venus* (1992) and refined as energetic polarities in essays such as on the Sisters of the Silver Branch web site (www.silver-branch.org/ssbcreations/ssbmfprinciple.html)
27. Johnson 243
28. See Lyotard's *Postmodern Condition* which presents modernity in terms of constant change in the pursuit of social and technological progress, and postmodernity as the culmination of those pursuits, along with the end of grand and normative meta-narratives.
29. Founded by Selena Fox in the late 1970s, Dennis Carpenter was co-executive director. The web site is www.circlesanctuary.org
30. Lewis 37. Quoted from "Green Spirituality," Spretnak's 1987 article in *Resurgence.*
31. Lewis 39
32. Griffin, "Postmodern Spirituality and Society."
33. Lewis 39
34. See Elgin's *Awakening Earth* and *Promise Ahead.*
35. Zell, interview, February 26.

36. One Star Trek film portrays an alien deep-space probe attempting to communicate, not with humans, but with humpback whales.
37. Zell, interview, February 26.
38. This term is used frequently in Star Trek, where Earth-life is repeatedly described as "Terran." From the Latin *terra*, meaning Earth.
39. Zell, interview, February 26.
40. See Swimme and Fox, *Manifesto for a Global Civilization*; Swimme, *Universe is a Green Dragon*; Swimme and Berry, *Universe Story*; Swimme, *Hidden Heart of the Cosmos*; Liebes, Sahtouris and Swimme, *Walk Through Time*.
41. Theories concerning the existence and origins of the universe and reality.
42. Again, Berry and Swimme's *Universe Story* epitomizes the ecospiritual cosmology emerging from the spirit-science synthesis.
43. Such as *Brief History of Time* and *Universe In a Nutshell*.
44. Zell, interview, February 26.
45. Ibid
46. Ibid
47. Ibid
48. This quantum physics term meaning all possible parallel universes and implying 'infinity' is used here to define the synthesis of universe (the observable physical-sensory realm) and cosmos (in its theological sense of Creation and the Creator), and to describe reality including both the material and spiritual, known and unknown, empirical and mystic.
49. Zell, interview, February 26.
50. See the work of Richard Bucke, Itzhak Bentov, William Tiller, and Ken Wilber
51. Zell, interview, February 26.
52. Ibid

53. See Dawkins' *Selfish Gene* and *God Delusion*, and Dennett's *Consciousness Explained* and *Darwin's Dangerous Idea*.
54. The Grey School of Wizardry is at http://www.greyschool.com/main.asp
55. From the *Stanford Encyclopedia of Philosophy*, available online at http://plato.stanford.edu/entries/evil/
56. See Liebniz' *Essais de Théodicée* (*Essays of Theodicy*, 1710) in which he coined the term 'theodicy' (the justice of God) as an attempt to reconcile the existence of suffering with the existence of a benevolent God. He addressed the 'underachiever problem' through the Principle of Sufficient Reason, which states that there must be sufficient reason to explain why this world exists in its form and not in another form. He also explained the 'holiness problem' through the *Philosopher's Confession*, in which he submits that God wills everything in the world, but His will for good is 'decretory' while His will for evil is merely 'permissive.' See also Murray's "Leibniz on the Problem of Evil" from the *Stanford Encyclopedia of Philosophy*.
57. See Swinburne's *Is There a God?*
58. Advaita, one of the major schools of Vedanta, identifies the Self (*Atman*) with the Whole (*Brahman*), suggesting that there's no distinction between the two. Since everything is a dream of God, nothing but Brahman is real, and everything else, including the material universe, is false (except on a strictly pragmatic level). Only because of ignorance is Brahman visible as the material world. All events, good or bad, are experiences of God; therefore, evil and suffering are divine. See Sharma's *Philosophy of Religion and Advaita Vedanta*.
59. Dvaita, the dualistic school of Vedanta, suggests a distinction between the Self and the Absolute. Everything is divided into two distinct categories: the individual soul (*jiva*) and God (*Ishvara/Vishnu*). Other divisions include

those between innumerable selves, God and matter, and self and matter. Only in the form of matter do evil and suffering exist. Therefore, they aren't in any way divine, but products of material fallibility and karma of the intrinsic soul. See Flood's *Introduction to Hinduism* and the related works of Madhvacharya.

60. Zell, interview, February 26. Oberon excludes "fun" pain such as BDSM.
61. Ibid
62. For instance, in the work of Alan Dershowitz, Peter Singer, and Tom Regan.
63. The New Testament contains many verses pertaining to salvation, one of the best-known being John 3:16: "For God so loved the world that he gave his one and only Son, that whoever believes in him shall not perish but have eternal life" (NIV). In my experience growing up in a Christian church and through studying it as a student and researcher, the saving power of Christ's death and resurrection are core Christian doctrine, whether emphasizing faith and good works (Catholic) or faith alone (many Protestant denominations).
64. In Islam, the belief is that all people possess a primordial nature (*al-fitrah*) which has been forgotten through negligence. Salvation, therefore, is the process of remembering and reclaiming this inner knowledge embedded in the self.
65. The Vedas suggest that salvation consists of the Atman's (soul, true self) liberation from Samsara (cycle of reincarnation/rebirth), resulting in release.
66. Buddhism also conceives of a liberation from the cycle of rebirth (and the suffering and ignorance inherent in life) through The Four Noble Truths, which are the path toward Nirvana (cessation of suffering).
67. Zell, interview, February 26.

68. The mystical experience is described variously as Samadhi (Hinduism), Jhana or Satori (Buddhism), Nirvana (Hinduism and Buddhism), De (Daoism), Theosis (Christianity), and fitra (Islam). Of course, the idea is that each of these are experienced and then reported by the mystic, rather than being ultimate states from which one doesn't return. One of my favorite Christian mystics is Julian of Norwich, the English anchoress whose *Showings* are beautiful and inspiring.
69. Zell, interview, February 26.
70. Ibid
71. Beginning as a philosophy with the ancient Greeks, ethics concerns what constitutes a satisfactory life, but also touches on matters of moral behavior, thus crossing the boundaries of secular philosophy and religion. Normative ethics – as explicated, for instance, by Kant (1787), Ross (2003), and Rawls (1999) – relate to determining right and wrong action using some (often religious) standard. Meta-ethics, as investigated by Garner and Rosen's *Moral Philosophy* is concerned with the meaning and nature of ethical judgments, and with truth-bearing and validating principles applied to ethical decision-making. Meta-ethics theories are divided into "Semantic," "Substantial," and "Epistemological." Applied ethics, as explained in Singer's *Practical Ethics,* attempts to apply moral philosophy in determining the correct course of action in specific contemporary issues facing society.
72. Especially as described in Lynn White's "The Historical Roots of Our Ecological Crisis" (1967).
73. From the online version of the *Stanford Encyclopedia of Philosophy* (first published in 2002, with revisions through 2008) accessible at http://plato.stanford.edu/entries/ethics-environmental. I appreciate *SEP* being made available free on the Internet and find in this sharing a reflection of the

ethical strivings of CAW towards altruism and generosity.

74. Leopold, *Sand County Almanac*.
75. Especially their work together on the "Religion and Ecology" series at Harvard, but including Tucker's *Worldly Wonder*.
76. Gottlieb, *This Sacred Earth*.
77. Reuther, *Gaia and God*.
78. Zell, *CAW Membership Handbook*, 24.
79. "If it harm none, do as you will"
80. An ethic of reciprocity, for instance in the Holy Bible, Luke 6:31: "Do unto others as you would have them do unto you."
81. Oberon and Morning Glory Zell, interview by author, June 18, 2006, Cotati, CA.
82. Ibid
83. Most CAW members maintain a vague belief in a New Age type of complex reincarnation and karma as the balance between 'good' and 'bad' actions over a lifetime (or many lifetimes)
84. See Szabados and Soifer's *Hypocrisy: Ethical Investigations*.
85. Referring especially to scandals involving televangelists such as Jim Bakker, (in 1986), Ted Haggard (in 2006), and Jimmy Swaggart (in 1991)
86. The thinking in CAW is that a mature person manages his or her ego and has no need for dishonesty, closed-heartedness, or artificiality. It has further been observed that persons considered spiritually enlightened (such as the Dalai Lama) seem to be genuine and unpretentious.
87. *Stanford Encyclopedia of Philosophy* (online), http://plato.stanford.edu/entries/rationalism-empiricism
88. Zell, interview, June 18
89. Zell, interview, June 18
90. For some CAW members, nature itself is the ultimate power and force in reality, without reference to the supernatural

or metaphysical. For others, nature reflects a higher, deeper, and broader spiritual reality.

91. *Stanford Encyclopedia of Philosophy* (online), http://plato.stanford.edu/entries/afterlife
92. The 'Summerlands' is typically a peaceful, beautiful, but Earth-like place in the spiritual realm where souls may go after death to refresh and rejuvenate themselves before moving on to another 'assignment'.
93. Zell, interview, June 18.
94. Zell, interview, February 26.
95. Ibid
96. This echoes the Buddhist belief that even Heaven and Hell are temporary.
97. Many members consider death a 'preventable illness' that will one day be 'healed.' They point to other seemingly miraculous advancements, in medicine, for instance, that would have seemed impossible and absurd to Neolithic people.
98. Zell, interview, February 26.
99. Many CAW members, like their NeoPagan brethren, copy out their "Books of Shadow" (or traditional Grimoire) by hand, but others use computers, and have in the past decade popularized the "Disc of Shadows" in electronic format.
100. Zell, interview, February 26.
101. Ibid
102. Ibid
103. Ibid
104. That is, humankind lives within nature and according to Earth's limits. This is not a pantheistic view, however, because humans have spirits – but spirits are natural, not supernatural. Panentheistic debates still rage in CAW about whether God/dess is exclusively immanent or is both immanent and transcendent of the empirical universe.
105. Zell, interview, February 26.

106. Ibid
107. Ibid
108. Ibid

Chapter 5 CAW's Practices

1. For a while, a member of the extended polyamorous Zell household.
2. Zell, "CAW Tradition".
3. The Sabbats are spaced more or less evenly throughout the year and consist of:
   - Yule (later Christmas) – the winter solstice, December 21
   - Imbolc – mid-winter, February 2
   - Ostara (later Easter) – the vernal equinox, March 21
   - Beltane – mid-spring, May 1 or 2
   - Litha – the summer solstice, June 21
   - Lughnasad – mid-summer, August 2
   - Mabon – the autumnal equinox, September 21
   - Samhain (later Halloween) – mid-autumn, November 1 or 2
4. More than one ritual I've attended segued into more intimate activities as a natural extension of embodied spirituality.
5. CAW's forms of worship include the physical, along with the psycho-sensual, emotive, and magical. It's this naked physicality that some find controversial, but only because most Western societies are heavily Christianized.
6. Zell, "CAW Tradition"
7. Probably influenced by Aleister Crowley's 1904 *Book of the Law*, The Rede was formulated in its present form in 1964 by Doreen Valiente, friend and High Priestess of Gerald Gardner
8. Examples of the "left-hand path" in NeoPaganism would include elements of Norse traditions such as Asatru and Odinism, but not Satanism, which is outside the NeoPagan

milieu.

9. Zell, "CAW Tradition".
10. Eliade, *Sacred and Profane.*
11. Ibid 20
12. See Sheldrake's "Hypothesis of Formative Causation".
13. Think of King Arthur's round table or a group gathered around a camp fire: no one is at the 'head'.
14. Zell, *CAW Membership Handbook*, 24.
15. Ibid
16. Zell, "CAW Tradition".
17. See Watkins' *Old Straight Track.*
18. Zell, "CAW Tradition".
19. The practice of voluntary possession by a spirit or deity is common and crosses religious and cultural boundaries: from Santeria and Voudoun to Pentecostalism and New Age channeling, spirit possession is accepting a benevolent force into one's body (and psyche), and thus providing a body for otherwise ephemeral beings.
20. For instance Esther Hicks/Abraham and Jane Roberts/Seth
21. Zell, "CAW Tradition".
22. www.caw.org
23. CAW's Annwfn website, http://www.annwfn.org/index.cfm?PageID=149andCategoryID=44
24. Zell, "CAW Tradition".
25. See Niebuhr's *Beyond Tolerance.*
26. I've witnessed, or led, Zazen-type meditation sessions, Roman Catholic-inspired "blessing for the animals" rituals, Evangelical-ish hands-on healing circles, and Native American-like sweat lodges and vision quests.
27. Zell, "CAW Tradition".
28. There have been a host of new books engaging the Gaia/Earth concepts, including Reuther's *Gaia and God*, Lovelock's *Gaia: A New Look at Earth*, Lewis' *Gaia Speaks*, and Harding's *Animate Earth.*

29. "Powerful" as in Starhawk's "power with" and "power within" rather than "power over"
30. Zell, "CAW Tradition".
31. 1 Kings 18:36, 1 Chronicles 17:26, Psalm 86:10, Psalm 90:2 and Acts 4:24 (KJV).
32. To "grok in fullness" (Heinlein, *Stranger in a Strange Land*) is literally to 'drink' the essence, energy, and whole reality of something or someone so that, like the body absorbing and essentially becoming the water, one has absorbed and thus completely 'knows' the thought, object, or person. I believe that the effort to 'grok' is synonymous with the effort to develop a tangible psychic link to others and the planet beyond anything presently conceivable, as part of the larger project of global transformation.
33. The metaphor within the book for developing the ability to *grok* is "learning Martian".
34. Zell, "CAW Tradition".
35. Even though they are controversial, Masaru Emoto's various books on the energetic of water (*Secret Life of Water, True Power of Water,* and *Hidden Messages in Water*) are typical of the CAW passion for this element.
36. See section one of the film "Zeitgeist," available at http://video.google.com/videoplay?docid=5547481422995115331
37. Zell, "CAW Tradition".
38. Ibid
39. The process is explained in the *CAW Handbook* section "So You Want to Start a Nest?" (29)
40. Zell, "CAW Tradition".
41. Since CAW is NeoPagan, Doreen Valiente's "Charge of the Goddess" and its statement – made by a speaking Goddess – that "all love and pleasure are my rituals," influences the Church consciously and profoundly in its hedonistic propensities.
42. Many religions approve of sex (much of Judaism comes

to mind), but exclusively within certain boundaries, often related to cultural norms. The Family (Children of God) used sex to attract adherents, but only CAW holds it as an integral part of its theology and argues for its inclusion (as sacred) based on pre-Christian and extant tribal values, and specifically directed in a sacred text (Charge of the Goddess).

43. Zell, "CAW Tradition".
44. Adler 283
45. See Heinlein's *Grumbles from the Grave,* consisting of the author's personal correspondences and a short biography by his wife.
46. Zell, "CAW Tradition".
47. There are several pertinent books on sacred sexuality, including Nelson and Longfellow's *Sexuality and the Sacred*; Eisler's *Sacred Pleasure*; and Feuerstein's *Sacred Sexuality.*
48. From Wikipedia, the free online encyclopedia, http://en.wikipedia.org/wiki/Polyamory. Wikipedia isn't always a reliable source of information, but in this case, it fits the criteria for the needs of this essay.
49. Morning Glory Zell, "A Bouquet of Lovers: Strategies for Responsible Open Relationships," Green Egg: the journal of CAW (#89, Beltane 1990). Available at http://www.caw.org/articles/bouquet.html
50. Robert Heinlein, *Stranger In a Strange Land* (New York: Putnam, 1961).
51. Those who have "shared water" in a ceremony initiating an intimate kinship relation using the element most precious on Mars.
52. Heinlein 290
53. Heinlein 336
54. Heinlein 345
55. Heinlein 343
56. Heinlein 345

57. Heinlein 346
58. Heinlein 347
59. Heinlein 347
60. Heinlein 348
61. Heinlein 371
62. From Feraferia's founder Fred Adams, who briefly worked with Oberon in the early years of CAW.
63. Zell, *Bouquet.*
64. Ibid
65. Ibid
66. Ibid
67. Ibid
68. Ibid
69. See Abraham Maslow.
70. Zell, *Bouquet.*
71. Zell, *CAW Membership Handbook*, 21.
72. See Laszlo's *Systems View of the World.*
73. Zell, *CAW Membership Handbook*, 21.
74. See Max Weber's sociology of religion and government in *The Protestant Ethic and the Spirit of Capitalism*, in which he suggests that capitalism evolved from an emphasis on hard work and personal responsibility for one's state in the world. The Protestant Ethic regards prosperity and wealth in this world as the result of, and reflective of, of divine blessing
75. Zell, *CAW Membership Handbook*, 21.
76. Not counting *biomimicry* or *bionics*, with all their startling possibilities. See the work of Janine Benyus or Kevin Passino.
77. The name of various starships in the Star Trek series.
78. As in Eisler's "Dominator/Partnership" model in *Chalice and Blade.*
79. Zell, *CAW Membership Handbook*, 21.
80. Ibid

81. Ibid
82. This was before Pluto suffered demotion to proto-planet
83. My personal equivalency chart comparing the two looks like this:

Circle	Academic Equivalent
1	Applicant
2	Freshman
3	Sophomore
4	Junior
5	Senior
6	Graduate
7	Doctoral
8	Postdoctoral (Professorial/Professional)
9	Post-academic (Transcendent)

84. Zell, *CAW Membership Handbook*, 32.
85. Ibid 32-33
86. Ibid 34
87. Ibid 35
88. Humorously referencing the James Bond 007 cycle.
89. Zell, *CAW Membership Handbook*, 36.
90. Ibid
91. See Martin's *Kingdom of Cults* and Singer's *Cults in Our Midst*.
92. Which is itself usually non-violent. The Satanic Temple, for instance, works for separation of church and state, and doesn't believe in a literal devil.
93. Bonewits' Cult Danger Evaluation Frame is available in his book *Real Magic* and online at www.neopagan.net/ABCDEF.html
94. See Hawkins' *Goddess Worship, Witchcraft, and Neo-Paganism* and, more generally concerning religion, Dennett's *Breaking the Spell*. Although some secular writers accuse all religions

of being exclusively sociological phenomena without divine content, the point is that NeoPaganism, being associated with anachronistic worship, is even more vulnerable to dismissal.

95. See, for instance, Ken Wilber's Four Quadrant integral system, in which 'magical self' (psycho-spiritual quadrant) and 'animistic-magical' (cultural quadrant) are second to last as a developmental stage. This system is graphically displayed and briefly described in the magazine What Is Enlightenment? (Issue 41, August-October 2008), 40.
96. These sentiments from conversations with various non-Pagans, including academic colleagues and skeptical friends, some of whom believe in God, but not miracles, or who accept divinity on Earth, but not magickal energy in nature. Such sentiments are part of the problem: if one is color-blind, how can one be convinced red exists?
97. These sentiments are based on personal experiences, mostly discussions with skeptics of Paganism and within Pagan groups who shared their experience of being called a "hippy church" as a pejorative.

Conclusion

1. Mainstream as for instance the history, philosophy, and religious traditions taught in US public schools and colleges and well known among the US populous.
2. See Benyus' *Biomimicry.*
3. See Shipley's *Intersensory Origins of Mind;* Morgan's *Emergent Evolution*; or Dowd's *Thank God for Evolution.*
4. For instance, Bunyan's *Pilgrim's Progress* (1678), a Christian allegory whose title includes "From This World to That Which is to Come".
5. See Hinde's *Burckhardt and the Crisis of Modernity* and Ivakhiv's essay "Resurgence of Magical Religion".
6. The debate over capital punishment has enlivened more

than one CAW conversation, with members on both sides of the issue. Some believe premeditated murderers have surrendered their right to life by their crime; others feel that no one has the right to kill another, no matter the justification, and that murderers should be compassionately imprisoned for life.

7. Many CAW members are carnivores, and the conversation on the right of individual animals (e.g., cows or pigs) to life continues. On one hand, the carnivores claim that beings on Earth eat each other, and this is a basic fact of nature. On the other hand, vegetarians claim that to "harm none" indicates the need to do as little harm as possible to other beings, and that vegetarian diet is more advanced for the body and planet. Generally, a sense of tolerance pervades the debate, and almost everyone agrees that no species should be pressured to extinction by humans, and that there may be a point at which species loss creates larger ecological problems.
8. See Oldmeadow's *Betrayal of Tradition.*
9. For instance, the European Union (EU), a political and economic entity of 27 member nations established by the Treaty of Maastricht in 1993. The EU has a standardized system of laws guaranteeing all members freedom of movement for persons, goods, services, and capital.
10. Traditional to CAW and probably gleaned from other NeoPagan sources. Each member signs the Pledge as part of the progression into the second Circle of CAW as a dues-paying member
11. Thompson, *Transforming History*, 10.
12. See Wilber's *Sex, Ecology, and Spirituality.*
13. See Bateson's *Mind and Nature* and Berman's *Reenchantment of the World.*
14. Thompson, *Transforming History*, 11.
15. See the various books by Hereward Carrington (e.g., *Your*

Psychic Powers) and the Psychic Research Center, Edgar Cayce, or such pop titles as Becky Walsh's *Advanced Psychic Development* (2007).

16. See Judith's *Waking the Global Heart.*
17. See Kroll's *The Mystic Mind* or Teasdale's *The Mystic Heart.*
18. See especially Pinchbeck's *Breaking Open the Head,* and almost all of the many works of Terence McKenna (e.g., *Archaic Revival*) and Ralph Metzner (e.g., *Expansion of Consciousness, Unfolding Self*).
19. Huxley, *Doors of Perception.*
20. From James' *Varieties of Religious Experience* and Otto's *Idea of the Holy* to Swinburne's *Faith and Reason,* the investigations of transpersonal psychology, and the ` in Time magazine (October 25, 2004).
21. Literally "home-place," from Callenbach's *Ecotopia.*
22. Solari 1965: 40
23. Stein 2012
24. Soleri 1965: 42
25. Ibid, 1995:168
26. Ibid, 1995:168

References & Suggested Reading

Adler, Margot. *Drawing Down the Moon: Witches, Druids, Goddess-worshipers, and Other Pagans in America Today*. Boston: Beacon Press, 1986. First published in 1979.

Arweck, Elisabeth. *Researching New Religious Movements*. New York: Routledge, 2006.

Barker, Eileen. *Of Gods and Men: New Religious Movements in the West*. Macon, GA: Mercer University Press, 1983.

———. *New Religious Movements: A Practical Introduction*. Blue Ridge Summit, PA: Bernan Press, 1990.

Barstow, Anne. *Witchcraze: A New History of the European Witch Hunts*. New York: HarperOne, 1995.

Bateson, Gregory. *Mind and Nature: A Necessary Unity*. Cresskill, NJ: Hampton Press, 1979.

Beck, Don Edward; Cowen, Christopher C. 2005. *Spiral Dynamics: Mastering Values, Leadership, and Change* (Hoboken, NJ: Wiley-Blackwell).

Bentz, Valerie and Jeremy Shapiro. *Mindful Inquiry in Social Research*. Thousand Oaks, CA: Sage, 1998.

Benyus, Janine. *Biomimicry: Innovation Inspired by Nature*. New York: William Morrow, 1997.

Berman, Morris. *The Reenchantment of the World*. Ithaca, NY: Cornell University Press, 1981.

Berry, Thomas. *The Dream of the Earth*. San Francisco: Sierra Club Books, 1990.

———. *The Great Work: Our Way into the Future*. New York: Bell Tower, 1999.

Berry, Thomas and Brian Swimme. *The Universe Story: From the Primordial Flaring Forth to the Ecozoic Era – A Celebration of the Unfolding of the Cosmos*. San Francisco: HarperSanFrancisco, 1992.

Birnbaum, Lucia. *She Is Everywhere!: An Anthology of Writing in*

Womanist/Feminist Spirituality. Bloomington, IN: iUniverse, 2005.

Boas, Franz. *The Mind of Primitive Man*. 1938. Whitefish, MT: Kessinger, 2007.

Bonewits, Isaac. *Real Magic: An Introductory Treatise on the Basic Principles of Yellow Magic*. Newburyport, MA: Red Wheel/ Weiser, 1989.

Bouma-Prediger, Steven. *For the Beauty of the Earth: A Christian Vision for Creation Care*. Ada, MI: Baker Academic, 2001.

Brodley, Ian. *God Is Green: Ecology for Christians*. Tracy, CA: Image Publishing, 1992.

Bunyan, John. *Pilgrim's Progress*. 1678. New York: Oxford University Press, 2003.

Callenbach, Ernest. *Ecotopia*. Berkeley: Banyan Tree Books, 1975.

Capra, Fritjof and David Steindl-Rast. *Belonging to the Universe: Explorations on the Frontiers of Science and Spirituality*. New York: HarperCollins, 1993.

Carpenter, Dennis. "Emergent Nature Spirituality: An Examination of the Major Contours of the Contemporary Pagan Worldview." In *Magical Religion and Modern Witchcraft*, edited by James Lewis, 35-72. Albany, NY: SUNY, 1996.

Carrington, Hereward. *Your Psychic Powers and How to Develop Them*. Whitefish, MT: Kessinger, 2007.

Christ, Carol. *Rebirth of the Goddess: Finding Meaning in Feminist Spirituality*. New York: Routledge, 1997.

———. *She Who Changes: Re-Imagining the Divine in the World*. New York: Palgrave Macmillan, 2004.

Chryssides, George. *Exploring New Religions*. London: Continuum International Publishing Group, 1999.

Church of All Worlds. "CAWeb – Green Egg Magazine," http://original.caw.org/greenegg/.

Crowley, Aleister. *The Book of the Law / Liber AL vel Legis*. 1904. Newburyport, MA: Weiser Books, 2004.

———. *Magic Without Tears*. San Ramon, CA: Falcon Press, 1973.

Dawkins, Richard. *The Selfish Gene.* New York: Oxford University Press, 2006. First published in 1976.

———. *The God Delusion*. New York: Mariner Books, 2008.

Dennett, Daniel. *Consciousness Explained*. Boston, MA: Back Bay Books, 1992.

———. *Darwin's Dangerous Idea: Evolution and the Meanings of Life*. New York: Simon and Schuster, 1995.

———. *Breaking the Spell: Religion as a Natural Phenomenon.* New York: Penguin, 2007.

Devall, Bill and George Sessions. *Deep Ecology: Living as if Nature Mattered*. Salt Lake City: G. M. Smith, 1985.

Devall, Bill; Sessions, George. 2001. *Deep Ecology: Living As If Nature Mattered* (Layton, UT: Gibbs Smith).

Dewitt, Calvin. *Earth-Wise: A Biblical Response to Environmental Issues*. Grand Rapids, MI: Faith Alive Christian Resources, 2007.

Dowd, Michael. *Thank God for Evolution: How the Marriage of Science and Religion Will Transform Your Life and Our World.* New York: Viking Press, 2008.

Driver, Thomas. *Liberating Rites: Understanding the Transformative Power of Ritual*. Boulder, CO: Westview Press, 1998.

Eisler, Riane. *Sacred Pleasure: Sex, Myth, and the Politics of the Body*. New York: HarperOne, 1996.

———. *The Chalice and the Blade: Our History, Our Future*. San Francisco: HarperCollins, 1998.

Elgin, Duane. *Awakening Earth: Exploring the Evolution of Human Culture and Consciousness*.

New York: William Morrow, 1993.

———. *Promise Ahead: A Vision of Hope and Action for Humanity's Future*. New York: Harper Paperbacks, 2001.

Eliade, Mircea. *The Sacred and the Profane*. New York: Harcourt, Brace, 1987. First published in 1959.

Ezzy, Douglas. "Religious Ethnography: Practicing the Witch's Craft." In *Researching Paganisms,* edited by Jenny Blain,

Douglas Ezzy, and Graham Harvey, 113–38. Walnut Creek, CA: Alta Mira Press, 2004.

Feuerstein, Georg. *Sacred Sexuality: The Erotic Spirit in the World's Great Religions*. Rochester, VT: Inner Traditions, 2003.

Flood, Gavin. *An Introduction to Hinduism*. Cambridge, UK: Cambridge University Press, 1996.

Fox, Matthew. *The Coming of the Cosmic Christ*. San Francisco: Harper and Row, 1988.

Fox, Matthew. 1983. *Original Blessing: A Primer in Creation Spirituality* (Santa Fe: Bear and Company).

Ferguson, Marilyn. *The Aquarian Conspiracy: Personal and Social Transformation in the 1980s*. Los Angeles: Tarcher, 1980.

Gardner, Gerald. *Witchcraft Today*. London: Ride, 1954.

———. *The Meaning of Witchcraft*. London: Aquarian Press, 1959.

Garner, Richard and Bernard Rosen. *Moral Philosophy: A Systematic Introduction to Normative Ethics and Metaethics*. New York: McMillan Press, 1967.

Gelderloos, Peter. *Consensus: A New Handbook for Grassroots Social, Political, and Environmental Groups*. Tucson, AZ: See Sharp Press, 2006.

Gibbons, Jenny. "Recent Developments in the Study of the Great European Witch Hunt." *Pomegranate* 5, Lammas 1998). http://www.kersplebedeb.com/mystuff/feminist/gibbonswitch.html.

Gimbutas, Marija. *The Goddess and Gods of Old Europe*. Berkeley: University of California Press, 2007.

———. *The Language of the Goddess*. London: Thames and Hudson, 2001.

———. *The Civilization of the Goddess*. San Francisco: HarperSanFrancisco, 1991.

Gottlieb, Roger. *This Sacred Earth*. New York: Routledge, 1995.

Greer, John. *A World Full of Gods: An Inquiry into Polytheism*. Tucson, AZ: ADF, 2005.

Grey, John. *Men Are From Mars, Women Are From Venus*. New

York: Harper, 2004.

Griffin, David Ray. "Introduction: Postmodern Spirituality and Society." In *Spirituality and Society*, edited by D. R. Griffin, 1-32. Albany, NY: SUNY Press, 1988.

Guiley, Rosemary. *Encyclopedia of Witches and Witchcraft*, 2nd ed. New York: Facts on File, 1999.

G'Zell, Otter. 1971. "The Gaea Hypothesis" *Green Egg*, Vol. 5(40).

Hansen, J.; Sato, M.; Ruedy, R. 1997. "Radiative Forcing and Climate Response". Journal of Geophysical Research 102: 6831.

Harding, Stephan. *Animate Earth: Science, Intuition, and Gaia*. White River Junction, VT: Chelsea Green, 2006.

Harris, Sam. 2014. *Waking Up: A Guide to Spirituality Without Religion* (New York: Simon & Schuster).

Harrison, Paul. *Elements of Pantheism*. Tamarac, FL: Lumina Press, 2004.

Harvey, Graham. *Animism*. New York: Columbia University Press, 2005.

———. *Contemporary Paganism: Listening People, Speaking Earth*. New York: New York University Press, 1997.

Hawken, Paul. *Blessed Unrest: How the Largest Social Movement in History is Restoring Grace, Justice, and Beauty to the World*. New York: Penguin Books, 2007.

Hawkins, Craig. *Goddess Worship, Witchcraft, and Neo-Paganism*. Grand Rapids, MI: Zondervan, 1998.

Heath, Duncan. *Introducing Romanticism*. Lanham, MD: Totem Books, 2006.

Heinlein, Robert A. *Stranger in a Strange Land*. New York: Putnam, 1961.

———. *Grumbles from the Grave*. New York: Ballantine Books, 1989.

Hinde, John. *Jacob Burckhardt and the Crisis of Modernity*. Montreal, Quebec, Canada: McGill-Queens University Press, 2000.

Hutton, Ronald. The Triumph of the Moon: A History of Modern Pagan Witchcraft. Oxford, UK: Oxford University Press, 2001.

Huxley, Aldous. *The Doors of Perception*. New York: Harper and Row, 1954.

Ivakhiv, Adrian. "The Resurgence of Magical Religion as a Response to the Crisis of Modernity: A Postmodern Depth Psychological Perspective." In *Magical Religion and Modern Witchcraft*, edited by James Lewis, 237-65. Albany, NY: SUNY, 1996.

Jacob, Jeffrey. *New Pioneers: The Back-to-the-Land Movement and the Search for a Sustainable Future*. University Park, PA: Pennsylvania State University Press, 1997.

James, William. *The Varieties of Religious Experience*. 1902. Vancouver, WA: Exposure Press, 2008.

Johnson, Elizabeth. *She Who Is*. New York: Crossroads, 2003.

Judith, Anodea. *Waking the Global Heart: Humanity's Rite of Passage from the Love of Power to the Power of Love*. Santa Rosa, CA: Elite Books, 2006.

Kaldera, Raven. *Pagan Polyamory: Becoming a Tribe of Hearts*. Woodbury, MN: Llewellyn Publications, 2005.

Kant, Emmanuel. *Critique of Pure Reason*. 1781. New York: Penguin Classics, 2008.

Kroll, Jerome. *The Mystic Mind: The Psychology of Medieval Mystics and Ascetics*. New York: Routledge, 2005.

Laszlo, Ervin. *The Systems View of the World: A Holistic Vision for Our Time*. 2nd rev. ed. Cresskill, NJ: Hampton Press, 1996.

Leland, Charles. *Aradia, or the Gospel of the Witches*. London: David Nutt, 1899.

Leopold, Aldo. *A Sand County Almanac*. Oxford, UK: Oxford University Press, 1949.

Levack, Brian. *The Witch-Hunt in Early Modern Europe*. New York: Longman, 2005.

Lewis, James, ed. *Magical Religion and Modern Witchcraft*. Albany, NY: SUNY Press, 1996.

Lewis, Pepper. *Gaia Speaks: Sacred Earth Wisdom*. Flagstaff, AZ: Light Technology, 2005.

Liebes, Sidney, Elizabeth Sahtouris, and Brian Swimme. *A Walk Through Time: From Stardust to Us*. Hoboken, NJ: John Wiley, 1998.

Leibniz, Gottfried Wilhelm. *Essais de Théodicée sur la bonté de Dieu, la liberté de l'homme et l'origine du mal*. 1710. Paris: Flammarion, 1999.

Lovelock, James. *Gaia: A New Look at Life on Earth*. Oxford, UK: Oxford University Press, 2000.

———. *Gaia*. Oxford, UK: Oxford University Press, 1990.

Lovelock, J. E.; Margulis, L. 1974. "Atmospheric Homeostasis by and for the Biosphere: The Gaia Hypothesis." *Tellus*. Series A (Stockholm International Meteorological Institute) 26 (1-2): 2-10.

Lovelock, James. 1987. "Gaia: A Model for Planetary and Cellular Dynamics." *Gaia: A Way of Knowing*, William Irwin Thompson, ed. (Great Barrington, MA: Lindisfarne Press).

_____. 2000. *Gaia: A New Look at Life on Earth* (Oxford: Oxford University Press).

Lyotard, Jean-Francois. *The Postmodern Condition: A Report on Knowledge.* Minneapolis: University of Minnesota Press, 1979.

McKenna, Terrence. *The Archaic Revival: Speculations on Psychedelic Mushrooms, the Amazon, Virtual Reality, UFOs, Evolution, Shamanism, the Rebirth of the Goddess, and the End of History*. New York: HarperOne, 1992.

Martin, Walter. *The Kingdom of the Cults*. Ada, MI: Bethany House, 2003.

Maslow, Abraham. *Motivation and Personality*. New York: HarperCollins, 1954.

Maslow, Abraham. 1994. *Religions, Values, and Peak-Experiences* (New York: Penguin Books).

Mead, Margaret. *Coming of Age in Samoa: A Psychological Study of Primitive Youth for Western Civilisation*. 1928. New York: Harper Perennial, 2001.

Melton, J. Gordon. *The Encyclopedia of American Religions*. 7th ed. Institute for the Study of American Religions. Wilmington, NC: Consortium Books, 1978. Detroit: Thomson/Gale, 2003.

———. "Perspective New New Religions: Revisiting a Concept." *Nova Religio: The Journal of Alternative and Emergent Religions* 10, no. 4 (2007): 103-112.

Metzner, Ralph. *The Unfolding Self: Varieties of Transformative Experience*. San Rafael, CA: Origin Press, 1998.

———. *The Expansion of Consciousness*. Berkeley, CA: Regent Press, 2008.

Miller, David LeRoy. *The New Polytheism: Rebirth of the Gods and Goddesses*. New York: Harper and Row,1974

Miller, Timothy. *The Hippies and American Values*. Knoxville: University of Tennessee Press, 1991.

Morgan, C. Lloyd. *Emergent Evolution*. Calcutta: Chandra Chakravarti Press, 2007.

Murray, Margaret. *The Witch-cult in Western Europe*. Oxford: Oxford University Press, 1921.

Nash, James. Loving Nature: Ecological Integrity and Christian Responsibility. Peabody, MA: Abingdon Press, 1991.

Niebuhr, Gustav. *Beyond Tolerance: Searching for Interfaith Understanding in America*. New York: Viking Press, 2008.

Nelson, James and Sandra Longfellow, eds. *Sexuality and the Sacred: Sources for Theological Reflection*. Louisville, KY: Westminster John Knox Press, 1994.

Oldmeadow, Harry. *The Betrayal of Tradition: Essays on the Spiritual Crisis of Modernity*. Bloomington, IN: World Wisdom, 2005.

Otto, Rudolph. *Idea of the Holy*. 1923. Whitefish, MT: Kessinger, 2004.

Paper, Jordan. *The Deities Are Many: A Polytheistic Theology*. New York: SUNY Series in Religious Studies, 2005.

Pike, Sarah M. *Earthly Bodies, Magical Selves: Contemporary Pagans and the Search for Community*. Berkeley: University of California Press, 2001.

Pinchbeck, Daniel. *Breaking Open the Head: A Psychedelic Journey Into the Heart of Contemporary Shamanism*. New York: Broadway, 2003.

Pinker, Steven. The Better Angels of Our Nature: Why Violence has Declined (New York: Penguin), 2011.

———. *Enlightenment Now: The Case for Reason, Science, Humanism, and Progress*. New York: Penguin Random House, 2018.

Quinn, Daniel. *Ishmael*. New York: Bantam, 1992.

———. *Beyond Civilization: Humanity's Next Great Adventure*. New York: Three Rivers Press, 1999.

, Liza Gabriel. *The Church of All Worlds Tradition,* pamphlet. Church of All Worlds: Cotati, CA, 2005.

Rawls, John. *A Theory of Justice*. Cambridge, MA: Harvard University Press, 1999.

Ray, Paul and Anderson, Sherry. *The Cultural Creatives: How 50 Million People Are Changing the World*. New York: Harmony Books, 2000.

Reclaiming, "Welcome to Reclaiming: a Community of People, a Tradition of Witchcraft, and a 501(c)3 Religious Organization in the San Francisco Bay Area," http://www.reclaiming.org/.

Reich, Charles A. *The Greening of America*. New York: Bantam, 1970.

Reuther, Rosemary Radford. *Gaia and God: An Ecofeminist Theology of Earth Healing*. San Francisco: HarperSanFrancisco, 1982.

Rifkin, Jeremy. *The Empathic Civilization: The Race to Global Consciousness in a World in Crisis* (New York: Penguin), 2009.

Sheldrake, Rupert. *The Presence of the Past: Morphic Resonance and the Habits of Nature*. South Paris, ME: Park Street Press, 1988.

———. *The Rebirth of Nature: The Greening of Science and God*. South Paris, ME: Park Street Press, 1994.

———. *A New Science of Life: The Hypothesis of Formative Causation*. South Paris, ME: Park Street Press, 1995.

Shipley, Thomas. *Intersensory Origins of Mind: A Revisit to Emergent Evolution*. New York: Routledge, 1995.

Singer, Margaret Thaler. *Cults in Our Midst: the Continuing Fight Against Their Hidden Menace*. San Francisco: Jossey-Bass, 2003.

Singer, Peter. *Practical Ethics*. Cambridge, UK: Cambridge University Press, 1998.

———. 1981. *The Expanding Circle: Ethics, Evolution, and Moral Progress* (Princeton, NJ: Princeton University Press).

Skrbina, David. *Panpsychism in the West*. Cambridge, MA: MIT Press, 2007.

Soleri, Paolo. 1965. *Paolo Soleri: Visionary Cities* (Santa Barbara, CA: Praeger Publishing).

Spretnak, Charlene. *The Politics of Women's Spirituality: Essays By Founding Mothers of the Movement*. Harpswell, ME: Anchor, 1981.

———. *States of Grace: The Recovery of Meaning in the Postmodern Age*. San Francisco: HarperSanFrancisco, 1991.

Starhawk. *The Spiral Dance: A Rebirth of the Ancient Religion of the Great Goddess*. San Francisco: Harper and Row, 1989.

———. *The Fifth Sacred Thing*. New York: Bantam, 1993.

———. *Webs of Power: Notes from the Global Uprising*. Gabriola Island, British Columbia, Canada: New Society, 2002.

Stein, Jeff. 2012. 'Arcology: Sustainable Hyperstructures' (TEDx Mission: "The City 2.0" https://www.youtube.com/watch?v=XCqdvLaBx50).

Sutin, Lawrence. *Do What Thou Wilt: A Life of Aleister Crowley*. New York: St. Martin's Griffin, 2002.

Swimme, Brian. *The Universe is a Green Dragon: A Cosmic Creation Story*. Santa Fe, NM: Bear and Co., 1984.

———. *The Universe Story: From the Primordial Flaring Forth to the Ecozoic Era – A Celebration of the Unfolding of the Cosmos.* San Francisco: HarperSanFrancisco, 1992.

———. The Hidden Heart of the Cosmos: Humanity and the New Story. Maryknoll, NY: Orbis Books, 1999.

Swimme, Brian, and Matthew Fox. *Manifesto for a Global*

Civilization. Santa Fe, NM: Bear and Co., 1982.

Taylor, Bron, ed. *The Encyclopedia of Nature and Religion*. New York: Thoemmes Press, 2005.

———. *Dark Green Religion: Nature Spirituality and the Planetary Future*. Berkeley: University of California Press, 2010.

Teasdale, Wayne. *The Mystic Heart: Discovering a Universal Spirituality in the World's Religions*. Novato, CA: New World Library, 1999.

Teilhard de Chardin, Pierre. *The Phenomenon of Man*. NY: Harper and Row, 1959.

———. *The Future of Man*. New York: Harper and Row, 1964.

———. *Toward the Future*. New York: Harcourt Brace Jovanovich, 1975.

———. 1959. *The Phenomenon of Man* (London: William Collins Sons).

Thompson, William Irwin. *Pacific Shift*. New York: Random House, 1986.

———. *Transforming History: A Curriculum for Cultural Evolution*. Great Barrington, MA: Lindisfarne Books, 2001.

———. *Gaia: A Way of Knowing* (Great Barrington, MA: Lindisfarne Press), 1987

Tucker, Mary Evelyn. *Worldly Wonder*. LaSalle, IL: Open Court, 2003.

Valiente, Doreen. "Charge of the Goddess." Self-published, 1950.

Walsh, Becky. *Advanced Psychic Development*. Berkeley, CA: O Books, 2007.

Watkins, Alfred. *The Old Straight Track: The Classic Book on Ley Lines*. Boothbay Harbor, ME: Abacus, 1994.

Weston, Jessie. *From Ritual to Romance*. London: Cambridge University Press, 1920.

White, Lynn. "The Historical Roots of Our Ecological Crisis." *Science* 155 (1967): 1203–7.

Wilber, Ken. "The Four Quadrants." *What Is Enlightenment?* 41 (2008): 40.

———. *Sex, Ecology, and Spirituality: The Spirit of* Evolution, 2nd rev. ed. Boston, MA: Shambhala Press, 2001.

———. *Sex, Ecology, Spirituality: The Spirit of Evolution* (Boston: Shambhala Publications), 1995.

Wilson, E.O. 2016. *Half Earth: Our Planet's Fight for Life* (New York: W. W. Norton).

Zell, Oberon, ed. *Church of All Worlds Membership Handbook*. 2nd ed. With the Church of All Worlds Clergy Council. Ukiah, CA: Church of All Worlds, 1995.

Zell, Oberon. "Theagenesis, the Rebirth of the Goddess." *Green Egg,* July 1971. http://www.caw.org/articles/theagenesis.html.

PAGANISM & SHAMANISM

What is Paganism? A religion, a spirituality, an alternative belief system, nature worship? You can find support for all these definitions (and many more) in dictionaries, encyclopaedias, and text books of religion, but subscribe to any one and the truth will evade you. Above all Paganism is a creative pursuit, an encounter with reality, an exploration of meaning and an expression of the soul. Druids, Heathens, Wiccans and others, all contribute their insights and literary riches to the Pagan tradition. Moon Books invites you to begin or to deepen your own encounter, right here, right now.

If you have enjoyed this book, why not tell other readers by posting a review on your preferred book site.

Recent bestsellers from Moon Books are:

Journey to the Dark Goddess

How to Return to Your Soul

Jane Meredith

Discover the powerful secrets of the Dark Goddess and transform your depression, grief and pain into healing and integration.

Paperback: 978-1-84694-677-6 ebook: 978-1-78099-223-5

Shamanic Reiki

Expanded Ways of Working with Universal Life Force Energy

Llyn Roberts, Robert Levy

Shamanism and Reiki are each powerful ways of healing; together, their power multiplies. *Shamanic Reiki* introduces techniques to help healers and Reiki practitioners tap ancient healing wisdom.

Paperback: 978-1-84694-037-8 ebook: 978-1-84694-650-9

Pagan Portals – The Awen Alone

Walking the Path of the Solitary Druid

Joanna van der Hoeven

An introductory guide for the solitary Druid, *The Awen Alone* will accompany you as you explore, and seek out your own place within the natural world.

Paperback: 978-1-78279-547-6 ebook: 978-1-78279-546-9

A Kitchen Witch's World of Magical Herbs & Plants

Rachel Patterson

A journey into the magical world of herbs and plants, filled with magical uses, folklore, history and practical magic. By popular writer, blogger and kitchen witch, Tansy Firedragon.

Paperback: 978-1-78279-621-3 ebook: 978-1-78279-620-6

Medicine for the Soul
The Complete Book of Shamanic Healing
Ross Heaven
All you will ever need to know about shamanic healing and how to become your own shaman…
Paperback: 978-1-78099-419-2 ebook: 978-1-78099-420-8

Shaman Pathways – The Druid Shaman
Exploring the Celtic Otherworld
Danu Forest
A practical guide to Celtic shamanism with exercises and techniques as well as traditional lore for exploring the Celtic Otherworld.
Paperback: 978-1-78099-615-8 ebook: 978-1-78099-616-5

Traditional Witchcraft for the Woods and Forests
A Witch's Guide to the Woodland with Guided Meditations and Pathworking
Mélusine Draco
A Witch's guide to walking alone in the woods, with guided meditations and pathworking.
Paperback: 978-1-84694-803-9 ebook: 978-1-84694-804-6

Wild Earth, Wild Soul
A Manual for an Ecstatic Culture
Bill Pfeiffer
Imagine a nature-based culture so alive and so connected, spreading like wildfire. This book is the first flame…
Paperback: 978-1-78099-187-0 ebook: 978-1-78099-188-7

Naming the Goddess

Trevor Greenfield

Naming the Goddess is written by over eighty adherents and scholars of Goddess and Goddess Spirituality.

Paperback: 978-1-78279-476-9 ebook: 978-1-78279-475-2

Shapeshifting into Higher Consciousness

Heal and Transform Yourself and Our World with Ancient Shamanic and Modern Methods

Llyn Roberts

Ancient and modern methods that you can use every day to transform yourself and make a positive difference in the world.

Paperback: 978-1-84694-843-5 ebook: 978-1-84694-844-2

Readers of ebooks can buy or view any of these bestsellers by clicking on the live link in the title. Most titles are published in paperback and as an ebook. Paperbacks are available in traditional bookshops. Both print and ebook formats are available online.

Find more titles and sign up to our readers' newsletter at http://www.johnhuntpublishing.com/paganism

Follow us on Facebook at https://www.facebook.com/MoonBooks and Twitter at https://twitter.com/MoonBooksJHP